837

FIELD MUSEUM OF NATURAL HISTORY
FOUNDED BY MARSHALL FIELD, 1893

PUBLICATION 274

ANTHROPOLOGICAL SERIES   VOL. XVII, No. 2

ETHNOLOGY OF THE MAYAS OF SOUTHERN AND CENTRAL BRITISH HONDURAS

BY

J. ERIC THOMPSON

ASSISTANT CURATOR OF CENTRAL AND SOUTH
AMERICAN ARCHAEOLOGY

24 Plates in Photogravure and 1 Map

BERTHOLD LAUFER
CURATOR, DEPARTMENT OF ANTHROPOLOGY
EDITOR

CHICAGO, U. S. A.

1930

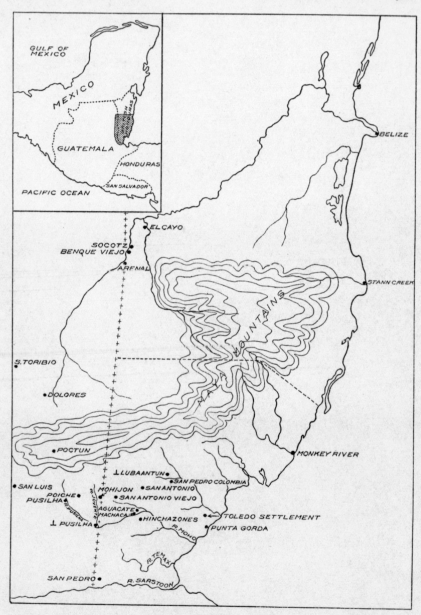

MAP OF SOUTHERN BRITISH HONDURAS AND ADJACENT GUATEMALA

Scale: 11 millimeters = 10 miles

FIELD MUSEUM OF NATURAL HISTORY
FOUNDED BY MARSHALL FIELD, 1893

PUBLICATION 274

ANTHROPOLOGICAL SERIES   VOL. XVII, No. 2

ETHNOLOGY OF THE MAYAS OF SOUTHERN AND CENTRAL BRITISH HONDURAS

BY

J. ERIC THOMPSON

ASSISTANT CURATOR OF CENTRAL AND SOUTH
AMERICAN ARCHAEOLOGY

---

24 Plates in Photogravure and 1 Map

BERTHOLD LAUFER
CURATOR, DEPARTMENT OF ANTHROPOLOGY
EDITOR

CHICAGO, U. S. A.
1930

PRINTED IN THE UNITED STATES OF AMERICA
BY FIELD MUSEUM PRESS

CONTENTS

LIST OF PLATES

27

PREFACE

This publication is the result of four visits paid to British Honduras. As archaeologist with the Second British Museum Expedition to Lubaantun, during the field season of 1927, I was able to obtain a certain amount of ethnological material, a summary of which is published in the report on the season's work (*Journal of the R. Anthrop. Institute*, Vol. LVII, pp. 295-323). It is with the permission of the British Museum that these first results have been incorporated into this publication. In the autumn of the same year a two months' stay in the village of San Antonio enabled me to gather further ethnological information. A short visit was paid to the ruins of Pusilha, where a number of stelae were discovered. In January, 1928, I returned to British Honduras as leader of the First Marshall Field Archaeological Expedition to British Honduras. Archaeological and ethnological work was carried on in the Cayo District and for a short period in the Corozal District. From December, 1928, to May, 1929, I was again in British Honduras as leader of the Second Marshall Field Archaeological Expedition to British Honduras. During this time two visits were made to San Antonio to collect ethnological information. A number of San Antonio Mayas were taken to work at the sites excavated by the expedition in the Cayo District. Several of these workers were very willing to give information. Possibly this was due to their absence from home.

I should like to record my deep sense of gratitude to a number of gentlemen resident in various parts of the colony for the help they so willingly furnished. The work in the Cayo District would have been very handicapped save for the aid and hospitality generously offered by Mr. Stuart Williams, manager of the Mengel Company's operations at that time being carried on at Camp 6. Mrs. Williams and the staff of the Mengel Company did everything in their power to make the visit a happy one. To Dr. Patterson of Cayo the expeditions are indebted for his timely aid on more than one occasion. Mr. and Mrs. Arthur Wolffsohn went out of their way to do all that was in their power to make my sojourn in Punta Gorda as pleasant as possible. Mr. and Mrs. Sydney Cuthbert helped the expeditions over many difficulties, and were always willing to do everything in their power to further the success of the work.

Father Allen A. Stevenson placed his very considerable knowledge of the Mayas, gained in the course of his many years' work as a missionary among them, at my disposal. He was able to aid considerably in clearing up several doubtful points. Father Stevenson is one of the few residents in the colony who have the interest and welfare of the Indian at heart.

At Field Museum Dr. Paul C. Standley, Associate Curator of the Herbarium, kindly aided in identifying a number of the plants used by the Indians. It would be unfair to pass by without mention the numerous Maya friends without whose information this publication would not have been possible. The chief of these are Agustin Hob, Faustino Bol, Cecilio Cal, and Tomas Chun of San Antonio, and Jacinto Cunil and Juan Cocom of Socotz.

The ethnological material gathered is somewhat meager. Had the work been initiated twenty years earlier, much fuller results would have been obtained. A few embers of the fire of Maya culture still continue to glow dimly. It has been my aim to gather these isolated sparks before all is trampled out by the onward rush of what we, in our insularity, call progress.

J. ERIC THOMPSON

ETHNOLOGY OF THE MAYAS OF BRITISH HONDURAS

I. HABITAT OF THE SOUTHERN MAYAS

The present population of British Honduras though small (estimated at 46,000 in 1923) is extremely variegated. The bulk of the population is negro. However, in the north of the colony, and to a less extent in the Cayo District, there are considerable groups of *Ladinos* (Spanish-Indian stock). Corozal and the neighboring towns were in fact populated by Mexican refugees from the war of the castes in Yucatan. The southern coastal region is settled by Caribs. A scattering of British officials and traders, odd groups of Chinese and Indian coolies, and a few Syrians and pure-blooded Spanish-Americans complete the sum of intrusive racial elements. The aboriginal American inhabitants form a small minority. They possess many villages in the northern districts, supplying most of the labor on the sugar estates. They are immigrants from Yucatan, who settled in and around Corozal during and after the war of the castes. There are a few Maya villages in the Cayo District. The Mayas of the western area are of mixed Peten and Yucatan stock with a small intermixture of Santa Cruz blood. Socotz has been taken as the type village of this district. The Belize and Stann Creek Districts possess no Indian population. In the Corozal and Toledo Districts alone are the Indians in any numerical strength.

Toledo is the most southerly, as well as the largest, of the six districts into which British Honduras is divided. To the northeast lies the Stann Creek District. The eastern boundary is washed by the Caribbean Sea. On the south the Sarstoon River forms the frontier with Guatemala. On the west a line drawn from the falls of Gracias à Dios to Garbutt Falls forms the western frontier of the colony with Guatemala, and to the northwest lies the uninhabited southern portion of the Cayo District.

The British claim to the colony of Belize as a whole is far from strong, but there seem to be no real grounds for the occupation of the Toledo District. By the treaty of London of July 14, 1786, the southern boundary of the colony was fixed by the Sibun River. Twelve years later took place the battle of St. George's Cay. In this fight the Spanish force under General O'Neil was defeated on attempting to capture Belize. On this victory lies the British claim to the land between the Sibun and the Sarstoon. To quote from the British Honduras Handbook, "The crushing defeat of the Spanish forces under the command of Field Marshal Arthur O'Neil, the Governor of Yucatan, on this memorable day, has added not only another laurel to British arms, but the colony of British Honduras, extending from Rio Hondo on the north to the river Sarstoon on the south, and from Belize on the east to Garbutt Falls on the west, to the great British Commonwealth of Nations by right of conquest."

Prior to the close of the eighteenth century the Toledo District was in all probability unoccupied. Possibly Cortez, on his memorable march from Mexico to Honduras, passed through the southwest corner of the district. At that time there were probably scattered settlements of Mopan and Chol Mayas in this area. However, between this day and the first colonization of the Caribs the district would appear to have been deserted.

The political and commercial capital of the district is the town of Punta Gorda, a small settlement of roughly 1,000 inhabitants, situated on the coast, and in communication by small coastal boats with Belize and the intermediate coastal towns as well as Puerto Barrios, the port through which passes most of Guatemala's Atlantic trade.

Punta Gorda itself is of some commercial importance. It serves the whole of the central area of the district, and at its two or three stores the Indians from the inland villages purchase all their simple requirements—soap, kerosene, cotton goods, etc., selling there in return their agricultural produce. With the exception of half a dozen whites and possibly twice as many *Ladinos* the whole population of Punta Gorda and the one or two other settlements along the coast is entirely Carib.

The term Carib is in reality a misnomer. The Caribs of the Bay of Honduras and the adjacent coastal towns are racially almost pure negro. Their history is of some interest. They are a cross between runaway African slaves and Carib women, their original home being St. Vincent. Thence, as a result of rebellion, they were deported to the Island of Ruatan by the British in the eighteenth century. From Ruatan they spread to the mainland, settling in small fishing villages along the coasts of Honduras and British Honduras. They have retained their native language, adding to it only a small percentage of French terms, dating from the era of the French occupation of St. Vincent, and a yet smaller number of English words. This possession of a distinct language is a great source of pride to the Caribs, and as a result they consider themselves superior to the Belize Negro. They keep within their own community, considering it a disgrace to marry an English-speaking Negro. Their chief industry is fishing. Expert sailors, they navigate their dories (dugout canoes) with great skill, crossing with regularity to the bay islands and the ports of Honduras. Many of them work in the lumber camps of the Toledo hinterland, and large numbers are employed in the various ranches of the Toledo settlement. For references to the Caribs see Lehmann, who gives a short bibliography, and Conzemius.

The Toledo settlement is one of the indirect results of the war of secession. At the close of that war a number of southern families resolved to leave their homes, rather than submit to the victorious North. Some were induced to make British Honduras their home. At that time (1868) the Punta Gorda hinterland was virgin forest (Swett). Most of the settlers, deterred by the hardships of pioneer life under such trying tropical conditions, soon abandoned their new homes, and either drifted back to the United States or wandered farther south to settle in Brazil. The few families that remained gradually developed the district immediately behind Punta Gorda. The forest was felled, and sugar-cane, maize, and cattle took its place. The colony prospered after a fashion. The soil was rich, the rainfall abundant, perhaps too abundant, and the sugar-cane grew luxuriantly for twenty or thirty years without replanting. There gradually developed a social order that was not unduly remote from that obtaining on the old southern plantations. Small settlements of Caribs grew up on each plantation, and Indian coolies drifted in in small numbers from the British West Indies and British Guiana. Since the world war, a cycle of bad years, due to the low prices fetched by sugar and the antiquated methods employed in the harvesting and preparation of the crop, has brought depression and decay upon the settlement. Stagnation is only too apparent, and many of the younger men, sons and grandsons of the original colonizers, have taken to mahogany cutting in the west of the district.

The settlement extends inland from the coastal fringe of Carib settlements, a matter of six or seven miles. Three or four miles farther inland this belt of rich soil of the type known as cohune ridge (from the large number of cohune palms [*Attalea cohune*] which thrive upon it) is replaced by a belt of pine ridge. The species of pine (*Pinus cariboea*) is indigenous to the colony, and yields an excellent timber not unlike American pitch pine. The soil on which the pine grows is of a poor coarse sand of little use for agricultural purposes, and at present is uninhabited. The word *ridge* is used in British Honduras to denote a belt of land, and has no reference to altitude.

Maya ruins are very seldom found upon pine ridge, for the Maya almost invariably sought the richest lands on which to build his temples and pyramids. So much so in fact that the modern Maya, searching for land on which to make his milpa, will use the presence or absence of ruins as criteria as to the richness of the soil in that immediate area.

Beyond the pine ridge is another belt of cohune ridge interspersed with low-lying land, which in the rainy season is converted into swamp, and is therefore useless for agricultural purposes. At a distance of some twenty miles from the coast the land begins to rise, and one enters the area of the Maya villages. The contrast in scenery is great. The monotonous flat forest-clad belt, rarely rising above the hundred foot contour, is replaced by hilly country gradually rising to an elevation of between fifteen hundred and two thousand feet on the western boundary of the district. The country is intersected by numerous rivers and watercourses, which, from the nature of the country, are fast flowing, and usually not navigable in their upper reaches.

The Rio Grande with its tributary, the Colombia, forms the northern boundary of the Maya settlements. Next comes the Moho River with its numerous affluents, the Rio Blanco or Blue Creek, and the Aguacate, both of which are in parts subterranean, the Machaca, also known as the Pusilha, and the Jobente, to mention the most important. To the south of the Moho flows the Temax, and again to the south, and forming the southern boundary of the colony, the Sarstoon.

The rainfall of the whole Toledo District is very high, giving rise to typical tropical rain forest and that high fertility associated with it.

The soil is of a clayey disintegrated limestone, black in appearance, which forms a covering for the limestone beds below. In many parts especially toward the Guatemalan border large outcroppings of limestone occur, often forming cliffs of considerable height. (For geographical description see Laws.)

The whole area is rich in valuable timber. A considerable quantity of mahogany is cut on the Colombia, Machaca, Blanco, and Sarstoon rivers. Besides mahogany (*tšikulte*), the following trees of commercial importance occur—sapodilla (*ya*), cedar, cabbage-palms, ramon (*oš*), and rosewood.

Although today the sapodilla is no longer cultivated, it appears that formerly it was purposely planted by the Maya. Aguilar (p. 98) states that this was the case. The sapodilla was one of the most useful plants known to the ancient Maya. It supplied excellent wood for building purposes, the majority of the wooden lintels in standing structures being of this material. Secondly, it yielded an excellent fruit, and thirdly, the gum was used in sacrifices.

For a lengthier discussion of the woods of the colony see E. Hummell's Report on the Forests of British Honduras.

The fauna is variegated. That proportion that is edible is listed under industry (p. 87). The outstanding non-edible animals are the jaguar (*balam*), the tapir, also known locally as the mountain cow (*ɔimin tše*), the ocelot (*sak šikin*, meaning "white ear"), the kinkajou, the local name of which is the night walker (*aqu maaš*), the mapache (*kululu*), the skunk (*pai*), the anteater (*luɔ* or *tšab*), the opossum (*otš*), the puma (*koh*), and the three-toed sloth (*saam?*).

Among the non-edible birds of prominence should be listed the sopilote or John crow vulture (*tš'om*), the king vulture (*batab tš'om*), hawks, all called *tš'ui*, and the ever present jay (*paap*).

Fish in fair quantities are found in the different rivers, of which bass are of most importance. Crocodiles are found in the lower reaches, but upstream have been exterminated by the Indians. Turtle are much sought after, supplying as they do such rich food.

Despite the richness of the soil, the abundant rainfall, the large numbers of edible species of fauna, and the good communications supplied by the rivers, there is no indigenous population, although at one time there must have been a considerable population as the large number of ruins demonstrates. Besides the two large sites of Lubaantun and Pusilha numerous small ruins are found scattered through the western half of the district, stretching up to the Maya Mountains. The aboriginal population, that today exists in this area, is entirely immigrant, having crossed over from Guatemala in the course of the last forty odd years.

These immigrant Mayas are of three stocks, Kekchi, Kekchi-Chol, and Mopan Maya. The Kekchi-Chol are the most numerous. They are immigrants, or descendants of immigrants, who have crossed into British Honduras from Cajabon, and the adjacent area to the northeast. The Cajaboneros are of mixed Kekchi and Chol blood, but they speak the Kekchi language with certain modifications, and in a somewhat sing-song manner. Even in historical times it would appear that Cajabon was Chol, racially and linguistically (Stoll, 1886, p. 359), and legends of Kekchi expansion against the Chols are given on page 152. However, at present the two races have completely merged. An attempt to differentiate certain customs of the two races is made on page 61, but generally when the word Kekchi is used in this publication, it must be understood to cover both the Kekchi and Kekchi-Chol.

The Kekchi immigrants are fewer in number. They hail for the most part from San Pedro Carcha, a small town lying a little to the east of Coban, and there are a few Kekchis scattered through the villages of the Toledo District from Coban itself.

The Kekchi-speaking Indians inhabit the following villages: San Pedro, Colombia, situated on the river of the same name and within a few hundred yards of the ruins of Lubaantun; Aguacate, situated a short way above the junction of the Aguacate and the Machaca; Machaca, situated a mile or two above this same junction, but on the Machaca branch; San Antonio Viejo, also known as Pueblo Viejo, situated near the source of the Aguacate on the Guatemala boundary. This town was originally settled by Mopan Mayas, but the small population is now Kekchi-speaking. Across the international frontier lie the villages of Pusilha, Mohijon, and Poite on the Pusilha and its affluents of the corresponding names. Between the Moho River and the Temax lies the little village of Hinchazones, which is inhabited for the most part by people from Aguacate. Farther south between the Temax and Sarstoon rivers lies the village of Dolores. Neither of these two villages was visited.

The only Maya-speaking village in the district is San Antonio. The Mayas of San Antonio are the descendants of immigrants from the Maya town of San Luis, Peten. San Luis was visited by Dr. Maudslay (p. 173) on his trip from Cajabon to Ixkun in 1887. He briefly narrates the story of the foundation of San Antonio. Karl Sapper (1897, p. 51) passed through San Antonio on his trip from Punta Gorda to San Luis in 1891.

The San Luis Mayas are in all probability descendants of the Mopan Mayas, mentioned by Villagutierre, and others. At the present time they inhabit the villages of San Luis, Dolores, lying about twenty-one miles as the crow flies north of San Luis, and San

Toribio, which lies about twenty-six miles in a straight line north-northwest of San Luis. The little village of Mohijon is of mixed Maya and Kekchi families. This small settlement is situated about halfway between San Luis and San Antonio. Santa Barbara Poctun was in all probability once San Luis Maya-speaking, and the little settlement of San Antonio Viejo was certainly so. The present decade is witnessing a gradual squeezing out of the Mayas in this district by the Kekchis. This fate has already overtaken the Chol and Pokomans at the same hands.

Nevertheless the area occupied within the last fifty years by the San Luis Mayas appears to coincide closely with that said to have been occupied by the Mopan Mayas in the sixteenth century.

It has been suggested that the Mayas of San Luis are descendants of the Itzas of Peten-Itza, but there are fairly cogent arguments against this theory.

The Mayas of Socotz and other Indian villages in the neighborhood are immigrants from the area around Flores, and they speak the same dialect as that spoken at San José on the shores of Lake Peten-Itza, which in turn is practically the same as that spoken in Yucatan. Furthermore among the Mayas of Socotz occur surnames such as Itza, Cocom, and Uk, which are Yucatecan. On the other hand no such names occur among the San Luis Indians, but one of the only five Mopan surnames known is met with in San Antonio (see p. 85). Furthermore the San Luis dialect differs to a considerable degree from that spoken on the shores of Lake Peten-Itza and in Yucatan. In pronunciation the *a* tends to become a *u* (e.g. *tšak* becomes *tšuk*, *šamatš* becomes *šumutš*). Final consonants such as *b* are very slurred over (e.g. *haleb* becomes *hale*). The plural termination is seldom used, the singular being used in its place. The consonant *d*, which is absent in Yucatecan Maya, tends to replace the *l* (e.g. *helo* becomes *hedo*). Many words differ in the two dialects, and there are certain grammatical differences. Nevertheless a San Antonio Maya can converse with a little difficulty with Socotz Indians. During the field season of 1929 the workers at Mountain Cow waterhole were drawn from both San Antonio and Socotz. They got on quite well together, chaffing each other about their strange ways of talking, and now and then floundering over some word that was not common to the two languages.

It would appear then that the Mayas of San Luis are in all probability descendants of the Mopan Mayas, and that the Mayas of San José are descendants of the Itzas of Tayasal, still living within a few miles of their original capital, as too are the Mayas of Socotz, who are immigrants from San José and neighboring villages.

Dr. Berendt collected a small vocabulary in the Peten in 1866-67. This was published by P. A. Means in his "History of the Spanish Conquest of Yucatan and the Itzas" (p. 188) as an appendix.

He groups a number of villages as speaking the dialect, which he calls Peten. This group includes the villages of San José, Dolores, San Luis, Yaxche, San Toribio, Santa Barbara Poctun, and Santa Ana. Now San José certainly speaks a different dialect to that spoken in San Luis, Dolores, and San Toribio. Furthermore the vocabulary and few sentences, that Dr. Berendt gives, show that he has obtained a mixture of the two dialects. All the phrases with one exception are San José Maya, and not the Maya of San Antonio. On the other hand a few of the words are definitely San Antonio Maya. The manuscript was apparently written in Sacluc, and possibly the vocabulary and phrases were obtained there too. Sacluc, which lies northwest of Flores, is right outside Mopan territory. Possibly Dr. Berendt obtained some of his information in some village of the Mopan-Pasion divide, and the greater part in the village of Sacluc. Hence the confusion. In Appendix I will be found brief notes on the San Antonio dialect.

The first settlement in British Honduras of Mopan Mayas is of some interest in helping to elucidate the psychology of the Indian. In 1883 some of the inhabitants of the Maya town of San Luis, Peten, irked by constant taxation and military service, resolved to cross the border and settle in British Honduras. A hundred or so eventually settled in the spot that is now known as San Antonio, after a short stop at the village which is now called Pueblo Viejo.

At first the new community did not prosper. The crops were bad, and fever was rife. A council was called to discuss the misfortunes that befell them. The unanimous decision was that the troubles were due to the fact that their old saints no longer protected them. Although many of the most important members of the community had migrated, those that had remained had insisted on retaining the village saints in the San Luis church. The council finally decided to raid San Luis and seize the saints so that they might be set up in the new church in San Antonio, where they would be able to see all the evils that were besetting the community and take steps to set them right. Preparations, which included the purchase of a barrel of gunpowder in Belize for the blowing in of the church door, if necessary, were carried out in complete secrecy.

Eventually on the chosen day San Antonio, to a man, set forth armed with guns, axes, machetes, and the barrel of gunpowder. The distance between the two towns is a matter of some forty-five miles. By the following evening the army had reached the outskirts of San Luis unobserved, and hiding in the forest awaited the dark. When by 9 P.M. San Luis in all innocence was soundly asleep in its hammock, the army marched silently forth. Half the force was left in reserve; the other half crept into the town and, reaching the church, had soon smashed in the door with their axes. The gunpowder was not needed. It was the work of a moment to seize the coveted santos and the church bells too and flee back to the reserve force. Before the people of San Luis had realized what had happened the invading army was scurrying back towards San Antonio. The return was rapid and by the following evening the saints had been installed in the little palm-thatched hut that served as church. The stolen bells chimed across the hills summoning the inhabitants to assemble to hear the story of the bloodless rape of the saints. An attempt by the outraged inhabitants of San Luis to recover their precious saints was to be expected. Measures of defence were taken, and a system of sentries instituted. Further the alcalde of San Antonio wrote to the Governor of British Honduras to the effect that for some totally unknown reason their neighbors of San Luis seemed to bear them ill-will, and they even feared attack. Would the Governor therefore supply them with arms with which to defend themselves against any unprovoked attack. The government at Belize, at that time as ignorant of the psychology of the Indian as it is now, replied with a consignment of lead to make bullets and a few old rifles.

When the counter-attack of the San Luiseños materialized, all the male population was absent in Punta Gorda. The women held off the San Luiseños until the men could be summoned from the coast. On their arrival next day the San Luis invaders were arrested and taken prisoners to Punta Gorda. After promising not to make any further attempt to attack San Antonio, they were released. It was obvious that the saints preferred their new abode. To this day San Antonio proudly displays to its infrequent visitors the famous saints. Needless to say disease abated, and the crops improved once the saints were made acquainted with the true state of affairs, and were able with their own eyes to see the troubles that beset their flock. Many of the documents referring to this incident in the history of British Honduras still repose in the hut of one of the ex-alcaldes in San Antonio.

At present San Antonio, together with the alquilos (groups of two or three families that live outside the village, but socially and politically form part of the community), has a population not far short of a thousand. Not all of these are Mopan Mayas, for in recent years a number of Kekchis have drifted in from across the border, or from the neighboring villages. They have had a decided effect in modifying religious beliefs, and they form the majority of the sorcerer class. Nevertheless they soon lose their language; few of the children born in San Antonio of Kekchi parents are able to speak Kekchi. A certain number of Kekchis had also settled at San Luis before the migration to San Antonio. They are probably the basis for the village being marked Kekchi on all the linguistic maps.

According to the British Honduras census of 1921 the Maya-speaking population for the whole colony is given as 7,806. This is divided up as follows:

Toledo	1,692
Corozal	2,660
Orange Walk	1,838
Cayo	850
Belize	377
Total for Colony	7,806

Unfortunately the census did not differentiate between the Kekchi and Maya languages. According to the 1911 census the population of San Antonio and the surrounding alquilos amounted to 707. By 1921 the population of the San Antonio area had risen to 1,119, but this figure apparently includes the village of San Pedro, Colombia, as this village had been founded between 1911 and 1921. However, the population of Colombia cannot amount to more than 200, if that. Accordingly the population in 1921 of San Antonio and the alquilos was probably in the neighborhood of 950. The Aguacate area shows an increase during this decade from 431 to 526 inhabitants. The remaining Indian population of Toledo is grouped around the area between the Temax and Sarstoon rivers. The total Indian population both of Toledo and the Colony as a whole is really larger than is shown by the above figures, as this is based entirely on language. There are a large number of Indians in the western and northern districts who have, unfortunately, lost their language and now speak only Spanish.

II. AGRICULTURE AT SAN ANTONIO

The Maya communities of southern British Honduras are typical of their nation in that their whole life centers round agriculture. Their very existence is bound up with their crops. The clearings on which they grow their produce are known throughout this area to the Spanish-speaking peoples as milpas (*kol*). A fresh milpa is cut every year. A milpa may consist of two, three, or even four manzanas, a manzana consisting of sixteen mecates, each twenty-four yards square; that is roughly an acre and a third. The word *mecate* is derived from the Aztec *mecatl* ("string") with which the milpa was measured. The average milpa is from three to four acres in area. Ten men working for one day can clear average forest off one manzana.

An old law of Cajabon prohibited milpas larger than four manzanas. This possibly contributed toward the migration of the Kekchis from that area into British Honduras.

In addition to the milpa, each family has a small patch of cleared land which is permanently under cultivation and in which perennials such as oranges and cacao mainly are cultivated. Where possible, the cultivator makes his milpa close to the permanent patch. A number of these perennials are also grown close to, or within the limits of, the village, but the ravages of the innumerable pigs kept by every family make their cultivation in the seedling stages a hazardous task. Furthermore the clearing of the forest from the village site has caused very considerable denudations.

The range of fruit trees, vegetables, and cereals grown by the modern Maya is wide, covering, as it does, in addition to the staple products of his pre-Columbian ancestors, a varied selection of plants introduced in colonial and more recent times. In Appendix II are listed the principal plants now cultivated by the Mayas, together with references from historical sources that throw light on the question as to which were known to the Mayas before the ___sh conquest.

___e agricultural year of the Maya of San Antonio may be said to ___mence in February. Until recent years it was customary for the ___le population of San Antonio to repair to the church on February 8 each year for an all-night vigil. This service appears to

41

have no connection with any ceremony of the Catholic church; in fact the Catholic priests were quite unaware that it took place. Within the last few years there has been an attempt to shift this service, which is an intercession for a successful agricultural year, to the first Saturday in February. The instigator of this change was an ex-alcalde, Janaro Chun, who had been educated in Belize, and was opposed to all the old customs that savored of paganism. There was considerable opposition to the change, and since Chun lost his post of alcalde, there has been a return to the old date of February 8. Until recent years attendance at the vigil was compulsory, and non-attendants were liable to a fine. At nightfall the whole village proceeded to the church, where fifty or sixty candles were lit. Prayers were offered to the Almighty and Huitz-Hok, the Mountain-valley god. The ceremonies were enlivened by the drinking of considerable quantities of rum. At midnight the more devout members of the congregation filed out of the church, and kneeling or standing, offered more candles and copal, as they prayed anew. The prayers have now, unfortunately, fallen into disuse except among a few of the older generation, and some of the people in the remoter alquilos. I was unable to obtain any texts, merely the statement that God and Huitz-Hok were invoked. One informant added that the morning star and the moon were appealed to as well to send good crops. All-night vigils are a part of many Maya ceremonies of aboriginal origin, and except for the fact that this inter-cession takes place in a church, and that the God of the Christians is added to the old list of pagan deities invoked, there is no evidence of the ceremony being of post-Colombian origin. This is the only ceremony of supposedly Maya origin that is fixed in the calendar. According to the Goodman-Thompson correlation of the European and Maya calendars, the days clustering around the position occupied by February 8 in the tropical year were more emphasized than any other date in the year during the Old Empire (Thompson, 1927). The position February 8 corresponds to April 11 in the correlation put forward by Herbert J. Spinden. There seems then a strong possibility that should the Goodman-Thompson correlation be correct, a matter that is by no means decisively settled, then this festival still maintained at San Antonio is the same as that ob over 1,200 years ago by the Mayas of the so-called Old Emp this same general area. Bishop Landa states that either in Ch Yax the temple of the Chacs was renovated, and their idols, bra and pottery were repainted or renewed. At the time of the conques these two months corresponded to the period January 2 to February 10 (Landa, chap. 40). The Chacs were agricultural gods, and therefore there might be some connection between the modern and the ancient ceremonies. However, in Bishop Landa's time it would appear to have been a movable feast. Among the Lacondones the ceremony of renewing the incense vessels commences in the middle of February and continues until nearly the end of March, but the time depends to a large extent on the ripening of the products of the milpa. However, among the Lacondones the ceremony appears to be primarily a thanksgiving for the past season. Only on completion of these ceremonies is the new milpa prepared (Tozzer, 1907, p. 106). In the Valley of Mexico February 2 is set apart as a day of intercession for a good harvest (Gamio, Vol. II, p. 408).

In the early part of the year each man marks out the spot where he intends to make his milpa (kol). This is a simple business consisting solely of cutting a narrow ride through the forest so as to include the area, usually three or four acres in extent, which it is intended to clean and cultivate. For the purpose of clearing and sowing the Mayas combine into groups of fifteen to twenty-five to help each other in their work. In this way the clearing of each man's milpa in turn is carried out by the whole group. This practice is definitely of pre-Spanish origin. Bishop Landa (chap. 23) writes, "The Indians have the excellent custom of helping one another in all their work. At sowing time those who have no one to do this work band together in groups of twenty, more or less, and all together they do the share of each individual, and they do not stop until each man's piece has been done. The land today is held in common, so he who first stakes out a claim is given possession of that piece of land." The communal groups vary in composition from day to day, each man arranging to exchange labor with his friends. Thus A and B are among those working for C. C in turn will have to work for A and B when they are making their respective milpas, but A may not necessarily work for B, and conversely B for A. That will depend on a private arrangement between the two. Once the contract to help each other has been agreed upon the engagement becomes a solemn obligation which no one will attempt to break. A substitute can be sent, but failing that the man as a point of honor must fulfill his part of the contract. Offers of money, however tempting they may be, will not induce any one to break his engagement.

Today it is no longer the custom for every man to make a plantation. A number who work in the lumber camps refrain from raising their own crops and pigs, buying the necessary corn from neighbors. As they can supply themselves with enough corn to last a year for ten dollars, the pay for about a fortnight's work, it is a wonder more do not follow their example. However, there appears to be a slight stigma attached to those who so break with tradition.

The site of the plantation may be any distance up to eight or ten miles from the village. After a long occupation of a village, virgin forest becomes scarce, and it is often necessary to walk two, three or even four leagues to obtain untouched forest land. After raising one crop the land is usually abandoned for seven or eight years to allow a heavy second growth of timber to form. Occasionally a piece of land may be sown two years in succession, but this is rare and regarded as unorthodox, and likely to result in a poor yield. However the real reason is probably to be found in the fact that secondary growth (Kat'ok) usually consists to a considerable extent of thorny plants that make work very unpleasant. The evening before felling is to start on each plantation, the members of the communal group gather at the house of the man whose land is to be cleared. There a vigil is kept up the whole night. Entrance to the wake is not confined to members of the group. Any friend of the owner may drop in, and on the other hand members of the group may be absent. Chicken, pig, black beans, tamales, tortillas, etc., are served, and cocoa, rum and posole are drunk. The man's wife and family attend the vigil. Accordions, harps, or marimbas are produced, and the hours till dawn are whiled away in music, conversation, eating and drinking. The writer was informed that one of the objects of the vigil was to prevent any possibility of the man having sexual intercourse with his wife.

At dawn the owner of the plantation sets out alone for the scene of the day's labor. The ceremonies that he has to carry out must be performed in private. The rest of the group, therefore, wait about twenty minutes before following him. On arrival at the spot which he has selected for his plantation, the man proceeds to where he judges roughly the center of the patch to be. Choosing a large tree as near this spot as possible, he places a few pieces of wood on a banana leaf or in a small hole in the ground at the foot of the tree. Setting light to it, he places on it a lump of copal incense (Pom), a resinous substance obtained from Protium copal, and extensively used by the Maya both in ancient and modern times. As soon as the fumes of the copal ascend he recites the following prayer, turning at the same time to the four quarters:

Ay dios,   *in na,*   *in yum,*   *Santo wiɔ,*   *Santo hoq,*   *Santo tše.*
O God,   my mother,   my father,   Lord Huitz,   Lord Hok,   Lord Che.

Ma biki   *balowa lu*   *yantala.*   *Alebe*   *tan in ɔek*   *a welte*
No impatience   just as thus   it has been.   Now   I am offering for you   to know

tan in tuksik   *a wol.*   *Yan*   *wala*   *muk*   *ya tikeni.*
I am molesting   your soul.   There is   perhaps   strength   to suffer it.

Bel in kah in   *qaskun-tetš,*   *bel in kah*   *in meya-tetš*   *tial*
I am going to   dirty you,   I am going   to work you   in order that

in kušlebal.   *Pero*   *ma in qati*   *ka*   *u*   *t'ul-en*   *mašqui*
I may live.   But   I do not wish   that   he   pursue me   none of

ti baaltšeil,   *maaštowa*   *kun,*   *maaštowa*   *sinaan,*   *maaštowa*
the wild animals,   not yet perhaps   snake,   not yet perhaps   scorpion,   not yet perhaps

šuš   *ka*   *u*   *yakunten,*   *maaštowa*   *tše*   *ka*   *u putšen,*
wasp   that   it   pay attention to me,   not yet perhaps   wood   that   it hit me,

maaštowa   *baat,*   *maaštowa*   *maska*   *ka*   *u*   *tšuken.*   *Etel tulakal*
not yet perhaps   the axe,   not yet perhaps   the machete   that   it   catch me.   With all

in wol   *bel in kah*   *in meya tetš.*
my soul   I am going   to work you.

One or two passages in this, as in the other prayers, are obscure.
I have preferred to leave them thus, rather than attempt to elucidate
them along lines that are possibly incorrect. Examples of dialectic
differences are *kun* for *kan*, and *maska* for *maskab.* The free translations have, possibly, too biblical a flavor, but it is difficult for us
to understand the mental attitude of the Indian when he prays,
without employing some close parallel in the religious phraseology
to which we are accustomed.

FREE TRANSLATION

O God, my mother, my father, Huitz-Hok, Lord of the Hills and
Valleys, Che, Spirit of the forests, be patient with me, for I am about
to do as my fathers have ever done. Now I make my offering to
you that you may know that I am about to trouble your very soul,
but suffer it I pray you. I am about to dirty you—to destroy your
beauty—I am going to work you that I may obtain my daily bread.
I pray you suffer no animal to dog my footsteps nor snake to bite
me. Permit not the scorpion or wasp to sting me. Bid the trees
hey fall not upon me, and suffer not the axe or knife to cut
with all my heart I am about to work you.

tly after the conclusion of the prayer the rest of the party
rs upon the scene, and the felling commences. The timber is
down in swathes, and as it is the task at which the Maya excels,

work proceeds rapidly. The branches of felled trees are cut into small sections so that they may dry the more readily. Exceptionally large trees are sometimes left standing, but many of these will be partially destroyed when the milpa is fired.

Many are of the opinion that in the days of Maya prosperity the forest land did not exist, but had all been cleared to permit of intensive cultivation. Cook has shown that forest growth in Central America is for the most part recent. However, this does not necessarily imply that all the forest was cleared at one and the same time. According to the Popol Vuh, the method of agriculture before the conquest involved, as it does today, the felling of forest. The divine twins, Hunahpu and Xbalanque, go out to prepare a milpa armed with axes and hoes. Thanks to their miraculous powers they are able to fell the forest in no time, but during the night the animals of the forest raise up once more all the trees, bushes, and lianas, and the work has to be done all over again. The early Spanish accounts are full of descriptions of the thick bush encountered in Yucatan. Peter Martyr (Decade IV, chap. 6) speaks of the inhabitants of Cozumel fleeing to the thick bush on the arrival of some of Cortez's men. As Cozumel was one of the leading sacred cities of the Maya, one would at least expect the surrounding country to be cleared if that was the general Maya practice. Even the thickly populated Mani district was heavily forested in 1547, according to Cogolludo (Book V, chap. 7). Landa speaks of Aguilar fleeing from his captors through the forest to a neighboring chief. The same writer, although he does not actually state that the Mayas used to fell the forest to make their milpas, implies that this was the case. He says that the working of the milpas consisted in collecting the rubbish and burning it, and that they were engaged in this work from the middle of January to April. If the land was already cleared, three months would not be required for collecting and burning the rubbish. Aguilar recommends that the Mayas should not be allowed to live in their milpas as that means they go to live in the forest four or six leagues from the town. He also speaks of the stretches of forest between Cabo Cotoch and Ascension Bay, and the forest between Tixhualatun and Chemax. Now Tixhualatun was the town where the Mayas were said to have kept their archives, and again one would not expect the surrou area to be heavily forested unless this was the general rule in tan. One may then conclude that in pre-conquest days the sar tem of clearing forest, and then abandoning the land for sev eight years was observed, and that the Maya Empire was alw heavily forested, and except in the immediate vicinity of the towns appeared the same as it does today—stretches of forest broken by a patchwork pattern of milpa clearings.

This system of agriculture necessarily implies a relatively small population. Estimates of a population for Chichen Itza ranging from half a million up to a million are surely grotesque. It is remarkable what a small population would be required to build even the largest Maya city, if one admits a rigorous system of communal slave labor working over a long period.

However, we have strayed somewhat from our description of the preparation of the modern milpa.

If the patch is not too far from the village, the women folk of the axemen usually journey out to the scene of operations with the midday meal, which is provided by the owner of the milpa. The day following the completion of one milpa, work starts on the land of some other member of the group, who in his turn holds a vigil, and proceeds alone to the milpa to burn copal and conciliate the spirits of the forest, and the Huitz-Hok, patrons of agriculture.

After cutting, the timber and bush are left about three weeks to dry before burning off. Heavy rain is very much feared at this period, as it may cause the felled timber to rot and accordingly make burning very difficult. Again, the night before burning is kept as a vigil. The usual chicken, cocoa, rum, etc., are consumed. As soon as the dew is off the ground, the owner repairs alone to his milpa, and placing copal on a leaf in the center of the cleared area, recites the prayer that is given below. Sometimes a friend or two will arrive shortly after and aid in the firing. The date of burning is not fixed, depending as it does to a large extent on the state of the weather. Usually it takes place in the second, third, or fourth week in April, but it may occur earlier or later.

PRAYER TO THE WIND BEFORE BURNING MILPA

Ay Dios,	Santo Iq,	alebe	in qati	ka	a	meeteten
O God,	Holy wind,	now	I desire	that	you	do for me

a ...eya.	Tubakaneeš	a	tšuk	iq,	a sik	iq,
your	Where are you	your	red	wind,	your white	wind,

a	A ma in	wel	tubakaneeš	tušul	kaan,
y	I do not	know	where you are,	in what part of	the heavens,

y	...utš wiɔ,	nukutš hok.	Alebe	in kati eeš
in the mi...	mighty hills,	or the great plains.	Now	I desire you

ka	utɔ	a bašul-eeš	tiki	itšil	in	meya.
that	it be possible	you play	well	within	my	work.

This prayer is fairly straightforward. Note as dialectical difference *tubakanen*, which is obsolete in Yucatan.

FREE TRANSLATION

O God, Holy wind, now I pray you do your work for me. Where are you red wind, or you white wind, or you whirlwind? I know not where you are—in what corner of the vault of heaven, or whether you be in the midst of the mighty hills or the far flung plains. Now I beseech you cause the flames to play amidst the fruits of my labor.

It is somewhat doubtful if one wind god is being addressed, or if the red, white, and whirlwinds are considered to be separate deities. Tubakaneeš is of course plural, but the pronoun *a* (your) is placed before each wind. The present-day Indians of San Antonio associate colors with world directions, but no longer know which color is associated with the different points of the compass. Among the ancient Maya red was associated with the North. Chacal Bacab—the red bacab—held up the north end of the world. Similarly white was associated with the West, and Zacal Bacab was responsible for that quarter.

Tozzer describes the rite invoking the wind gods among the Maya of Yucatan. Posol is offered to the wind gods, and a little is sprinkled to the four quarters, but no prayers are offered. A similar offering is made after the corn has been planted (Tozzer, 1907, p. 162).

After firing, the milpa is covered with a thick layer of ash in which lie scattered a number of the largest trunks. These, because of their great bulk, have not dried out entirely, and therefore resist to a certain extent the onslaught of the flames even when the red and white winds, issuing from the farthest corner of the vault of heaven, do their utmost. A light rain is now required to lay the ash and soften the ground for sowing. This is usually forthcoming as the first week in May can be relied upon to produce a storm.

The night before the milpa is to be sown those that are to help gather at the house of the owner of the milpa for an all-night vigil. At one end of the hut a cross is set up and before that on a table or a strip of bark are placed the sacks of maize that are to serve as seed. Mixed with this seed is the seed that was last gathered at the previous harvest. This seed contains Santo Ixim, the maize spirit. The maize is believed to be inhabited by a maize spirit who is the vitality of the crop. When the crop is being harvested, Santo Ixim is gradually driven out from his haunts until he takes refuge at last in the last sections to be gathered. When these alone remain the other workers retire, and the owner of the milpa alone gathers the ears from this area. These ears he takes home with him, for in them is imprisoned the maize spirit. They are sprinkled with the blood of a chicken and are set aside for the following sowing. They are also sprinkled with a little lime dust, but the object of this is merely to preserve them from weevils. Every plant has its spirit, but in no case is so much attention paid them as in the case of maize. Beliefs in an indwelling corn spirit are almost world-wide in their distribution. James Frazer (chaps. 43-50) has dealt with the subject at length and described almost similar practices from various localities in the Old World. By mixing the seed of the last cobs to be gathered in the previous year with other seed the new crop is assured of the presence of Santo Ixim. Should this seed containing the maize spirit not be mixed with the other seed to be sown the Indians believe the crop will be a failure.

Returning to the vigil, the seed to be sown is placed on the table before the cross and one or two candles are lighted and placed in front of it. Then a calabash containing a little cacao and ground maize is placed before it between the candles. A censer containing copal incense (*pom*) is lighted, and with that the seed is liberally censed by the owner of the house or by some brujo (*pulia*) who happens to be present. The man with the censer then proceeds around the outside and inside of the hut censing the whole building. Meanwhile the wife of the owner of the house, assisted by the wives of one or two of the men present, prepares a meal of chicken and rice and tortillas, which with cacao and ground maize is served at midnight. The rest of the night is spent in conversation or music. Sometimes a visit is paid to the church to pray for a successful crop. The object of this all-night vigil is twofold. First, it is a religious observance, and penitential rite, such as was commonly observed throughout the Maya area in pre-conquest days. Second, it has the additional purpose of removing all possibility of sexual intercourse on the part of those that are going to sow. Sexual intercourse immediately prior to, and for some time after sowing, is considered by the majority of the Indians of the Toledo District to be very harmful to the new crop. The interval of sexual abstinence is not a definite one, as among the Kekchis of the Alta Vera Paz, but may be said generally to extend from a few days before sowing to some fifteen days after. At the end of this period cohabitation may be resumed, but care must be taken that as little movement as possible is made. It is believed that if the hammock or the body should move too much, the stems of the young plants will be broken by violent winds. A directly opposite custom is observed by a minority of San Antonieros of Kekchi-speaking descent. No vigil, to which all the fellow sowers are invited, is kept. Instead, at midnight, the owner of the milpa that is to be sown the following day and his wife get up and strip off all their clothes. They lie down at each corner of the hut in turn with their heads to the north. Barely effecting penetration, the man simulates the movements of intercourse. As in the former case, both parties are as passive as possible. My informant, a man from the alquilos, was very intoxicated when he gave me this information, and further spoke very bad Spanish. However, he seemed to wish to say that at the last corner of the hut the sexual act was consummated. As explained on page 61, this may be an old Chol survival. No meal is eaten in the morning before starting out to sow.

The owner of the milpa proceeds alone to his land to be followed a half hour later by the rest of the sowers. On arriving at the center of the milpa, he burns copal and sows seven handfuls of maize in the form of a cross to the four world directions. He then recites the prayer given below:

Ay dios,	*in mam,*	*in tšitš,*	*Santo Wiɔ,*	*Santo Hok,*
O God,	my grandfather,	my grandmother,	Holy Huitz,	Holy Hok,

Santo Quh,	*tan in ɔekeeš*	*in*	*silol*	*etel*	*tulakal*	*in*	*wol.*
Holy Kuh,	I offer to you	my	offering	with	all	my	soul.

Ma biki sa han wal tetš u men	*in*	*halal*	*dios*	*etel*
Not impatient for the sake of	my	true	god	and

Kitšpana.	*Yan a*	*ɔekten*	*tiki*	*tikitšpan*	*tulakal*
the Virgin.	You must	give me	fine,	beautiful	all

a ku ben in kah	*in pukul*	*itšil*	*in meya*	*itšil*	*in kol.*
I am going	to sow	in	my work	in	my milpa.

Ka kunumteten.	*Ka bilahten,*	*maaštowa*	*ku(?) kutilul*
Guard it for me.	Watch it for me,	let nothing yet perhaps	happen to it

habištowa	*ka hokoko*	*balotowa*	*hasta*	*ben kah*	*in molo.*
just as	I put it in	so yet perhaps	until	I go	to collect.

One or two phrases in this prayer are somewhat obscure, notably the two commencing *Ma biki* and *maastowa ku.*

FREE TRANSLATION

O God, my grandfather, my grandmother, Lord Huitz-Hok, god of the hills, and the plains, Lord Kuh, god of the milpa lands, with all my heart, with all my soul I make this offering to you. Be patient with me in what I am about to do for the sake of God Almighty and the blessed Virgin Mary. I pray you give to me an abundant return for all the crops I have sown, for all the work I have done in my milpa.

Guard it for me, watch it for me, let nothing damage it. May I harvest from all that I have sown.

Another sowing prayer, which was presumably translated straight from the Kekchi, is used by a few of the San Antonieros of Kekchi descent:

Ay Dios Santo,	in yum,	in tšitš,	Santo Iɔam,	Sr. Kahwa,
O Holy God,	my father,	my grandmother,	Holy Itzam,	Sr. Kahwa,

Sr. Coha,	in mam,	in yum,	šucanen,	Dios Señor,
Sr. Coha,	my grandfather,	my father,	Xucanen,	Lord God,

Santa Cruz,	ben k' in	lomah	tas yelo.	In qati	paq	samal.
Holy Cross,	I am going	to strike	your covering.	I wish	to sow	tomorrow.

In mam,	in tšitš.	Ay dios Santo.	Kusa	bin k'	in mat
My grandfather,	my grandmother.	Ay Holy God.	Excusa(?)	I am going	to penetrate

a booy	matan	Sr. Kesab.
your shadow	bounty	Sr. Kesab.

The informant gave the translation "I am going to strike your breast." This is undoubtedly the idea behind the word *tas*. The Mam are being addressed, and as the body of the Mam is the earth, making holes in the earth to sow the seed could very well be described as striking the Mam's breast.

Another very similar sowing prayer also of Kekchi origin is as follows:

Ay Dios Santo,	in yum,	in tšitš,	Santo Iɔam,	Sr. Kahwa,
Ay Holy God,	my father,	my grandmother,	Holy Itzam,	Sr. Kahwa,

Sr. Coha,	in mam,	in yum.	Solanen	Dios
Sr. Coha,	my grandfather,	my father.	I kneel before	God

Señor Cruz.	Talen	ti cielo	Santo Luum.	Ben k' in
Lord Cross.	I have come	to the heavens,	Holy earth.	I am going

lomah	a	t'an.	In qati	paq	samal.	In mam,
to strike	your	face.	I wish	to sow	tomorrow.	My grandfather,

in tšitš,	Ay Dios, Santo Quh	z'in mat	a booy	in mat
my grandmother,	Ay God, Holy Kuh,	I am penetrating	your shadow,	I am penetrating

a booy,	Sr. Kesab.
your shadow,	Sr. Kesab.

Shortly after the conclusion of the prayer offered in the milpa the rest of the party, who are to help in the sowing, arrive, and the sowing commences. The sowers are armed with sharp pointed sticks (*akte*), and with these they make small holes in the ground at intervals of two or three feet. Into these holes four or five grains of maize are dropped, and the earth is then heaped up into a slight hillock on top of them. An interval of about three feet is left between the lines. In this manner the whole field is traversed, exactly the same process being followed in the succeeding swaths.

Attention has already been drawn to the identity of the ancient and modern method of aiding one another which the Indians practised. The modern method of sowing, too, corresponds exactly to that practised before the arrival of the Spaniards. This method of sowing is illustrated in both the Dresden and Troano-cortesiano codices. Bishop Landa (chap. 23) writes, "When they have prepared their land they do nothing but collect the rubbish and burn it in preparation for sowing. They are engaged in this from the middle of January until April, and then when the rains break they sow. This they do carrying a bag on their shoulders, and making holes in the ground with a pointed stick. In these holes they place five or six seeds, covering them up with the same stick."

After the milpas have been sown, they are not touched again until ready for harvesting. No attempt is made to keep the plants free of weeds. As a matter of fact, the young plants usually get a good start on all weeds, and there is no particular need to hoe the rows. Sometimes when there is no rain after sowing the crop is destroyed and has to be replanted. The milpas are occasionally damaged to a considerable extent by different pests.

When the crops are being devoured by locusts, they are saved by driving away the locusts in this manner. Thirteen of them are caught in a milpa and taken to the church, where, shut in a receptacle, they are placed on the altar. Four large black beeswax candles are lit, and a service is held. After the service the thirteen locusts are returned to the milpa from which they were taken. Presumably this is done so that they may carry the message to their fellow locusts, that they must leave.

Also the owner of the milpa will say to the locusts:

Saq	ma ko hante	in nul.	Kasuk.
Locust	do not eat	my green corn.	Go away (?).

By substituting tš'o the prayer can be addressed to the rats, which do considerable damage to the milpas.

Should there be any shortage of rain short prayers such as the following are offered to the powers that control the rains:

Ay Dios,	Santo tšak	qato	wa	qašuk Santo ha,
O God,	Holy Chac	desire	perhaps	that it rain holy rain,

	in qat	in bilah	kitšpan	in puqul.
	I wish	to see	beautiful	my sowing.

FREE TRANSLATION

O God, Lord Chac, spirit of thunder and lightning, I pray you cause the holy rain to descend so that my crop may be good.

Ay dios	*qato*	*wa*	*qašukten*	*ha*	*Santo ha*	*ti meya*
O God	pray	perhaps	that he rain upon me	rain	holy rain	for the work

ka	*in bilah*	*bikilil*	*in*	*meya.*
that	I may see	beautiful	my	work.

FREE TRANSLATION

O God, I pray that Lord Ha, spirit of the rain, may shower down his rain for me upon the field that I have prepared so that my harvest may be good.

Qato would appear to be an imperative, though of a form unknown in Yucatan. *Puqul* is dialect for *paqal*. *Qašukten* (*Qašaki-ten*) is the indefinite future. Tozzer (1921, p. 70) states that this form, which is always contracted in Yucatan, is found only with the root *bin* of the verb to go. A future would naturally be expected after the verb *qat*.

The sun, Santo kin, is never prayed to under any circumstances, for it is believed that were he invoked he would not stop short, but would burn up the crops entirely.

If the prayers for rain are not effective, the Mayas call the attention of the saints to the drought. Any saint from the church is taken outside and placed well in the sun, so that he or she may be convinced how parching are the hot rays of the sun. Undoubtedly in earlier times a statue of one of the rain gods was the victim of this irreverent treatment. At present no statues of the old gods survive and the Christian saints have to suffer in their place. Sometimes the saint is taken out of the church and marched around the building, while prayers are offered to Huitz-Hok and Santa U. The previous night is passed in vigil. The crop is ready for harvesting toward the end of September. Again groups are formed to gather it as when it was sown. No ceremony is performed. The women folk of the gatherers repair to the hut of the owner of the milpa, where they help prepare the evening meal, as the owner is under an obligation to feed those who are assisting him. The gathering of the last cobs has already been described. The maize, with the exception of that containing the maize spirit, is neatly stored with its covering still adhering in small thatched shelters adjacent to the milpa. From there it is carried on the back in large netted bags (*bai*) to the house as required. Granaries such as these are described by Bernal Diaz (chap. 178). Speaking of a reconnaissance party of which he was a member not many leagues from the area under discussion, he notes, "We found four houses full of maize and beans." No doubt the early Spanish invaders suffered frequently from hunger because they found only scant provisions in the villages, whereas no doubt if they had sent foraging parties to visit the milpas they would have been well rewarded.

The Maya is not very mindful of past favors, and it is not therefore strange to find that no thanksgiving service such as the primicia service (p. 115) occurs in the milpa at harvest time. An annual harvest festival is held in the church by the visiting priest, but this is not considered an important function; and, if the size of the collection is any criterion, the god of the Christians receives scarcely any more concrete gratitude than the old local deities.

A second crop is frequently sown. This is smaller than that sown in the spring. The autumn crop is sown in November or December, and is ready to harvest in March or April. Among the Maya of the Toledo area the practice of bending down the ears of corn so that the rain runs off them and they thereby dry better is not observed. The following terms are those in general use at San Antonio:

Corn in general	*išim*
Seed	*paqal*
Corn just sprouting	*top'en išim*
Plant a foot high	*išmenul*
Green corn	*šmunŭl*
Harvest	*hotš or mol*
Dry ear of corn	*nŭl*
Beard of corn	*uɔuk*
Shelled corn	*bŭkŭl*
Milpa	*kol*
Flower of corn	*topnil išim*

Maize is far and away the most important crop of the Mayas, and consequently the ceremonies connected with its sowing are of more importance than those associated with the planting of any other food-plant. Until a couple of decades ago, or even more recently, prayers were offered to the Huitz-Hok when beans, cacao, tobacco and other important products of the soil were sown, but, unfortunately, within the last few years these have fallen into disuse together with many other of the old customs. Beans are believed to have their own in-dwelling spirit, similar to that of the maize crop. The same ceremony of capturing the bean spirit was observed as in the case of maize. However the bean spirit is believed to dwell in the first plants to be harvested, not in the last as in the case of maize. The reason for this difference apparently lies in the fact that the last beans to be harvested tend to be of poor quality, and therefore are no fitting abode for the spirit of the crop. Formerly sowing was preceded by an all-night vigil, during which the seed was censed, and prayers, similar to those offered when maize is sown, were recited and copal burnt.

Cacao, too, is believed to have its own spirit, which guards the trees, but no ceremonies connected with the cultivation of the plant now survive. The night before sowing root crops such as sweet potatoes, yams, cassava, etc., the sower sleeps on the ground. This is an example of sympathetic magic. The object appears to be to ensure that the plants will develop roots that are both deep and wide-spreading. The idea appears to be, although my informant did not actually say so, that as the body of the sower is spread out on the ground, and not up in the air, as would be the case if he slept in a bed or hammock, so the roots of the plant will cling to the soil, and not tend to expose themselves above the surface. When sowing these root crops no chili nor black pepper must be eaten. No intoxicants must be drunk either, only cocoa and sugar without the addition of the usual black pepper. The reason given by my informant (a Kekchi) for this practice was that if these restrictions were not carried out grubs would destroy the roots. Sweet potatoes must be sown at midday.

In actual fact such abstinence dates back to pre-conquest days. After sowing tobacco a chicken is eaten that grubs may not harm the young plants. Dieseldorff (1928-29, Vol. V, p. 333) mentions a number of ceremonies connected with sowing, some of which are listed above as practised in San Antonio.

The Mayas tend to sow their crops on, or within a day or two, of special feast days. Tobacco, for instance, is sown on, or close to, St. James' day (July 25). Squashes are sown in April when the moon is full. The day of Holy Cross (May 3) marks for many milpa owners the time when the maize crop should be sown. On Good Friday chili should be sown. Aguilar (p. 95) writes that the Mayas used their calendar to find out when to clear, burn, and sow. In the "Relacion de Campocolche y Chocola" it is stated that the priest told the people when to sow. Accordingly the fixing of times to sow by Christian festivals is, in all probability, a survival of, or rather a mutation of, a pre-conquest custom.

III. RELIGION AND MAGIC AT SAN ANTONIO

The Mayas of the Toledo District, like their brothers in Yucatan, are, and have been for a considerable time, in name at least, Catholics. Each village has its church, and the whole group is under the spiritual care of the Jesuit mission at Punta Gorda. Father A. Stevenson of that mission is directly in touch with the different villages, making a visit on an average once every three or four months. During these visits baptisms, marriages, confessions, and masses are performed. Very occasionally the bishop, too, makes his diocesan round, confirming the young people. Further, the school teachers, Carib Negroes educated in the mission college, instruct the school children in religious subjects during school hours. Father Allen Stevenson has reduced the creed, the Lord's prayer, etc., to the Maya and Kokchi tongues, and the children are taught these together with hymns both in Latin and Maya. Christian influence then may be said to be much stronger here than in Yucatan. Nevertheless, the doctrines of Christianity are very poorly comprehended even by the younger generation. They can recite parrot fashion what has been taught them, but if one asks them any simple question such as who was crucified on the cross and why, the majority are unable to answer. However, the teaching in the schools and churches is rapidly overthrowing what remains of the old Maya religion, and a new generation is growing up quite indifferent to all religion, with merely a vague belief in a Supreme deity, a host of minor deities and an after-life. The religious ideas of the Indians given below must then be considered to be those of the older generation.

A definite fusion of the two religions, paganism and Christianity, has taken place resulting in a form of polytheism. At the head of the Pantheon stands the Dios of the Spaniards, who has become the Zeus of their deities. He is superior to the other gods or spirits, and they must obey his commands. Huitz-Hok, the gods of the mountains and plains, for instance, are very powerful, but they can do nothing if God is opposed. On the other hand, Dios is so remote that little atten is paid him. He has to look after the whole world, whereas the o Maya gods are essentially local. This attitude can be paralleled b the treatment meted out to Hunabku, the creator of the Mayas at the time of the conquest. He was considered to be too remote to be worth propitiating to any considerable extent. Below Dios are the

56

Morning Star and the Mam, known also as Huitz-Hok. With the latter have been fused the Chacs, the thunder gods, and finally the Ik, the wind gods. After these comes a mixed assortment of saints of the Christian church, the Virgin Mary, St. Anthony, St. Louis, etc., and minor Maya deities such as U, the moon, Kin, the sun, Ha, the water, Kuh, guardian of milpas, Che, the forest spirit, and the Cuchcaan, the holders up of the heavens. Finally there are the purely passive spirits of vegetation such as the spirit of corn, cacao, etc.

The Mams are the most important deities in the Maya Pantheon, although inferior in rank to God and the Morning Star. The name *Mam* is a generic term meaning grandfather, common to almost every dialect of the group of Mayance languages. The Mams are innumerable. However there are four of prime importance, who are associated with the four directions of the world and the four colors. Of these four one stands out in importance—the White Mam, who is ruler of all others. The Maya conceives the Mam as one single individual or four or as innumerable. In fact his conception of the Mams is not unlike that of an orthodox Christian in regard to the Trinity.

The Mams are also known among the Kekchi as Tzultacaj, and among the Mayas as Huitz-Hok. The term in both languages means the same, "Mountain-valley." The Tzultacaj have been treated at some length by Sapper (1897, p. 267) and Dieseldorff and mentioned in brief by Maudslay (p. 168) and other writers.

The Chuj, too, according to verbal information supplied by Oliver Le Farge, have a Mountain-valley deity, Witz-Ailik, the word meaning again "Mountain-valley." Possibly too, the Tzeltal may be added to this group. In all probability many of the highland tribes will eventually be found to have the same religious concepts. Unfortunately there is a great paucity of ethnological studies of Maya tribes and therefore comparative material is not at present available.

However, mountain worship was of very great importance among all branches of the Mayas. The single possible exception is supplied by Yucatan for the simple reason that in Yucatan there are no mountains. However, Cogolludo (Book IV, chap. 6) speaks of a hill outside Merida, which was worshiped.

The Mams are gods of the mountains, of the plains, of the underground, of thunder and lightning, and, by extension, of the rain. They are, too, gods of hunting and fishing and agriculture, although in this branch they are not the sole patrons. Hunting, fishing and agriculture are under the special protection of Venus as Morning Star, who has delegated his authority to the Mams who are his

servants (p. 125). The special interest of the Mams in agriculture is
well brought out by legends such as those on page 142.

Their essentially benevolent attitude toward man is recognized by
the Indians and emphasized again and again in the legends. Only
when they are not accorded their due share of incense and prayer are
they hostile (p. 141). Although the chief Mam is said to be very old
physically, others are not necessarily so. I believe the word Mam,
grandfather, conveys the idea of their having been in existence before the creation of the world and of being creator gods. This is
borne out by their being addressed as grandfather and grandmother,
a title given to the creator gods of the Quiche, the Aztecs, and
numerous other American Indian tribes. At least they are credited
with the introduction of agriculture (p. 135), and the teaching of it.
They first gave animals to the world (p. 145) and fish to man (p. 144).
Furthermore they are thunder and lightning gods (p. 134), who
throughout the new world are associated with agriculture.

They are of both sexes, although primarily looked upon as male.
The Female Mams are called *tšitš*, which means grandmother. I
suspect that the Maya in a hazy way consider them to be dual both in
nature and sex. Their duality in nature is shown by the manner in
which they give rain. Some rains are beneficial, others, at other times,
do considerable harm. The winds, which they probably control,
bring the rains but they may also blow down the young plants. This
applies too to Mexico. For example, the dual nature of Mexican gods
is depicted in the Codex Borgia (p. 56), where Quetzalcoatl and the
death god sit back to back. In the same manner they are dual in sex.
Itzam, one of the four great Mams, is one moment considered male,
at the next female. Similarly duality is shown over and over again
in Mexican mythology. Centeotl, the Totonac maize deity, is described as both male and female.

The Mams are said to reside in the middle of the hills, but at
the same time they are everywhere. As patrons of agriculture they
are the recipients of the prayers given on pages 45 and 50, when the
milpas are cleared and sown. They are also invoked to cure sickness
and at burials.

Nothing is known of the appearance of the Mams or their clothing
save references to the fact that the chief Mam wears sandals of moleskin and has the carapace of an armadillo as his seat (p. 142).

The Kekchis of the Toledo district have brought with them from
the Alta Vera Paz their local names for the four chief Mams, which
are at the same time mountains in that region. The chief Mam is

Yaluk. He is white and associated with the West. The second Mam is called Coha. He is the lord of the seas and associated with the South. Itzam is the ruler of the warm country and rules over the East. Xucaneb is the lord of the cold weather and the North. These last three are associated with the colors yellow, red and black, but it is not now clear which Mam is associated with which color. However it is interesting to note that the same association of white with the West prevailed in Yucatan at the time of the conquest. They stand at the four corners of the earth, and always shake themselves in June thereby causing the rain.

Kitzan or Itzam is claimed to be both male and female. As a woman she is said to be the wife of Coha (although Dieseldorff states that she is the wife of Xucaneb who in turn he says is the chief Mam). It is said that formerly she died every seven years and with her died all creation, coming to life again after a short interval. One would not naturally expect a mountain god to be associated with the sky, but Itzam according to one informant once ruled the sky. In connection with this it is interesting to note that the Yucatecan sky god was named Itzamna. Furthermore the death and return to life every seven years is reminiscent of the somewhat obscure reference in the legend of Venus, the Sun, and the Moon (p. 119) to previous suns that lasted seven years.

Dieseldorff devotes nearly the whole of his book "Kunst und Religion der Mayavölker" to the Mams and Tzultacaj. He endeavors to show that they are distinct deities. His theories may be summarized briefly as follows:

The Kekchis possess two principal deities, Tzultacaj and the Mam, who are always in opposition to each other. The Tzultacaj are benevolent. They are personifications of maize and consequently patrons of agriculture, protecting the young crops from the animals. They are young and they are the surface of the world. They play with the lightning and rule over the first 360 days of the year. The hot springs are considered female Tzultacaj. The Mam on the other hand is malevolent. He destroys the maize crops and causes famine. Consequently he is very much feared and his name must not be pronounced out loud. The rumblings to be heard below the earth at the beginning of the rainy season are caused by the Mam, who, being tied under the ground, is awakened by the coming and going of the people, and turns in his bed. He likes to eat people and rules over the five unlucky days at the end of the year.

From this brief account it will be seen at once that there are wide differences between the theory set forth above that the Mam and

Tzultacaj are distinct and biologically opposed and that which my informants stated emphatically time after time that the Tzultacaj and the Mam were one and the same.

The possible explanation of this divergence may be found in the fact that the Kekchis of the Toledo District are for the most part immigrants from, or sons of immigrants from, Cajabon and the neighboring villages. Now these towns, though now Kekchi speaking, are by race to a considerable extent Chol, and it is possible that different Chol beliefs have survived here, making Tzultacaj and Mam one and the same, whereas at Coban the beliefs given by Dieseldorff are held.

Personally I do not believe that the Mam of the Kekchis and the San Antonio Mayas has any connection with the Mam who ruled over the last five days of the year. Cogolludo (Book IV, chap. 8), in describing these, writes, "They had a piece of wood, which they dressed like those figures of boys made of straw that are used in bullfights and placed on a stool on a mat. They gave him food and gifts during the feast known as Vayeyab. When the feast was finished they undressed the idol and threw the piece of wood on the ground without troubling to reverence it any more. And they called it Mam, grandfather, whilst the offering and feast lasted."

From this one gets the impression that here we are treating of a ceremony that symbolizes the passing of the old year and the beginning of the new, just as we in the twentieth century represent the old year as a doddering old man and the new year as a young child. In the same way the Mayas symbolized the last five days of their year as Mam. If the Mam of the old year was the same as the Mam of the mountains, surely he would not be treated with the disrespect shown Mam at the close of the old year.

Sapper describes the Tzultacaj as living in a hammock of serpents (*Crotalus homdus*). He is lord of agriculture, water and fever, and punishes people by the stings of serpents for their sins. He is the lord of the lightning. The thunder is the noise he makes when he strikes a tree with his stone axe. Floods are the signs of the feast he holds in the bowels of the earth. He is often worshiped in caves (Sapper, 1897, p. 267).

This description, I believe, demonstrates what I have tried to point out above; namely, that the Tzultacajs and the Mams are one and the same. For Sapper emphasizes the bad side of the Tzultacaj whereas according to Dieseldorff Tzultacaj is benevolent, although at the same time he states that the Tzultacajs are lords of fevers and

are much feared in their guise of hot springs. Further, Sapper writes
that the Tzultacaj live in the bowels of the earth and cause the
floods. According to Dieseldorff, it is the Mam who live below the
ground and cause the floods. Sapper obtained his information from
Coban Kekchis, which would indicate that the difference between the
religious concepts of the Kekchis and Mayas of San Antonio and
those of the Kekchis of Coban is not due to the Chol blood and tradi-
tions of the former, but to Dieseldorff having misunderstood the
beliefs of the latter.

The question next arises as to whether the San Antonio concept of
Mam is a recent borrowing from the Kekchis or an earlier borrowing
from the Chol people. Unfortunately, no opportunity presented itself
of visiting Santo Toribio or Dolores where there has been no Kekchi
influence. If the Mayas of these two villages, who belong to the same
(Mopan?) Maya stock, are found to share this belief in the Mams, it
would be fairly strong evidence that the cult antedates the arrival of
the Kekchi immigrants, and is in all probability due to an earlier
Chol cultural expression. The Chol certainly possessed mountain
gods, as Remesal (Vol. II, chap. 19) writes that they drew blood to
the woods, mountains, and rivers. San Luis was visited, but this
town, where the Mam cult is as strong as in San Antonio, has also
come under Kekchi influence, though to a much lesser extent.

That there were two cults of Mam, one followed by the Kekchis,
and the other possibly by the now submerged Chol, is suggested by
the two diametrically opposed sexual practices observed in connection with the worship of Mam before the sowing of the corn (see
page 50). Dieseldorff (1928-29, Vol. V, p. 332) notes that the practice of cohabiting before sowing is observed in Chahal, whereas
around Coban abstention is maintained. Now Chahal is right in the
center of the old Chol territory, and these practices may well have
formed part of a Chol cult of the Mams, whereas in the Kekchi
worship abstention would have been observed.

As a final complication we have the identification of the Chacs
with the Mams. The Chacs among both the ancient and modern
Mayas were lords of thunder and lightning and the rains. By extension they are lords of the milpas. Again there is a chief Chac among
four principal ones, who are associated with the four corners of the
world and the four world colors. In addition to this there are innumerable minor Chacs. They are also said to be of great size.
They, like the Tzultacajs, carry stone axes; when lightning strikes
a tree, the Chacs are said to have cut it with their stone axes. The

Chacs live on the hill tops, and are also associated with the winds. By extension they were probably once gods of fevers, as natural fever is invariably attributed to bad winds. It is obvious that the Chacs are the lowland Maya equivalent of the Mountain-valley gods of the highland tribes.

The Mayas of San Antonio recognize the Chacs and the Mams as being one and the same, but the blending of the two sets of deities is not complete; two or three of the legends that deal with the Chacs can be attributed without hesitation to the Maya culture. The association of frogs with the Chacs, as, for example, in the Cha Chac ceremony of northern British Honduras and Yucatan or in the pleasing legend given on page 149, is not known to have an equivalent among the Highland tribes, although this is probably due to lack of ethnological information, as the connection existed in Mexico in the case of the Tlalocs.

The Mams as gods of pestilence were formerly honored in San Antonio by a special feast. It has now been discontinued in the village, but in some of the San Antonio alquilos still survives. No one seems to remember with certainty the date of this ceremony, but the general consensus of opinion favors May or June. The feast was known as Tzen Huitz (ɔen wiɔ), the feeding of Huitz, and was essentially a feast made by the old women to guard the community from sickness and wild beasts. The old women gathered in the Cabildo (the town hall) at midday and prepared turkeys and *atoles* made of maize and honey. At the same time four rough shelters were erected at the outskirts of the town, one to the north, one to the west, one to the south, and one to the east. In the evening the old women formed a procession, burning copal, and visited the four shelters where, at each in turn, one quarter of the turkeys and *atoles* was placed on a table or the bark of a tree. The old women then proceeded to the church where they spent the night in prayer and vigil. At midnight they came out of the church and kneeling down outside, prayed to Huitz for their protection as they burnt copal.

Meanwhile the Mams were supposed to visit the shelter and spiritually regale themselves with the offering. In the morning the old women repaired once more to the shelters, and gathering up the offerings returned to the village, where they had a feast of the material food that remained after its spiritual content had nourished the Mams. No young girl was allowed to be present at these ceremonies, as it was believed that should she partake of the feast death would soon overtake her. A few special men were allowed to take part in the feeding of Huitz, probably those of political and religious importance —councillors and witch-doctors. This ceremony was also practised at San Luis, the original home of the people of San Antonio. The Indians of the Toledo District possess no idols of Mam, or, for that matter, any other of the old deities, nevertheless many consider the little saints of the Catholic churches that are found in many of the houses to be Mams. On one occasion when I asked the owner of a house why he had no image of a Mam, he replied, pointing at a statuette of Saint Joseph, "But I have, there he is." The Mams in addition to the prayers in connection with the milpas, hunting, fishing, and sickness receive prayers on the completion of a new house or pigstye.

The Morning Star is a deity who ranks next to the Christian God in power, but in importance is below the Mams, and might be described as sharing second place in the amount of attention paid to him with the Christian God. He is known as Santo Xulab (šulab, star) or Noh Ich or Nohoch Ich (Noh or nohotš, great; Itš, eye or face). In connection with the latter name it is interesting to recall that the Aztecs used to depict a star as an eye, and this practice may have been introduced into Yucatan in late times. Dr. Spinden (1913, p. 209) illustrates a conventionalized eye from Chichen Itza, which he believes may very well have represented a star.

Xulab is the patron of agriculture, hunting, and fishing, particularly the last two. As already explained he has delegated his authority to the Mams as brought out in the legend of the Sun, the Moon, and Venus (p. 125). This practice of offering first to Xulab at dawn, and later to the Mam is still maintained by the more orthodox of the Toledo Indians (pp. 88-89).

Just before dawn the deer and other inhabitants of the forest are astir in search of food and water, and this possibly accounts for the adoption of the Morning Star as a patron of hunting, for the Mayas say when Ah Nohoch Ich rises his children rise too. Xulab is considered to be bearded and very ugly, and this accords with the depiction of his Mexican counterpart, Quetzalcoatl.

The belief that the Morning Star is the real patron of agriculture, hunting and fishing, but has delegated his power to the Mams, is probably the result of an attempt made by the priest astronomers to substitute their pet deity, Venus, for the Mams. The attempt to suborn the soil-loving peasants from their earth gods failed, and the result was the present compromise. In all probability the Mam cult dates back to "archaic times," whereas Venus worship would not have been introduced until the Venus calendar was in full swing.

The modern Mayas no longer distinguish Venus from the other planets, and the worship is accorded whichever planet happens to be the Morning Star. However, when more than one planet is visible in the eastern sky before dawn Venus is recognized by its greater size. No attention is paid to the evening star, nor is Venus recognized as Evening Star. The astronomical knowledge of the Maya of the old Empire times has been entirely lost. For example in the legend of the Sun, the Moon, and Venus (p. 138), the youngest brother is believed to have become one of the planets, but my informants could only say that he was not the Morning Star, and after some hesitation suggested that he became the Evening Star. One of them, Cecilio Cal, a particularly intelligent and well-educated San Antonio Maya, said that he thought he had become Jupiter, but cross-examination revealed that he was unable to distinguish Jupiter from any of the other planets, but by naming it solely tried to show that another planet other than Venus was indicated.

The worship of the moon (U) in San Antonio would appear to have been introduced by the Kekchi immigrants in recent years. From the Mayas she is the recipient of scant attention, although the Kekchis consider her a deity of some importance, and worship her under the name of Po. They do not consider the moon to be the patroness of anything in particular, but invoke her, apparently more or less as an afterthought, on any occasion. The passing generation of Kekchis used to burn copal to the new and full moon. When the moon is new, the flesh of all animals is believed to be tender. The people of San Antonio say that there is a rabbit seated in the moon. This belief they share with the Aztecs. It is also stated that there is a woman in the moon.

Kin (*Qin*), the sun, is of scant importance. He is rather dreaded, and is never addressed in prayers. It is believed that were he asked to shine down with more force upon the earth, he would comply, but to such an extent that the crops would be burnt up by his fierce rays. There is seldom any need for more sunshine, although at times there may be too much rain.

In the Corozal District of British Honduras the sun is invoked under the name of Kankin (yellow sun) during the *Cha Chac* or rain-making ceremonies. The climate of Yucatan is drier than that of the Toledo District, and drought is more frequent. At first it would seem strange to invoke the sun during a rain-making ceremony, but the sun's name is casually brought in with SS. Isidro and Lorenzo, the wind gods, and the virgin of Guadaloupe (Gann, 1918,

p. 47). Among the Lacondone, too, the sun (*Qin*) is one of the lesser gods (Tozzer, 1907, p. 98).

Kuh (*Quh*) is associated in some unrecognized way with the milpa, but he is also invoked in the prayers of the hunters. Today he is little more than a name associated with Huitz-Hok on occasions. Among the Mayas of Yucatan the spirits of the milpas are known as Kuhs (*Quhob*). They are believed to live in the fifth heaven. The word *Kuh* is also used in Yucatan to express god in general, or temple or pyramid.

The Cuchcaan are four in number. They stand at the four corners of the world and hold up the heavens, their title, in fact, meaning "the holders up of the sky." They are associated with the four world colors, and correspond to the Yucatecan Bacab. They are accorded no worship, and play no part in the religious life of San Antonio.

Ha (water) is the water spirit both of rain and of water upon the face of the earth. However, Ha is looked upon as essentially a passive god with little actual power himself and more or less under the strict authority of the Chacs. He has authority over the fishes and crocodiles, and so we find him invoked when fishing parties take place (p. 91). His closest parallel is Ixim, the maize spirit; both have but little control over nature, and are at the mercy of more active deities.

Che (forest or wood) is the spirit of vegetation. He again is purely passive. He controls to a certain extent the wild game living in the forest, but his functions are largely usurped by Huitz-Hok, and Nohoch Ich. These spirits or deities bear the current names of the forces of nature they personify. With the destruction of the old priesthood with their knowledge of the calendar and the esoteric side of Maya religion, there perished all but the elemental quasi-deities connected intimately with the daily life of the Maya peasant. Nevertheless, in the survivals we have the vestiges of the religion of the layman in the days when the Maya yet ruled. Esoteric religious concepts such as that of Kukulcan have entirely disappeared among the Yucatecan, the Lacondone and the Maya of the Toledo District.

There are a considerable number of disembodied spirits who roam the forests on the outskirts of the villages. They are not so feared as are those of Yucatan by the Mayas of that state.

The Tabai or Xtabai (*štabai*) are the best known and are the most malevolent. They have human features, but no flesh. Their backs are covered with hard bony scales. They are very mischievous, and are always planning harm to humans, or causing humans to do evil. If they meet any one in the forest they catch him, upon which he usually falls down in a faint. Later he develops a terrible headache, after which madness gradually overcomes him until at last he dies. The Xtabai, who are feminine tabai, can assume any form. A widower of San Antonio is said to have gone out into the forest with his daughter. He was desperately in love with another girl, and as he walked along a Xtabai came towards him in the form of this girl. The man rushed up to the Xtabai and embraced it thinking it was the girl. As he touched the bony back of the Xtabai, he fell down vomiting. He was taken home, but not long after he went mad and eventually died. The young girl, his daughter, said that her father had rushed out and embraced a tree trunk. Xtabai among the Lacondones is a goddess who resides in the rocks of the forest. Among the Maya the name is also given to a class of demons of snake form who seize men and carry them to the underworld or hurl them into a cenote. They are sometimes female in form (see also Gordon, p. 104). For legends of the Xtabai see pages 156 et seq.

Chentun (*tšentun*) is a guardian of morals, as he only appears to those with evil intentions. He wears the bark of the Mahaywa tree, and is always extremely filthy. He will appear to any one who is contemplating evil either in the forest or in the deserted parts of a village. His first appearance is in the form of a warning, but if the person disregards the warning he may appear again and even squeeze the life out of his victim. His wife is known as Siwanahwa. She lures people into the forest and then kills them.

The Chel are the bad spirits of dead brujos. The souls of bad brujos cannot go to Meknal (the old Maya underworld) as the Kisin, ruler of the underworld, is afraid they will bewitch him. They can't go to heaven either as God won't have them there. Accordingly, they go and hang on the walls and roofs of the homes of the wind gods. They can't do them any harm as the winds are invisible. They are very repulsive to look at. When there is a strong wind they are loosened and fly away and do a lot of damage to houses and trees and milpas. Those that are recently dead have no rest. They are being blown about all the time, but a strong wind is required to move those who have been dead a long time as they have already paid for much of the evil they did when alive. They rest on trees and the trees fall down afterwards under their weight.

After a very heavy wind two men once went out to look for fallen trees with honey. Many trees had fallen. As they passed through a ravine, they heard a wailing coming from under a mass of fallen branches. They looked, but could see nothing. The voice said, "O friend! I am so unhappy here. I tell you you must do no evil. When I was living I used to practice black magic. Now see how terribly I suffer. Now I am just resting a while till another heavy wind whirls me up into the air again." The Chel was buried under the fallen branches.

Mahanamatz (*Mahanamaɔ*) is the name given to a gorilla-like mythical animal. This animal is also known as Sisimito, which appears to be a Spanish word. The termination, at least, is the Spanish diminutive. The Mahanamatz are slightly larger than men and have the same features except that they are extremely hairy. They live in rocky areas in the remotest parts of the forest, and stand upright. However, they are said to walk with their big toes turned backwards. The females are friendly, but the males hostile. If a male catches one he tears one open with his huge, shaggy paws. It is useless to shoot him, as the shot will not penetrate his thick coating of hair. The only hope of salvation lies in setting fire to him. When he approaches to tear one apart, one strikes a match and applies the flame to his hairy coat which will burn up like dry tinder. The Mahanamatz is mentioned in the legend of the Chac on page 147.

There exists among the Kekchi a curious belief in a monster that closely resembles the classical centaur. These monsters are said to be a cross between Germans and mares. In the Alta Vera Paz there are a considerable number of German coffee-planters, who are said to mistreat their Kekchi laborers, and this, or the fact that Guatemala entered the world war against Germany, may be the reason why the Germans are saddled with the paternity of these monsters. Possibly this belief in centaurs is not due to Spanish stories, but has its origin in the first garbled accounts of the Spanish cavalry, that must have spread like wildfire all through Central America within a few weeks of the first use of the horse in warfare in the new world. The centaurs are believed to reside only in the Alta Vera Paz, and apparently are quite harmless, and not gifted with any occult powers.

The souls of the dead are known as *pišan* eight days after death. They seldom or never trouble the living and scant attention is paid them.

Kisin is the god of the underworld, and earthquake deity among the Maya of Yucatan. Among the Mayas of the Toledo District he is little more than a name. He has become merged in the devil of the Christians and his name today is usually employed as a swear-word. Hell is known among the San Antonio Mayas as *Meknal*.

Beliefs in the next world among the Indians of the Toledo District are strictly Catholic. In San Antonio I could find no belief such as exists still in Yucatan in a series of heavens one above the others although this belief once existed among the Socotz Mayas (p. 173). Funeral customs are described on page 81.

The sorcerers are known as *pulia*. Throughout the area, even in the Maya-speaking village of San Antonio, they are Kekchis. The office of sorcerer is never the sole career of a man, as most of the work he performs is unpaid, and he cannot by any possible means maintain himself by the occasional trifling sum he may gain as a doctor. The sorcerers are not easily distinguishable. Some men are said to have a considerable knowledge of herbs and remedies, while others, on the border line, will, behind their backs, be referred to as sorcerers, although all they may know may be the ceremonies connected with curing the simplest fevers. No one openly acknowledges himself to be a sorcerer, but is referred to by others as such often with a slight suggestion that thereby he is perhaps outside the pale. The office of sorcerer is not necessarily heritable. Any one with an inclination that way can become one provided he can find some one willing to teach him and initiate him into the ritual.

Initiation as a brujo is obtained by a small payment to some one already initiated into the craft, usually a friend or relation of the initiate. The length of the initiation will depend upon the amount of knowledge the initiate wishes to acquire. The following description of an initiation was given me by an informant, who had been initiated into a few of the minor secrets of brujeria, and ranked as a very junior *pulia*. The description had been given him by his instructor, and is probably the traditional hokum, used to impress the initiate into the great knowledge of the instructor.

The instructor and the initiate retire to a hut in the bush for a month so that there may be no eavesdropping. During this period the initiate is taught by his master all the different prayers, and practices used in causing and curing sickness. At the end of that period the initiate is sent to meet Kisin. Kisin takes the form of a large snake called Ochcan (*otškan*), which is described as being very big, not poisonous and having a large shiny eye. When the initiate and the ochcan meet face to face, the latter rears up on his tail, and approaching the initiate till their faces are almost touching, puts his tongue in the initiate's mouth. In this manner he communicates the final mysteries of sorcery. This meeting usually takes place at or close to a nest of the leaf-cutting ants, as the ochcan is said to reside in these nests. Attention is called to the Socotz legend of an initiation ceremony to brujeria on page 109 where again the snake imparts the information by licking and then swallowing the initiate.

The duties of a sorcerer are fourfold. As a priest he dedicates new houses, and acts as leader in prayer where a number are seeking divine aid. For example, he will recite the prayers on a hunting or fishing expedition. As a priest-sorcerer he will cure sickness. As a diviner he will discover who has caused sickness. Finally as a pure sorcerer he will practise black magic and divination. When a new house is built it must be consecrated before it can be inhabited. During my first stay in San Antonio I occupied a brand new hut that had just been completed. After I had been there ten days or so, the owner, who lived outside the village in the alquilos, arrived one day and announced that that evening the house would be consecrated. To carry out the consecration he chose a man living next door, a Kekchi, who had a reputation for being a sorcerer on a small scale, but was not of first rank. About 5:00 P.M. the whole of the family arrived from the alquilo. The men, the father and two sons, took possession of the new hut, while the women, the mother and young daughter, together with a younger son went to the house of the sorcerer next door. From that time till midnight the owner of the hut, the sons, the sorcerer and I wiled away the time in conversation and listening to my phonograph. A number of other men dropped in for an hour or so. At one time there were perhaps fifteen in the hut, but gradually the others left and by 10:30 P.M. there were only the five of us left. At midnight the wife of the quasi-sorcerer arrived armed with five white candles of European manufacture, a lighted censer of the type shown in Plate XVIII, Fig. 8, a lump of copal, and a small piece of raw meat that appeared to be chicken liver. The sorcerer lighting the candles placed one on top of the beam at each corner post and one in the center of the middle beam. This was the only occasion on which I found five directions observed. When this task was completed he placed the lump of copal (pom) on top of the smouldering fire in the censer, and as soon as the incense ascended he passed round the hut censing the six main posts, swinging the censer as he muttered prayers beneath his breath. After this he took the piece of meat and smeared it on each one of the corner posts in turn, again mumbling a prayer. After smearing the center of the middle beam he placed the piece of meat on top at the side of the lighted candle. When this was completed, he took a modern pail containing a very weak mixture of water and ground maize, and using a stick passed round the hut both inside and out asperging the walls and posts. Subsequently, his wife also censed the six main posts without, however, praying, and the ceremony was then completed.

I was unable to get any information on the prayers recited, but was informed they were directed to Dios and the Huitz-Hok. The food was for the consumption of the spirit of the posts and the Huitz-Hok. The hut was then vacated for two hours, in order, I was told, that the spirit of the wood and the Huitz-Hok might be able to take their spiritual sustenance undisturbed. We adjourned to the sorcerer's house next door, where the women had been engaged in preparing a meal of chicken, rice, chili, tortillas, and cacao mixed with ground corn and black pepper. After the meal which was eaten without ceremony, the men in one group, the women in another, we continued talking till about 2:30 A.M. We then returned to the new hut, where a desultory conversation was kept up till dawn, when the candles were blown out and the ceremony was concluded.

The same ritual is employed when a new hen-house or pigstye has to be consecrated. It is believed that failure to make the offerings of food and incense and to maintain a sleepless vigil until dawn would result in sickness and ill-luck. Consecration of new houses was known to the Maya prior to the Conquest, as Cogolludo (Book IV, chap. 4) states, "Whenever they make new houses, which is every ten or twelve years, they won't enter or live in them until an old sorcerer comes from a distance of one, two, or three leagues to bless them with his silly charms." Ponce (p. 9) gives a description of a house-consecration ceremony from Mexico, which is not dissimilar.

All cases of illness among the Mayas are not attributed to black magic, although undoubtedly a very large number are. The son of the quasi-sorcerer mentioned, a boy of about eleven years, had been suffering to a considerable extent from a number of deep suppurating sores that had at one time covered nearly all his body. A spell in the hospital at Punta Gorda had improved his condition vastly, but one leg was still badly wasted away by two large open sores one just above and the other below the knee, with the result that he was unable to walk. Another sorcerer had been giving him a course of treatment, and I had the luck to attend one of the sessions.

The session commenced, as on all such occasions, at sundown. There were present the sorcerer, the father of the boy, a friend and myself. In the back room the mother was busy in preparing the midnight supper. A younger brother of the patient spent his time flitting from one room to another. No move was made until midnight. Shortly after twelve o'clock the boy's father fetched a censer, a candle, some water and some small fish in a half calabash. The fish, which had been caught during the day by the younger brother, were a kind of small minnow and were still alive. The candle was lighted and passed to the patient, who held it in his left hand. The sorcerer then proceeded to hold lightly for perhaps half a minute the boy's ankles, then his legs just below the knees, then above the knees, and subsequently his wrists and temples, the while he muttered in a very low voice what were probably prayers. Next he touched these same places and the boy's chest lightly, making a sign which was probably the sign of the cross. When this was concluded, placing copal in the censer, he put it directly below the hammock in which the young patient was lying. A little water was then sprinkled on the bad leg, and subsequently two of the fish were placed on the leg, one above the other, below the sores. They were held there for some minutes by the sorcerer, who all the time kept up his mumbled prayers or incantations. Next he appeared to replace the fishes with some pieces of the hot, charred wood from the censer, but the patient did not wince nor show any evidence of pain, nor subsequently was there any sign of burning at the spots where the charcoal-like substance was applied. After this the sorcerer gathered together the fishes, the calabash of water, the calabash containing the small fish, and the censer, and left the hut. At the end of five minutes he returned with the utensils empty. I was informed that he had gone to the outskirts of the village where he had thrown away the contents. This concluded the ceremony. Bishop Landa describes a ceremony called driving out the evil spirits which was practised in Yucatan in pre-Columbian days. At the conclusion of the ceremony, the censer and the rope that had been used by the Chacs, together with some wine, was given to a man to take out of the town. The bearer was forbidden to drink or look behind at the load he was carrying. Thus they said the devil was cast out (Landa, chap. 30). After the sorcerer had returned in our case of throwing out the evil, we adjourned to the usual meal of chicken, rice, and chili, washed down with cacao mixed with ground corn and black pepper. The vigil was continued until dawn, when all were free to sleep.

In only one case did I find a sorcerer willing to impart to an outsider the prayers or incantations they practised when curing a sick person. However, I was informed the prayers were addressed to Huitz-Hok. In the case described above no drink was taken by the sorcerer. As a rule, however, sorcerers refuse to act unless they have drunk a considerable quantity of rum. This drinking of rum is entirely ceremonial, and is no doubt a survival of the ceremonial drinking of pre-conquest days. The payment for the Chachac ceremony of Yucatan is $1.50 (Mexican), two chickens, two loaves and two bottles of anise rum. A frequent method of curing illness at San Antonio is to pass tiny tortillas made of the blood of a hen, maize, and copal, seven or nine in number, over and under the body of the sick man (cf. the curing of the man in the legend of Chac, p. 149). These tortillas are kept for three days, at the end of which period the sorcerer takes them far out into the forest and, lighting copal, either burns them or throws them away. The tortillas are said to draw the evil out of the sick man's body.

Sometimes a fox or a carrion crow or some other animal is seen near the spot where the tortillas are thrown away. Any animal or bird thus seen is said to represent the spirit of the sickness come to receive it back. Another method of curing sickness is somewhat similar. Seven tiny tortillas are made of maize mixed with blood, ground cacao and copal. If the patient is a man the blood is from a hen. If the patient is a woman a rooster's blood is employed. These tortillas are placed on the patient's body as follows: one each on the forehead, heart, the small of the back, each wrist, and each ankle. After remaining there some time they are carried off and thrown away in the forest.

Similarly, a child can be cured by passing lighted copal nine times under and over the hammock in which it lies. Another method of curing a sick person is to make a little figure of black beeswax in the shape of the sick person. This figure is given the name of the sick person and addressed in these words: "You, so and so, are going to get well."

An informant treated a child with fever at Uaxactun on payment of two dollars with the following prayer:

In watah	*in mahantik*	*a suhuyil*	*in peɔe*	*sui venas,*
I have stood up	to beg the loan of	your virginity	to press	the (flesh) around the pulse,

sui šitš,	*su sui*	*ot*	*fulano de tal,*	*wiqaletš*
the (flesh) around the vein below the elbow,	the flesh next to	the skin	of so and so,	you wind

išpakil.   *Tubak a*   *talel?*   *Wa tumen*   *u yiqaletš*   *ha*
(that is) trembling.   Whence do you   come?   Perhaps   his wind you are   the water

Wa tumen   *u yiqaletš*   *luum?*   *Wa tumen*   *ti ku*
perhaps   his wind you are   the earth?   Perhaps

Kuštahetš   *wa tumen.*   *Bel in kah*   *in*   *wutš*
I have found you   perhaps.   I am going   to   unlock

u yabehil   *u yok,*   *u yabehil*   *u puksiqal.*   *In hoksikal*
the key of   his foot,   the key of   his heart.   I am plucking out

wiqal   *špaqilob.*   *Bolonten*   *kin*   *oš*   *t'antik,*   *Santas animas,*
the wind of   the sicknesses.   Nine times   may I   thrice   call you,   holy spirits,

purgatorio,   *Santa Marta,*   *Santa Lucia,*   *Señora de Carmen.*
purgatory,   St. Martha,   St. Lucy,   Our Lady of Carmen.

Iɔlak hokol   *t'*   *u*   *yabehil*   *u yok.*   *Iɔlak*
Come out   from   his   the key   of his foot.

iɔlak   *kah hokok*   *t'*   *u*   *yabehil*   *u puksiqal.*   *He,*
Come out   from   his   the key of   his heart.   You there,

yiqaletš   *špaqilob*   *wa tumen*   *excellente*   *yaniletš.*
you wind   of the sicknesses   perhaps   excellent one   you exist.

Ka oš walahen   *in hokseš.*   *Hokineš*   *Hokineš*   *Amen.*
Three times I stand   to pluck you out.   Come out   Come out   Amen.

FREE TRANSLATION

I am standing up before you to beg your saintly aid as I hold so and so's pulse, his veins, and his flesh. You evil winds that cause him to tremble, whence do you come? Perhaps it is you, the wind that blows over the water. Perhaps it is you, the wind that comes over the earth. I have found you out. From where you lie hid in the patient's foot, or in his heart I am going to drag you out, you evil winds of sickness. Thrice nine times I call upon you in the name of the holy spirits, purgatory, St. Martha, St. Lucy, Our Lady of Carmen. Come out from where you lie hid in his foot, or in his heart, come out, you evil wind. I know you are there. Three times I stand to cast you forth. Come out. Come out.

The word *yabehil* is the Spanish word *llave*. This prayer reveals the attitude of the Maya toward illness. It is caused either by an enemy or the evil winds. The Mayas themselves are somewhat vague as to these winds. Some say they are spirits, or rather winds with a mentality capable of thought, who wander over the face of the land in search of someone into whose body they can enter. Others say they are incapable of action by themselves, but are sent into a man's body either by the *Tabai* (p. 66) or by a sorcerer. They are quite unconnected with the four big winds (*iq*) from whom they are distinguished by being called *iqal*. Some references to the evil winds will be found in the section dealing with Socotz, and also in the legend entitled "The Source of Sickness in Socotz" (p. 166).

Blood-letting was formerly practised. A piece of pointed glass was fixed onto a short stick with a piece of wax. In the case of a headache this was placed against the patient's temple, and the end of the stick was given a flip with the finger to drive the glass into the flesh. Blood-letting in the arms and other parts of the body was also practised. This was to let the bad blood out.

No one will openly admit the crime of practising black magic, but most cases of illness are attributed to its practice. A favorite method of harming an enemy is to get a sorcerer to "send" a rat or, more frequently, a toad with a red head into the former's stomach. Unless quickly treated with the correct counter-measures this will infallibly cause your enemy's rapid decease. A rather amusing case of black magic came up during the course of my stay at San Antonio. The daughter of the alcalde had recently gone mad, and her mother-in-law had been taken ill at the same time. The alcalde for some time previously had been trying to induce his son-in-law to take up his residence with him but without success. It was soon noised abroad that the alcalde had had his daughter and mother-in-law bewitched either out of spite or to induce his son-in-law to fall in with his wishes. A good informant of mine, a certain Francisco Assi, a sorcerer, and so of course a Kekchi, divined that the sending had been arranged by a certain old woman at the instigation of the alcalde. It was claimed that the old woman had received a payment of eight dollars to cast the spell. Such a scandal arose that the alcalde found himself called on to clear himself. He summoned the court and the case was held, the alcalde doubling in the roles of prisoner and judge. He found himself not guilty, but fined the wretched Francisco Assi $5.75.

That almost world-wide method of making an image of the enemy and then maltreating it is employed in the Toledo District. An image of the man that it is desired to harm is made in wax, and a cord smeared in chili and lime is tied tightly round it so as to pass over the heart. Just as the image is constricted by the cord, so the victim will suffer, the chili and lime causing inflammation. The image is often slipped into the house of the victim. A more interesting variation of this is also employed. A waxen figure is again made. In its left hand are placed any of the nail-parings or hair of the victim that can be procured. In its right hand is placed a stone. The sorcerer then maintains a vigil of five nights. The following day he places the wax figure on top of the door lintel of the victim's house. At the end of three more days the spell begins to work. In the course of the night the wax figure throws the stone he holds in his hand at the victim. Every night for a month he will continue to throw a stone a night. Gradually the victim grows ill, as he is struck night after night, until finally he dies at the end of the month. Clay images are used in Yucatan to harm one's enemy. Chili is rubbed on, and they are buried in the doorway of the victim's hut. (Tozzer, 1907, p. 159; see also "The Source of Sickness in Socotz," p. 166.) A black wax candle given the name of your enemy and allowed to burn upside down is also equally efficacious.

Divination is practised to a limited extent. The sorcerers claim to be able to find out who has been casting a spell by feeling the pulse and examining the veins of the victim. I found no one willing to speak freely on this subject, but I gather the divination which is accompanied by mumbled prayers partially points to the sender, but that divine inspiration largely supplements the evidence supplied by the veins and pulse. In the story about the alcalde given above Francisco Assi claimed to have discovered the identity of the sender solely by the veins and pulse of the mad daughter-in-law.

Another form of divination, not however confined entirely to the sorcerers, is known as Xoc Kin (šok qin). This term means the reading of or counting of the days, and is used to prophesy the kind of weather that will be met with during the year. The Xoc Kin takes place at the beginning of the year, embracing the whole of January. The first twelve days of January are taken to represent the months. If for example January 1 is a rainy day that is a sign that January will be a wet month. Similarly January 2, if a dry day, indicates that February will be a dry month. So the days of January are counted off till January 12 is reached. This day represents the month December. From January 13 to 24 the count is renewed, but this time backward. January 13 represents the month of December again, January 14, November, January 15, October, and so back through the months until January 24 again represents January. Then the different prophecies are compared and checked off one against the other. The days from January 25 to January 30 are then used to help settle any outstanding differences. As these days are only six in number, they are divided into two halves, the first half of the day until midday (tšunqin) representing one month, the other half of the day from midday to sunset representing another month. In this way January 25 until midday prophesies the weather in January, January 25, midday to sunset, the weather in February, and so on until January 30 is reached. The morning of this day shows the weather for November, and the afternoon indicates the weather for December. As a final check the twelve hours of daylight on January 31 are counted off, one for each month. It would appear that the Xoc Kin is in all probability a survival from the old Maya calendar, where probably the first *uinal*, or possibly lunar month, was employed as the basis for the divination during the coming *haab*. A similar divination is practised in the Valley of Mexico (Gamio, Vol. II, p. 405). An experimental Xoc Kin is given on page 77.

1st Count January	Weather	2nd Count January	Weather	3rd Count January	Weather	4th Count Jan. 31	Weather	Month	Will be
1	Wet	24	Showers	25 Morning	Dry	6 A.M.	....	January	Wet
2	Wet	23	Showers	25 Evening	Dry	7 A.M.	Wet	February	Wet
3	Showers	22	Showers	26 Morning	Fine	8 A.M.	Showers	March	Showers
4	Fine	21	Fine	26 Evening	....	9 A.M.	....	April	Dry
5	Fine	20	Showers	27 Morning	Showers	10 A.M.	Fine	May	Fine
6	Fine	19	Wet	27 Evening	Fine	11 A.M.	Showers	June	Showers
7	Wet	18	Showers	28 Morning	Wet	12 A.M.	Rain	July	Showers
8	Wet	17	Dry	28 Evening	Fine	1 P.M.	....	August	Wet
9	Showers	16	Wet	29 Morning	Showers	2 P.M.	Wet	September	Wet
10	Fine	15	Showers	29 Evening	Showers	3 P.M.	Showers	October	Showers
11	Fine	14	Fine	30 Morning	....	4 P.M.	....	November	Fine
12	Wet	13	Showers	30 Evening	Dry	5 P.M.	Wet	December	Wet

IV. SOCIAL LIFE AT SAN ANTONIO

Each of the important Indian villages of the Toledo District has its alcalde (mayor). A new alcalde is elected each January. The men of the village are summoned to the cabildo (the town hall), usually the most pretentious hut in the village. Names of candidates are proposed by the older men, and the voting is conducted by a show of hands. Any man or boy over the age of about seventeen is free to vote. As a rule there is no contest, only one name being proposed. The alcalde is paid a salary of four dollars a month. He is responsible for the conduct of the village. He must furnish men for clearing the trails or any other task that the district magistrate may detail. Finally he acts as local magistrate. All cases of crime or misconduct are brought before him. He has the power to impose a fine of not more than twenty-five dollars, and can imprison up to seven days. The prisoner has always a right of appeal to the district magistrate at Punta Gorda. All serious cases that cannot be dealt with adequately by the alcalde's range of punishment are also referred to Punta Gorda. The alcalde is aided in the discharge of his functions by a segundo-alcalde (vice-mayor) and eight policemen. The police are paid no salary, but are paid twenty-five cents for every arrest that leads to a conviction.

The daily life of a San Antonio Maya is really remarkably free from ceremony or religion. Almost all his religious devotion seems to be concentrated on his milpa. There appear to be no ceremonies of any kind connected with childbirth except that the placenta and umbilical cord are wrapped in leaves of *bihau* and taken away and buried. The couvade is not practised. Babies are kept at the breast for a long period. Bishop Landa (chap. 30) notes this too, stating that often the children are not weaned until they are three or four years old.

The *Hetz* ceremony (p. 110) is performed, but the four and three month periods are not observed. Children, after this ceremony, are invariably carried astride the hip. At a young age the children are set to work, feeding the pigs and chickens. By the time they are seven they are already carrying light loads of corn or other fruits from the milpa to the home in the usual Maya fashion; that is, in a net on the back, the greater part of the weight of which is supported by a piece of bark or liana passed across the forehead. It has been suggested that this method of carrying loads initiated so young in life may be to a slight extent responsible for the very pronounced brachycephaly of the modern Maya.

Nominally attendance at the school is compulsory, but in actual practice there is a good deal of truancy. The children obtain the day off to work in the milpa or to stay at home and mind the younger children while the parents are away in the milpa.

There are no puberty ceremonies of any description.

The men usually marry before the age of twenty. The girls are, as a rule, married before they reach their sixteenth birthday, but many boys of sixteen and girls of fourteen are already married. The age would in some cases be even lower were it not for the refusal of the church to marry anyone under fourteen. Sexual intercourse between the young men and the unmarried girls is common, but there is no organized prostitution. Often an illicit affair between an unmarried couple is followed by marriage, especially if a child is born or is expected. A young man who intends to marry a girl who is no longer immaculate is usually warned of her condition by the man responsible for her moral downfall. Courtship is almost non-existent.

The young man, who has decided that he would like to marry some particular girl, sends a representative to ask her parents for her hand with or without first consulting her. The representative, who is usually the boy's father or uncle or elder married brother, visits the girl's parents and says that the boy would like to marry their daughter. No reply is then given, but after a few days the boy and his representative visit the girl's parents again to receive the reply. Actually, they have been unofficially notified so as to give the boy time to prepare a feast in the event of acceptance. On arriving at the hut, the men are asked to sit down, and the father says that so far as he is concerned, there is no objection to the marriage. He then asks his wife whether she is agreeable. The reply being in the affirmative, he asks the girl whether she is willing to marry the boy. Whatever her private opinion of her suitor may be, she invariably replies that she is willing to marry him, her parents' decision being practically binding. Personally I had the experience of several cases where a boy and a girl were in love and had intended to marry, but another had applied for the girl's hand before her lover. The girl had to follow the custom of the village and obey her parents' decision that she should marry the other boy. However, in more than one case the first boy became her lover after her marriage.

On acceptance a feast is held to celebrate the betrothal. The suitor pays all the cost of this, including a hog, a gallon of rum, tortillas, and cocoa, and in addition gives the girl presents of clothing and hair-oil. Once he has been accepted as the girl's future husband, he must supply her with all her food and wood, bringing the supplies to the girl's hut. However, he continues to eat at his own house. For this reason betrothals are usually of short duration at San Antonio.

On the next occasion that the Catholic priest visits the village the couple is married. This, too, is the occasion for a feast to which all are invited. The boy again has to foot the bill. However, he does not make any present to the girl's parents. The cost of marriage is somewhat high. The two feasts will cost the boy about seven dollars apiece. In addition he has to pay the priest for the marriage, buy the girl clothes, and pay for the food and wood if not in actual cash at least in labor, which he might otherwise employ to more profitable use. Finally there is the cost of building a new hut and furnishing it with hammock, bed, pots, comal, etc.

Most couples set up a house of their own on marrying in the event of both parents being alive. If, however, only one parent of either the boy or the girl is living, and there are no other unmarried brothers or sisters, it is usual for the young couple to make its home with the parent.

There is no social organization or trace of totemism, and consequently any one is free to marry within the laws of the Catholic church; that, of course, means that first cousins may not marry. There is no objection to marrying a person of the same name, although in Yucatan in former days that was taboo. Marriage almost without exception is performed in the Catholic church. The priest is apt to raise objections to baptizing the children of couples who are living together without the church's sanction; and the parents, fearing for the eternal welfare of their children, almost invariably have the marriage solemnized in the church.

A number of relationship terms still survive (see also Breton):

MAN'S		WOMAN'S	
watan	wife	witšam	husband
mehen	son	wal	son
mam	grandson	mam	grandson
iš-tšupmehen	daughter	wal	daughter
tšitš	granddaughter	tšitš	granddaughter
tat	father	tat	father
na	mother	na	mother
mam	grandfather	mam	grandfather

tšitš	. . . . .	grandmother
na	. . . . .	maternal aunt
natšin	. . . . .	paternal aunt
tata	. . . . .	maternal uncle
tata	. . . . .	paternal uncle
sukun	. . . . .	elder brother
kik	. . . . .	elder sister
wiɔ'in	. . . .	younger brother
wiɔ'in	. . . .	younger sister
as above 4	. . . . .	cousin
as above 4	. .	cousin once removed
mehen	. . . . . .	nephew
ištšupmehen	. . . .	niece

tšitš	. . . . .	grandmother
na	. . . . .	maternal aunt
natšin	. . . . .	paternal aunt
tata	. . . . .	maternal uncle
tata	. . . . .	paternal uncle
sukun	. . . . .	elder brother
kik	. . . . .	elder sister
wiɔ'in	. . . .	younger brother
wiɔ'in	. . . .	younger sister
as above 4	. . . . .	cousin
as above 4	. .	cousin once removed
wal	. . . . . .	nephew
wal	. . . . . .	niece

Polygamy, of course, is never practised. Divorce is unknown, but desertion is common. Men fairly frequently take another woman, usually a widow, and abandon their wives. Cruelty is not uncommonly shown towards women, but never to children. Wives are beaten by a considerable number of their husbands. Man is certainly very much the head of the family. One young Maya of San Antonio was off to Punta Gorda to buy fifteen bottles of rum for the Easter festival. I asked him if his wife was going to get drunk as well, to which he replied that she didn't earn any of the money, so he wasn't going to spend any of it on buying rum for her. I tried to point out that she was doing her share by cooking his food and mending and washing his clothes, but he could not see that that entitled her to have any of the money he had earned spent on her amusement.

Bishop Landa (chap. 22) describes how at the big feasts of the Mayas, to which men alone were invited, drinking carousals were indulged in to a large extent, and the wives waited outside to help their drunken sottish husbands home. The same scene can be witnessed today in the Maya villages of the Toledo District at the big feasts at Christmas, Easter, and on other occasions, although today the women are present at the big dances and feasts, but usually in a retired position. They are always waiting until they can persuade their drunken, shouting husbands to go home, often dragging or half carrying them home.

The ceremonies connected with death and burial are simple. The corpse is buried as soon as possible, usually without any prayer. A coffin is seldom employed as it is believed that when the last trump sounds every one will rise from his grave as he is and will march to heaven. The Indians say that a man buried with a coffin will have to carry it all the way to heaven, and that would be very tiring. Until very recently the personal possessions of the dead man and food were buried with him, but this custom is gradually dying out. However, among many families it is still customary to throw away a little food at the end of the third day after death. To do this the relative or friend of the deceased proceeds a short way into the wood and throws the offering away. The food thus offered to the spirit of the dead man is the food which the man would normally eat plus possibly one or two foods of which the dead man happened to be particularly fond. This ceremony is repeated on the eighth day after death. The offering on the third day might have a Christian origin. According to another informant, on the occasion of a death one prayed to Huitz-Hok, the Mountain-valley god, and U, the moon. The ghost of the dead man is believed to stay on this earth until the eighth day when he goes to the other world. He may appear to people during these eight days, but no one I questioned had ever seen the ghost of a dead man, or even knew of any one who knew some one who had seen a ghost. Thirty or forty years ago people were often buried beneath the floor of their houses, and this custom, I was informed, is still practised by the Kekchi around San Pedro Carcha, Alta Vera Paz. It is believed that when a corpse is thus interred in the floor of the hut, the soul of the deceased will re-enter the body of the next child to be born in that or any other hut. This is, apparently, a Chol custom. Bishop Landa (chap. 33) states that the Mayas often buried their dead in or behind their houses. When this occurred the huts were often abandoned if the occupants were few in number. The dead are vaguely believed to return to this world on All Souls' Day. On that day candles are lit at dawn and at dusk, and are placed in the four corners of each house, and a little copal is burnt. There is no belief that the souls of the dead can enter the bodies of animals or take animal shape. In Colombia the dead are frequently buried in half canoes. This would appear to be a recent innovation based on expediency, as the Kekchi people, in their Alta Vera Paz homes, make little use of canoes owing to the lack of rivers.

Feasts held in celebration of the most important celebrations in the calendar of the Catholic church are frequent. There are about ten altogether in the course of the year. Of these the most important are: the New Year, St. Joseph, Easter, Holy Cross, St. Anthony (patron of the village), St. Louis (patron of their original home—San Luis), and Christmas.

These feasts are only religious celebrations to a very small degree. They serve primarily as an excuse for a communal bout of drinking. In a way these bouts are to a certain extent ceremonial, and a survival of the pre-conquest custom of honoring the gods with ceremonial drinking. This ceremonial drinking also survives in the curing of sickness as the sorcerer will seldom attempt to cure his patient until he has drunk a bottle or half bottle of rum, supplied to him by the patient.

The feasts are the occasion for a series of reunions. Everyone has procured an abundant supply of rum from Punta Gorda, and groups pass round the village, bottles in hands, to visit their friends, relations, and compadres. In the evening a big feast is held to which everyone in the village is invited. For each feast there is a guild consisting of nine, or in some cases, thirteen members. One guild will be responsible for the feast at Christmas. Another guild will have the feast for St. Joseph in its keeping. In this manner there are eight or nine guilds each with its feast for which it is responsible.

Membership in the guild is entirely honorary, and confined to married men. The chief member of the guild is known as *Nohoch Priosti*. The word *Nohotš* is Maya for big, but the word *priosti* would appear to be a corruption of a Spanish or Latin word. The other members of the guild are known as *ka ɔ'ik, oš ɔ'ik..........
bolon ɔ'ik*, which can be freely translated as second messenger, third messenger..........ninth messenger. The *Nohoch Priosti* holds his position for as many years as he wishes. He is directly responsible for the feast. On becoming *Nohoch Priosti* he will build a particularly large hut which will serve as his home, and at the same time as the place where the feast will be held. On him falls all the financial cost of the feast. This he can recuperate by charging for the rum he supplies at the feast, the profit going to the church, or he can decide to supply the rum free, thereby obtaining a great deal of popularity. The position of *Nohoch Priosti* is one of considerable honor, especially if the feasts he gives are free. He has under his orders the other members of the guild, the messengers, whose sole function is to carry out his orders and help with the arrangements for the feast. All the members of the guild, as stated above, must be married so that their wives may be available for the work of cooking the hog, making the tortillas, etc. Should the *Nohoch Priosti* decide to retire, his place is filled by the *ka ɔ'ik*, and every other member of the guild moves up one place. All the members of the guild invite some married man to become a member of the guild to fill the vacancy caused by the retirement of the *Nohoch Priosti*. The man is urged to join, and is told that it is his duty to the community to belong to one or more guilds. On entering the guild he becomes the ninth or thirteenth messenger according to the membership. A

man may, and in fact often does, belong to more than one guild. The guild of the Holy Cross feast has recently ceased to exist. The reason given is that the *Nohoch Priosti* died during his term of office.

Life is very placid in San Antonio, except when a feast is being celebrated. For this reason the feasts are very unpopular with the Catholic fathers, who are doing all in their power to suppress them. So far they have had little success. The previous District Magistrate at Punta Gorda also did what he could to put an end to the only remaining amusement of the village, but during 1928 he was transferred to another District, and his place taken by Mr. Alcoser, who speaks Maya, and is a real friend of the Maya.

Anyone who has been in close contact with the Maya cannot fail to like him, and in practically every case where the Maya is maligned the author is found to be someone who has never been in close personal contact with him. It would be hard to find a more libelous and unfair description of the Maya character than that given by Mendez. The Maya, when not contaminated by European influence, is extremely honest, and considers stealing a serious crime. During my visits to San Antonio the door of my hut was never locked, and the villagers used to stroll in and out as they wished. Nevertheless nothing was ever stolen, although there were many things in my possession, which they very much envied. It would be wrong to say that theft is entirely unknown; a few cases have been reported from time to time. The Maya is not very scrupulous in living up to his word, if by breaking it he causes someone else no actual financial loss. For instance, he will sign on as a laborer, and take an advance of salary. Later he will repent of his decision, and return the money advanced. Murder is not uncommon. The cause is almost invariably found to be jealousy over a woman. Cold-blooded murder is infrequent, murders being almost invariably committed when the murderer is under the influence of drink. Rape and incest are extremely uncommon, and the only case of homosexuality of which I heard involved only half-caste Mayas.

The Maya will lie fluently to save himself or his questioner trouble, but such lies as a rule are more in the nature of "white lies." He is very good tempered, cheerful, fond of a practical joke, or an obscene story, and by no means the morose silent Indian of the adventure stories. He is affectionate, and gives his friendship readily where he thinks it will be reciprocated. Love, in our sense of the word, undoubtedly exists between a large number of Maya married couples, probably as large a proportion of married couples as among Europeans. Maya parents treat their children with great indulgence, and, to the best of my knowledge, never thrash them. Personal quarrels are usually ventilated at the different feasts, where both parties, when drunk, seek each other out to continue a quarrel started months or even years ago. In this manner they will cherish some insult for a long period, until under the influence of drink they feel the urge to fight. Such fights are usually decided by bare fists, or rocks and kicks. Occasionally a machete will be used, but this is considered a serious matter, whereas the usual rough and tumble is looked upon as a necessary accompaniment of any feast, as long as no more damage than bleeding noses, cut lips, or black eyes results. Drunkenness is undoubtedly the most serious source of degradation, financial and physical, to the modern Maya. Drunkenness is deemed the natural condition of a man during any feast, and not in the slightest degree a cause for shame. A man, who although married has no children, is to a certain degree looked down upon by the rest of the community. Children are a very useful adjunct to every family in a Maya village, because of the help they can give in the milpa, and in the raising of hogs and fowls.

The list given below comprises practically all the surnames in use in San Antonio. In some cases the spelling is doubtful as several of the names are based on the spelling used by the Carib schoolmaster, who does not differentiate very carefully between Maya letters. Only two names appear to be definitely Kekchi—Rash and Tzir. None of the other names occur in any list of Kekchi surnames known to the writer. However, there is a strong possibility that some of them are of Chol origin. Cano mentions a Mopan chief of the name of Tezecum (Means, p. 98). This might well be an ancestor of the present day Tesecums of San Antonio. The surname Pop, which is very common in San Antonio, is held by people of Alta Vera Paz origin, though whether of Kekchi or Chol origin I do not know. The suggested meanings of the names were not given by their owners, but were obtained from a dictionary. However, many of them recognize the meanings of their surnames, as, for instance, in the case of Buul.

Assi	. . . .	*Hob*	. . . .
Bo	. . . .	*Hola*	. . . .
Bol	. . . .	*Ico*	. . . .
Bolon	. . . . . . nine	*Ixim*	. . . . . . maize
Buul	. . . . . . bean	*Kanche*	. . . . wooden seat
Cab	. . . . honey: earth	*Kukul*	. ripe fruit that is hard
Cal	. . . .	*O or Oh*	. . . .
Chal	. . . . . . resin	*Paquul*	. . . .
Chen	. . . . . . well	*Pop*	. . . . . . mat

Chiac (Chiaac)	turtle mouth(?)	Rash	green (Kekchi)
Ch'o	rat	Salam	half(?)
Chub	yellow cotton	Shoh	half rotted maize
Chun	base, bottom, trunk	Sib	wood-rot
Co	ocelot	Tek	manatee or dugong
Coh	crazy, tooth	Tesecum	
Coq	......	Tzac	a kind of small fish
Cum	jar	Tzip	......
Cus	little dog	Tzir	......
Ho	five	Yaxcal	......

There is considerable danger of inbreeding at present at San Antonio. As can be seen from the surnames, there are not many distinct families, and almost everyone can claim relationship with half the village. Inbreeding has to a certain extent been avoided by the introduction of fresh Kekchi blood. Unfortunately for the future of the people of San Antonio this small stream of immigration has dried up in recent years. I had hoped to have been instrumental in introducing new stock into San Antonio from Socotz. During the field season's work at the ruins of Tzimin kax, some of the unmarried workers considered marrying girls in Socotz, as they hoped thereby to avoid the heavier expense of a San Antonio marriage. Their hopes were dashed to the ground by the shortness of their stay in Socotz, as during the half day they were there it was not possible to woo and marry the maidens of Socotz, who are of a retiring disposition. There is one half-Carib in San Antonio, the son of a Maya mother, who left the village to live with a Carib in Punta Gorda. After her death the boy returned to San Antonio to be raised by his grandmother, and is accepted by the village as a Maya. What strain of white blood may have been injected into the race in earlier days is uncertain. It was probably thin. At all events the present-day Mayas of San Antonio keep themselves racially pure. There is one girl in the village, whose parentage is invariably attributed by gossip to an American resident of the Toledo settlement, but she is an obvious albino with pure Maya features.

The Mayas display a curious lack of ambition for wealth, or even prestige. Almost all are equally poor, and seem to have no desire to be wealthier than the other members of the community. The one or two who have a very few dollars stored away, are not envied, nor do they receive any more respect. Respect seems to be entirely reserved for those of considerable age. I failed to see any ambition among the Mayas, save to have a good milpa, and consequently sufficient food to live comfortably, and raise a few hogs to sell for clothes and rum. The exception is supplied by the desire to shine as a *Nohoch Priosti* (p. 83).

V. INDUSTRY AT SAN ANTONIO

The most important activity of the Indians after the milpa is hunting. Game is now growing somewhat scarce in the vicinity of the villages, and it is often necessary to make journeys of some length to obtain a good bag.

Below is given a list of the more important animals and birds hunted for food in the Toledo District:

qeqentše . peccary (*Tayassu angulatun*)		št'ut . . . . parrot
kitam . . . . . . warree		yaš kuɔ . . . . . wild turkey
keh . . . . . . large deer		koš . . . . . . qualm
yuk . . . . . . small deer		bale . . . . partridge
baaɔ . . . . howling monkey		batš . . . chachalaca or pheasant
maaš . . . . . spider-monkey		qambul . . . . curassow
haleb . . . . . . tepizcuintle		kubul . . . cacique or grupendula
ɔimintše . . . . . . tapir		naatš haas or *puun* . toucan or pito
wetš . armadillo (*Tatu novemcinctum*)		real

Snares are employed to a large extent by those who live in the remoter districts, where game is abundant. These bear a very strong resemblance to those portrayed in the codex Troano-cortesiano. A strong sapling is planted firmly in the ground, and the end is bent down and held down by a piece of liana lightly attached to a piece of wood on the ground, thus forming a noose. These snares are placed on the runs of wild game. As soon as an animal by running his head into the noose moves it slightly, it is released and flies upward with the force of the sapling to which it is attached.

A type of dead fall trap (*peɔ'*) is also employed. This is open at both ends, the sides consisting of a series of stakes. The roof consists of three sticks running lengthways, on top of which are placed heavy stones and rubble. The trap is sprung by the animal running against a stick in the center of the runway. This topples over another stick against which it leans, and which in turn allows a third stick to fall to the ground. This third stick supports the weight of the roof and on its collapse the whole roof falls to the ground imprisoning the animal.

The Mayas hunt with modern single-barreled shotguns, which they obtain in Punta Gorda. However, the blowgun (ɔontše) is also employed to a limited extent for shooting birds. It would appear to have been introduced to San Antonio by the Kekchi immigrants. The Kekchis of the Alta Vera Paz use it constantly, but it is unknown in Yucatan. However, in the sixteenth century it was in use there for shooting birds (Relación de Tequite, p. 110, and Breve relación, Vol. LVIII, p. 409) and it still survives at Socotz as a children's toy. The blowgun figures in the Popol Vuh, as well as in the legend of Venus, the Sun and the Moon (p. 120). Cortez, in his second letter, mentions that Moteuhzoma gave him a dozen painted blowguns and that the balls used in it were of gold. In all probability the blowgun was introduced into the Maya area from South America. However, only in the Isthmus of Tehuantepec are arrows used. The blowgun used by the Kekchis and Mayas of the Toledo District ranges from four and a half to six and a half feet in length. The wood from which it is constructed is known as *komoltše*. A section of wood is chosen and placed under water in the river. It is left there till the soft inner core rots away. A dab of chicle gum serves as a sight. The missile is a small pellet of baked clay, which is placed in the blowgun by means of a piece of hollowed bone. Sometimes hard seeds are employed instead of the clay pellets. The blowgun is useless for shooting anything except birds.

Bows and arrows are occasionally manufactured in San Antonio, but they are used only for sport. Nails bound onto the shaft by cotton thread serve as arrow points. Until recently the bow and arrow was also used for shooting fish, but this custom has become obsolete.

Hunting parties of two to eight or nine men are organized. They usually travel far afield. Leaving the village early in the afternoon they reach the area where they intend to hunt before nightfall. Here camp is made. Before retiring to their hammocks a small space near the camp is cleared of undergrowth and copal is burnt, and the Huitz-Hok are asked to give their animals to the hunters. The names of those animals which it is hoped will be obtained are specially mentioned. Another informant gave me the following prayer that is said on this occasion, but no mention is made by name of the game that is desired.

Ay dios,   *Santo Wiɔ,*   *Santo Hok,*   *Santo Quh.*   *Tan in ɔek,*
O God,   holy Huitz,   holy Hok,   holy Kuh.   I make an offering,

tan in tuqsik a wol,   *tan in manul t' a*   *witš,*   *tan a wiliken,*
I am molesting your soul,   I am passing over your   face,   you see me,

tan a tšantiken,   *ma biki patš*   *wal oɔilil.*   *Tan in manul in kuš-te*
you catch sight of me,   be patient on account of   great poverty.   I am passing to find

a walaq.   *Ka saten*   *kaš huntul,*   *kaš katul,*   *ma tin hobsik*
your animals.   Give me   although it be one,   although it be two,   I am not finishing

boon a yantetš.   *Biki in cumah*(?)   *ka maniken etel*   *in kitšpanil.*
how many you have.   Make the animal come   that it may happen   my goodness.
                              to me(?)   to me with

The last sentence of this prayer is very obscure. Several dialectic forms are noticeable: *tuqsik* for *taqsik, manul* for *manal,* etc.

FREE TRANSLATION

O God, Lord Huitz-Hok, God of the hills and valleys, Lord Kuh, spirit of the milpas, I am making you this offering of copal, I am about to molest your very heart, I am about to tread upon your face. Your eyes are upon me, you see my every movement, but I only disturb you on account of my great poverty. I am treading upon your surface in search of your children. Give me of them although it be but one or two. They are few in number, the few I slay will make no difference. Make the animals come toward me(?) that my hunting trip may be successful.

About three o'clock in the morning the hunters rise and await the rising of the morning star. As it rises, or at the time when it is judged it should rise, copal is burnt to it, and the following prayer is recited:

Ay dios,   *Santo šulab,*   *in mam in tšitš,*   *Santo Quh,*   *Santo šulab.*
O God,   holy star,   my grandfather, my   holy Kuh,   holy star.
                                 grandmother,

Katu wa   *saten*   *a walaq,*   *in mam,*   *in tšitš.*   *Tan in*
I desire perhaps you give me your animals,   my grandfather,   my grandmother.   I am

tuqsik   *a wol*   *etel a walaq,*   *lalic yan a ɔecten*   *ka in yalte.*
molesting   your soul   and your animals,   as always you must give me   that I may try.

            Ma tin hobsik   *boon a*   *yantetš.*
             I do not finish   how much   you have.

FREE TRANSLATION

O God, holy star, my grandfather, my grandmother, holy Kuh, holy star, give unto me of the denizens of the forest, who are your children. My grandfather, my grandmother, I am about to molest your very heart, I am about to disturb your children. As is your wont you must give me some of your animals to try. They are many in number, the few I slay will make no difference.

As soon as the prayer is concluded, the hunt begins. Until recent years the women, who, of course, had remained behind in the village, aided the men in their hunting by a very neat example of sympathetic magic. When the men were judged to be engaged in the hunt, the wives of the hunters sought out a sleeping hog, and proceeded to march round and round it, burning copal. It was believed that just as the sleeping hog was tame and quiet, so the wild animals in the forest would likewise be tame and accessible.

Fishing, too, supplies the villages with food. Fishing with hook and line is rare. Copal is burnt while the hooks are being made. Occasionally fish are shot with a gun or killed with a spear in addition to the use of the bow and arrow described above. The point of the spear, for which the Spanish name *lanza* is used, is made of iron or glass. The fishers go out in pairs in a canoe, one man gently paddling, while the other stands in the bow with his spear raised, looking down into the water for fish. Nets are not employed for trapping fish except when poison is used as described below.

The most usual method employed to obtain fish is to poison the water. The poison is obtained from a number of different plants. The most common of these is the root of a liana (*Serjania goniocarpa; lab*). Another common poison is obtained from a species of palm with fan leaves, that grows in the swampy land and the trunk of which is covered with prickles (*kuum*).

Another plant which is highly efficacious is *Salmea scandans*. The Maya name *ik lab* (*chili lab*) refers probably to the effect caused by masticating it. It is said that if placed in the mouth, the whole of the mouth goes dead. This plant is used all through Central America as a fish poison under the Spanish name *Salta afuera*, as it is said to be so strong that it causes the fish to jump out of the water.

As many as sixteen or twenty men may take part in fish-poisoning. They pass the night in vigil at the hut of any one of the party, partaking of chicken and rice. Candles and copal are lighted, and an offering of cacao is set aside during the course of the night. At dawn all proceed to the river, taking copal, one large candle and four small ones of black beeswax. A section of the river has already been decided upon. The candles are first lit, and subsequently two light logs of wood are placed in the river, one at each bank at the uppermost point of the section to be poisoned. On each of these logs a small fire is kindled, and lumps of copal placed on top of them. The two logs are then floated down stream as soon as the smoke of the copal begins to wreathe upward. An attempt is made to keep each log to its own side of the river. As the logs float down stream the following prayer is recited:

Ay dios,	*Santo Ha,*	*bin kin tuqetš*	*a wol.*	*Bel in kah*
O God,	holy Ha,	I am going to molest	your heart.	I am going

in qaskontetš	*yoqlal*	*a walaq.*	*Ma biki*	*patš*	*wal*
to dirty you	on account of	your animals.	Be patient	on account	of heavy

oɔilele, pero	*bik u yakunten*	*kaš*	*yan a*	*ayin*	*ka u*
poverty, but	take care that he love me	if by chance	there be a	crocodile	that he

kušte	*u qultš-il*	*a ku biki*	*u*	*haqes*	*in wol*
seek	his lair,	beware lest	he	to frighten	my heart

maaša	*kun*	*ka*	*u*	*yakunten*	*ka*	*in mete ti*
may it be	the snake	that	he	love me	that	I may work

kitšpan	*ka*	*kimik*	*leek*	*a boon*	*a yantetš.*
well	that	may die	just	as many	as you have.

FREE TRANSLATION

O God, Lord Ha, spirit of the water, I am about to molest your very heart, I am going to stir up the mud in your limpid pools because of the fish in your keeping. I do this on account of my great need. See, I pray you, that the crocodile harm me not, bid him seek his lair, that he frighten me not. May the snake not bite me, so that I may work in peace. Permit that I kill all the fish that are here in your keeping.

On the conclusion of this ceremony nets of henequen fiber are stretched across the river at the top and bottom of the reach that is to be worked. The pieces of the poisonous liana wood, four in number, are thrown into the water. Soon all the fish in the reach are floating dead upon the surface.

The capture of fish by poisoning is widely practised in the Amazon area, and possibly was one of the cultural traits introduced from South America via Panama, where it is a common practice.

San Antonio houses, *na* (Plates IX-X), resemble closely those of Yucatan, except that they are usually oblong instead of slightly oval in shape, and are practically never plastered (see Thompson, E. H.). The materials used are cabbage-palm leaves (*šan*) for the roof, sapodilla for the main posts, and a wood known in Spanish as *manteca* and in Maya as *luwin* for the remaining poles, and a liana known as *suk aq*. The distinguishing feature of the Maya hut is to be found in the fact that the walls do not take the weight of the roof. This is supported by six, or in the case of a small house only four, heavy posts (*okom*). In Plate X these are numbered 1.

The tops of these posts have a square notch cut out of them in which rest two horizontal beams (3). These two beams are known as *patš na*, meaning the back of the house, for they are the ones that carry the whole weight of the roof. On them rest six forked beams

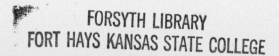

(5) that rise three on each side immediately above the *okom* to the *pol na*, meaning the head of the house, which is the ridge-pole (7). In addition there are four more beams, or in the case of small houses two only, that rise transversely from the same points to the ridge-pole. These (6) are known as *šol*. These twelve poles, or in the case of small houses, eight poles, carry all the weight of the ridge-pole. The weight of the bottom of the roof is carried by a horizontal pole on each side (4), which rests on the transversal beams marked 2. The inward thrust of the center of the roof is met by three crossbeams (8). The top two are known as *qubak*, the one beneath as *lekep*. The crossbeam below this is known as *peɔhol*.

The roof itself consists of a series of horizontal rows of light sticks on which the cabbage-palm leaves are forked. They in turn are held by a number of light vertical poles at short intervals called *siktše*. These vertical poles in turn are held by the ridge-pole and the beams marked 4. In some cases the cabbage-palm leaves are replaced by cohune-palm leaves (*Attalea cohune;* Maya *tuɔ*). These leaves are split down the stem, and are laid with the leaves hanging down and overlapping the row below about three or four inches. The roof when newly constructed is often nearly two feet thick.

The walls of the houses are aligned with the six main posts. They consist of small posts or sections of cohune leaf-stems. There are no windows, but light enters through the open doors and the interstices between the posts and sticks of the walls. The doors consist of four or five light poles tied together with liana. One end is attached to the wall in the same manner, and they are locked by passing a piece of cord around the outside pole of the door and the corresponding pole of the wall. The floors of the houses are of beaten-down earth. No stone is employed in house construction.

Each household occupies either one large house of this type or two small ones. In the latter case, one house is the living room, which serves as men's sleeping quarters and men's visiting house; and the other is the kitchen and women's quarters. Married couples sleep in the living room. Where there is only one house, a flimsy partition sometimes divides the kitchen from the living room, in which case the kitchen is usually the inner room. However, there is really no true sex segregation; merely a tendency of the women visitors to congregate in the kitchen, while the men spend most of their time apart from meals in the living room.

The fire-place is a primitive affair, consisting merely of three stones on which are placed the griddle or pots. As the cooking is naturally woman's work, three, the number of hearth-stones, is woman's sacred number. In the same way four, the number of corners of the milpa, is man's sacred number (p. 110). Ovens are not used.

The furniture consists of numerous hammocks, which when not in use are knotted up, and a few gasoline boxes in both living room and kitchen. The living room often contains a bark bed; this consists of four low posts driven into the ground over which the outer bark of a tree is stretched. In the kitchen, besides a number of domestic utensils of pottery, calabash, and iron, there are low seats consisting of blocks of wood four or five inches high hollowed out beneath (qaantše). One or two home-made tables are usually found in the kitchen. A few poles thrown across the crossbeams supply a storage attic in which are placed ears of corn and other vegetable produce, old clothing and odds and ends. A notched pole is employed to reach this (illustrated by Sapper, 1905). Altars such as are described by Gann (1918, p. 27) and Tozzer (1907, p. 152) exist in a few of the houses, but are not generally found. Every house has, too, its pigstye, which is merely a miniature house.

The hammocks are manufactured in the village. The material employed is usually henequen fiber, though cotton or imported rope-cord is also used occasionally. The hammocks are intermediate in size between those used by the Yucatecans and those made by the Lacondones. They are woven in the same way as the hammocks of Yucatan. The henequen leaves of either *Agave sisalana* or *Agave fourcroydes* are cut down and then either sun-dried or passed rapidly over a big fire. After being put aside for three days, they are scraped with a machete. The shavings are then rolled between the hands or on the leg in the same way as cotton is twisted as it is run on to the spindle. The preparation of the fiber and the manufacture of the hammock (qaan) is man's work. The hammock is generally said to have been imported into the Maya area subsequent to the Spanish conquest. Bishop Landa (chap. 20), in his description of the interior of a Maya house, speaks of beds consisting of wooden stakes with matting on top, and says that the Mayas slept on these, cotton mantles serving to cover them. On the other hand, in the one truly romantic story of the conquest, "The Temptation of Aguilar," the hammock is mentioned. This may be due to a little romantic coloring supplied some time after the event (Torquemada, Book IV, chap. 3). Peter Martyr, the second writer to mention the Mayas, who wrote his account as early as 1526, speaks of hammocks in the houses of Cozumel. He writes, in the sixth chapter of Decade IV, as follows, "The inhabitants (of Cozumel) fledunto the thicke woods, and forsake their towne for feare, our men enter their desolate and emptie houses, and feede upon their country victualles, and found there furniture for houses of divers colours, rich and costly hangings, gar-mentes and coverlets, which they call *amaccas* of gossampine cotton."

Although this passage is somewhat obscure, I believe it may be assumed that the coverlets called *amaccas* are indeed hammocks.

A more authoritative statement that the hammock was known in Yucatan prior to the Spanish conquest is to be found in the account given by Oviedo (Book XXXII, chap. 3) of Montejo's invasion of the Peninsula. This account is very full and is based on that of an eye witness. It states that when the Spaniards arrived at Loche, the chief of that town refused to come out to meet Montejo. Montejo went into the chief's house and found him reclining in a hammock. The chief only addressed a few words to him, but whenever he opened his mouth two of his attendants raised a cloth in front of him, hiding his face from Montejo. Sanchez de Aguilar (p. 99), writing a century later, remarks that the Mayas manufactured hammocks.

Oviedo (Vol. I, Plate I) illustrates a hammock, which from the context must be of West Indian origin. This seems to be the only information of the type of hammock used in this area. It is similar to the hammocks used by most of the modern Carib and Arawak tribes of northern South America, from whom the culture of the West Indies was derived. All these hammocks show a different technique to that employed by the modern Maya of British Hon-duras and Yucatan. They are woven on looms by the women, where-as the net hammocks of the Maya are made of henequen by men and are not woven (Plate XI). Where the hammocks of the Caribs and Arawaks are not woven, the woof is replaced by a series of cross-bars. This is the technique shown in Oviedo's illustration. This type of hammock is unknown in the area under discussion. The hammock is reported from the Talamancan region at the time of the conquest, and there seems a possibility that it reached the Mayas through Central America, and was not introduced, as supposed, by the Span-iards from the West Indies. The fact that the bed is reported from Yucatan at the time of the conquest does not necessarily imply that the hammock was unknown. The Mayas at the present time use their beds for sleeping in when at home, but possess hammocks for travel-ing and for resting in their huts. Further, the hammock was no novelty to the early Spaniards in Yucatan, as they had become acquainted with it in the West Indies, and for that reason it might very well have been passed by without mention.

Tozzer illustrates a section of Lacondone hammock, which resembles that used in northeastern South America, having regular cross-bars (Tozzer, 1907, Plate XII). Possibly this is a local development. On the other hand Central American tribes, such as the Bribri, use the netted technique (Skinner, p. 57).

Pottery is made in all the villages of the Toledo District. The quality of the material is good, and the shapes are by no means unpleasing, and are even and regular. A light polish is usual, but no paint is used. The Kabal, that supposed missing link between primitive and wheel-made pottery, is unknown in the Toledo District, and the coiled method is employed. The making of pottery is, as nearly everywhere where the wheel is unknown, the work of the women. The clay is mixed with ground snail shell (*huti*) or ground calcide of a very crystalline type. The woman places a banana leaf on top of a low wooden stool and, sitting on the ground, takes up a large lump of the clay mixture after first dusting her hands with fine lime. She first makes three long sausage-shaped rolls of clay. These she makes into three separate rings by joining the ends of each one together. These rings are placed on top of one another so as to take the form of a hollow barrel. The top one is slightly smaller than the two below. The three coils are then smoothed down on the inside. For this only the hand is employed. Subsequently the outside of the pot is smoothed over until the separate coils are no longer visible (Plate XIII). At this period the clay contains much moisture and barely retains its shape. It is then put aside for four or five days to dry in the shade of the hut. By then the clay is still pliable, but much of the moisture has evaporated. The bottom is then made, the rim is shaped, and handles, if any, are added. The bottom is made separately and welded on to the jar, which is now shaped as required. The bowl is then placed on one side for another seven or eight days, and then fired at home. No decoration of any sort is applied either before or after firing.

A series of the most typical shapes are shown in Plates XVII and XVIII. Figs. 1 and 2 represent water jars (*p'ul*). Of these two shapes 1 is by far the commonest type. Fig. 3 is also used for storing water and possesses a high polish. This is far and away the best ceramic product of San Antonio. Fig. 4 is the comal (*šumutš*), which is employed to bake tortillas. Fig. 5 is the *šok* used for roasting cacao beans. It is interesting that, as far as I know, no complete comal has ever been found in a Maya ruin, although metates, either whole or fragmentary, are frequently found. Nor are sherds of flat ware found in large quantities. Bishop Landa definitely states that maize was ground and toasted. However, it would almost seem that the Maya must have toasted their tortillas placed on leaves, or some such substance, and laid in the ashes of a fire. For if the comal had been used undoubtedly very large quantities would be excavated on every house-site as the whole Maya culture centers around maize. Fig. 6 is a typical cooking pot (*kum*), and Fig. 7 is used as a drinking cup (*hai*). As the shape indicates it is based on a half gourd. Fig. 8 is the vessel used for burning copal.

Wickerwork baskets (*šak*) are made usually almost dish-like in shape. The warp elements are thirty-two in number, and are always placed singly. No designs are employed; in fact, one can say without fear of contradiction that the modern Maya-speaking people of the Toledo District are entirely lacking in any artistic sense. However, the Kekchis still retain a certain artistic touch, though they, too, since their immigration into the colony, seem to have lost much of it. For example, around Coban gourds are decorated with pleasing incised and painted designs. In the Toledo District no designs are ever employed.

Weaving is no longer practised by the Maya-speaking peoples of San Antonio, although one or two Kekchi women still occasionally weave simple pieces. In San Pedro Colombia weaving is practically extinct. In Aguacate alone is it a live industry. Coarse cotton is spun locally, but is only employed in the manufacture of bags. Finer cotton, but of poor quality, as well as all the colored thread is imported from Coban, Alta Vera Paz. This is brought by Kekchi peddlers overland, the round trip taking as much as a month. The loom (Plate XII) is a simple contrivance of the usual rod-heald type. The top is tied to a post and the bottom held by a band around the woman's waist. Among the Kekchis of the Alta Vera Paz this band is of hide; in the Toledo District it is of liana. The loom is thus held in an almost horizontal position. The strips of cloth woven are usually about three feet long and slightly over a foot wide. Three strips of this cloth will thus make one woman's blouse. The alternate warp strands are raised together by means of a heddle. This consists of a number of cotton loops connecting the alternate warp strands with a wooden rod, by lifting which the threads to which it is attached are likewise raised. The designs are applied in a manner similar to tapestry as the cloth is in process of being woven. The patterns are purely of Alta Vera Paz origin, birds, men, chevrons and other geometrical patterns being most frequently employed. There is a vague, but not particularly close resemblance between some of these designs and those shown on the lintels at Yaxchilan (Menché). The spindle and spindle whorl are of some hard wood, probably sapote. No Maya names survive at San Antonio either for the loom or any of its parts. The raw cotton is called *tumun*, and the thread *quš*. A needle is called *puɔ*. In Kekchi the loom is called *pot*. Within a few years the weaving industry will probably be extinct in the Toledo District. Coarse cotton is also obtained from the seed kernel of the ceiba tree (*Bombax ceiba, yaštše*). This is used for mending clothes, but its use is fast disappearing in face of the invasion of cheap manufactured cotton goods from Europe and the United States.

Canoes (*tšem*) are used by all the villages except San Antonio, which alone is not situated close to the banks of a navigable river. The canoes, which are without exception of the dugout type, are usually made of the wood of the cedar tree (*Cedrela odorata*), the mahogany (*Swietenia macrophylla*), the ceiba (*Bombax ceiba*), or the San Juan (*Vochysia guatemalensis*). They vary in size from about six feet in length to nearly twenty feet, and are propelled by cedar paddles or long poles. They are chiefly used to carry maize, beans, etc., down to the coast, and to bring back purchases. On the coast the Carib Negroes use sails in their dugouts, but among the present-day Maya these are unknown, probably because their travelling is largely confined to the rivers. At the time of the conquest the Mayas and neighboring Indians probably used the sail. Bernal Diaz relates how a scouting party was sent forward to find the route to Olid's settlement during Cortez' famed march to Honduras. When close to the present southern boundary of British Honduras they espied a boat hugging the coast and driven by oars and a sail. The scouting party captured it when it put in to shore at night time. It belonged to an Indian trader, and was carrying a cargo of maize and salt (Diaz, chap. 168).

Tump lines (Spanish *mecapal*, Maya *hool*) are in San Antonio invariably made of bark. The bark usually employed is that of the tree known in Maya as *kampaq*, although any tree with a tough and easily removable bark may be employed. The Indians of the Kekchi villages use leather or cotton tump lines. The netted bags (Plate XI, Fig. 3) are called *bai*.

The bark of the Moho tree known in Maya as *Huhul,* which is probably *Belotia campbellii,* is used for making beds. The bark of the tree is slit down the required length, and softened by being beaten with the back of the axe, and then stripped off by wedges. It is taken home, and placed in water for a day or so and then beaten again all over with a heavy stone or hammer until well softened. The strips of bark are held down in a horizontal position with stones until dry, or tied to the walls of the houses. A rough wooden frame consisting of four short posts and cross sticks is made, and on this the bark is laid, forming a primitive and somewhat hard bed *(tš'ak).* No mattress of any sort is employed. In some of the Kekchi villages of the colony, notably Aguacate, rush mats, imported from Coban, are used for beds, but they are unknown in San Antonio.

These strips of bark are also used as cacao bean driers (Plate XIII) and to a limited extent for making tump lines or *mecapals.*

Clothes of bark cloth were made by the ancient Mayas, and they have only fallen into disuse within the last eighty years among the Mayas of San Luis. This same bark of the Moho tree is said to have been used. According to others the leaves of Chichicastor, a species of stinging nettle, supplied the fiber for these clothes. The bark of the *poitše* tree is also used for beds, and cacao bean dryers.

The majority of the dyes now used in San Antonio are bought in Punta Gorda, but one or two native dyes are still in use. Logwood is unknown in the southern part of the colony. Its place is taken by a plant called *tšuktšemutš* (*Calderonia salvadorensis*). This is a red dye used for coloring the masks used in the Cortez, and other, dances. A yellow dye is obtained from a root called *škantia.*

The clothing worn by the men is all of European manufacture. Cotton trousers (*eš*) and a shirt (*koton*), the tail of which is worn outside the trousers, constitute the sole garments of the men, with the exception of a soft hat, or less often a straw hat of local manufacture. Boots are worn only on state occasions. Frequently men and women will be met travelling from one village to another carrying their shoes in their hands. They are donned at the entrance to the village. Sandals (*šanap*) are falling into disuse. Usually the women go about naked to the waist. However, young girls of marriageable age usually wear blouses, as do too the older women when strangers are about. The skirts worn are often four or five in number. They are home-made of trade piece goods (Plate XIV). The men as a rule choose their wives' clothes. Necklaces of green and red beads are much worn in addition to earrings and long chains of imitation gold, and children often wear necklaces made out of pierced Guatemalan coins. A shawl is sometimes used to cover the head. The introduction of this is probably due to the Catholic priests, as women are not allowed to enter the churches bareheaded. In the Kekchi-speaking villages, and to a less extent in San Antonio, short, highly embroidered blouses, wrongly called *huipils*, are worn. These are brought by Kekchi Indians from Coban, and are of native manufacture. The traders often spend a month on their selling trip, travelling all the way on foot. In addition to these, simple blouses of coarse white imported cotton are made. They have simple embroidered patterns around the neck and the sleeves. Strips of cotton are embroidered by hand with simple patterns of birds, flowers, and geometric patterns in black thread, and then sown onto the blouse (Plate XXIV).

The tortilla (*wa*) is the Maya equivalent of bread. It is universally eaten from New Mexico to Panama. Corn is placed overnight to soak in a solution of lime and water. Early in the morning the housewife washes the grain in clean water. The lime has softened the shell, which is easily removed. The corn is then ground on the metate by means of the rubbing stone. The metates (*ka*) are imported from Honduras, being made of the famed Esquipulas stone. They are three-legged without any decoration. The sides are slightly raised and the rubbing stone is a very flat oval in cross section (Plate XV). The woman stands at the end of the metate, which, standing on a table, is level with her waist. The grain is ground and reground until it is a fine flour. As soon as it is all ground to the satisfaction of the woman, she places it on a low stool or block of wood. Then squatting down on the floor, she takes a chunk of the damp dough, and placing it on a piece of banana leaf, proceeds to flatten it out with her fingers. In this manner a very thin layer of the dough is obtained, not unlike a pancake, save that it is considerably thinner. Each tortilla as it is made is placed on the comal to roast. The comal (*šumutš*) is shown in Plate XVIII, Fig. 4. In recent years it has been largely replaced by the flat iron griddle. A very little grease is smeared on the griddle to prevent the tortillas from sticking to it and being burnt. The tortillas cook slowly as only a very low fire is maintained below. Each tortilla, as it is cooked, is placed in a large round calabash of the kind called *lek*, over the top of which is placed a cloth. This is to conserve the heat. Another favorite method of serving maize is in the form of tamales (*pootš* or *šnawa*). The corn is ground in the same manner as in the preparation of tortillas. It is next stuffed into the husk.

It is then tied up with a few hairs of the beard, and boiled. Often the center contains in addition mashed beans, in which case the tamal is called *buuliwa*. When the center is made of calabash seeds the tamales are known as *tutiwa*. Tamales are also made with chicken and chili, or almost any ingredient that suggests itself.

Maize is also the basis of many drinks of which *posol* (*Royem*) is the commonest. The grain, after being steeped in a solution of lime and water, is washed and boiled until a thickish liquid, like arrow-root in appearance, is obtained. Another form of posol is made by grinding the softened grain and adding hot or cold water. Pinol is made by first roasting the grain on the comal and then grinding very fine. Sugar is added. In this form it is carried on journeys, as for drinking all that is required is the addition of a little cold water. Food is served in calabashes (*luts̆*) or in small pottery vessels that are of the same form as the half calabashes. These are called *hai* (Plate XVIII, Fig. 7). Food is eaten with the fingers, but in recent years tin plates, knives, forks, and spoons have been adopted to a small extent.

Little gourd supports (*ts̆'uyu*) are made of circles of dyed henequen straw (Plate XI, Fig. 3). The cords for carrying these are also made of henequen. Small rings of coarse pottery are also employed as supports. The Maya is rather irregular in his meals. As a rule he eats three times a day. The women of the household are up long before daybreak preparing the tortillas. At about 5 A.M. the men have their breakfast of tortillas, either dipped in chili sauce, or eaten plain with anything that may have been left over from the previous meal. Posol or, more rarely, coffee is drunk. When the men have finished and departed to their work, the women sit down to their meal. This is not necessarily a case of sex avoidance, but is primarily due to the fact that the women are busy heating the tortillas on the comal to keep up a constant supply of hot tortillas for the men. If the men expect to be away all day, they carry with them a supply of tortillas or tamales to eat at midday. For long journeys a special kind of tortilla is carried. These are more thoroughly cooked and are of a larger size. They are known to the Spaniards as *totoposte* (Nahuatl *totopochtli*). The Maya name is *op'* or *suk pet*. Posol is also carried either to the work or for long journeys.

When the day's work is short, the men return about half-past two or three o'clock in the afternoon. They then eat the principal meal of the day. Again tortillas will form the main dish, but other fruits will be eaten such as plantains, okra, coco, etc. Occasionally meat also will be eaten. The average Maya household eats meat about three times a week. As cattle are not kept, beef is almost unknown to the Maya, and pork is the meat most usually eaten. All game, including monkey, parrot, and iguana, is considered somewhat of a luxury. Food is cooked either by boiling or broiling in, or at the side of, the ashes. Ovens are unknown, and frying is practically never employed. Sometimes another meal, similar to that eaten in the early afternoon, is consumed at sundown. Posol, pinol, cocoa, coffee, and even tea are drunk with, or between, meals. The Mayas of San Antonio are fond of eating small lumps of lime. They say that it tastes good, and is good for one. However, they do not chew lime with tobacco and chili, as is the custom of the Tzeltals (Starr, 1901, p. 133).

By no conceivable stretch of imagination could anyone describe the Mayas as musical. Practically never do they sing or whistle. Occasionally a Maya, who has been in contact with *Ladinos*, will pick up the words of some Spanish song, but he will either recite the words or give them to the accompaniment of a dreadful howling which bears no resemblance to the original tune. However the Mayas possess a number of musical instruments which they play with little regard for tune or harmony.

The musical instruments used by the San Antonieros are all homemade. Of these the most important is the harp-drum, *paš* (Plate XVI). This, like all the musical instruments used, is of very primitive workmanship. The harp itself is a clumsy imitation of the usual European type. The base, however, is formed by a wide resonator. While the harp is being played by a seated individual, the hollow base is beaten by another individual seated at its base in the same way that the old Maya wooden drum (the *tunkul*) was probably beaten; that is to say, with the wrist and fingers. A deep booming sound is given forth which can be heard at a considerable distance. Simple violins are also used. The strings are of henequen with the result that the notes are very far from melodious. The musical bow (*paštše*) is also used in San Antonio. There are two varieties. The first consists of a piece of flexible wood (*kampaq*) the ends of which are joined by a piece of henequen cord. The cord is placed in the mouth, which serves as a resonator, without, however, touching any part of it. The music is obtained by the vibration of the cord against the teeth when struck with a small stick. At present a thin wire frequently replaces the henequen cord. In the other variety a gourd serves as the resonator. The musical bow would appear to be of aboriginal origin (Saville, 1897; Brinton, 1897). At the present time there is one small dilapidated marimba in San Antonio. The marimba is the most universal musical instrument now in use in Central America. Nevertheless, despite its probable African origin, it is practically never played by the Negroes in Central America. The marimbistas are invariably of *Ladino* stock. Simple four-hole flutes (*šol*) are in use in all the Maya villages. The mouthpiece is made of a piece of henequen leaf, causing a sound not unlike that of bagpipes.

Kettle drums of the typical European shape are employed for official business, such as summoning the town council. They are made of hollowed sections of wood, over the ends of which are drawn pieces of raw-hide. To the edge of the raw-hide are attached short cords, which are twisted around short sticks and rest against the under edge of the rim. The true *tunkul* is no longer in use.

Small rattles similar in shape to those shown in the Dresden Codex are used in masked dances. However, today they are made of old tin cans with seeds or pebbles inside, attached to wooden handles (Plate XVI, Fig. 2).

A small bull-roarer is also used by children as a toy. Although there is no evidence of the use of this world-wide instrument among the ancient Mayas, it was known to the Aztecs.

Important feasts, such as Easter, the day of the patron saint of the village, or the day of Holy Cross, are often marked by masked dances. These are, with one possible exception, of Spanish origin. They owe their origin to the Kekchi immigrants from the Alta Vera Paz. The early Spanish missionaries were offended at the paganism or occasionally indecency of the Indian dances. They hit on the plan of substituting dances that would point a moral or make the audiences more acquainted with the glorious history of the spread of Christianity in other countries. The Indian was already too well acquainted with the mercies of the Christian deity vouchsafed to him through the tender treatment of Spanish monk and adventurer. Accordingly subjects such as the overthrow of the Turks with the miraculous aid of St. James were turned into dances for the Indians. Sapper (1905), Lothrop (1925, 1927a, 1929) and Gann (1925, p. 203; 1926, p. 160) have already described and illustrated several of these play-dances. They are somewhat uncouth and certainly extremely wearisome. The performances extend over a number of days and the dancing is kept up with few intermissions from morning to far into the night. The costumes, which are hired from one village to another for the dance, are gaudy and essentially European.

"The devil dance," "The monkey dance," "The Cortez dance," "The Moor dance," are all of Highland origin. However, there is one dance, which though known to the Kekchi, is danced chiefly in San Luis Peten and San Antonio. This is the deer dance (*Oqot keh*). It is danced at San Antonio in honor of San Luis, *ci-devant* former patron saint of San Antonio. The dancers are twelve in number. One represents a tiger, the second a deer, three and four dogs, five and six two old men painted black, and the remaining six are by way of being the chorus. The old black men are known as *bes* (*betš*[?]), which means the stupid ones who know nothing.

All wear wooden masks, of which the most interesting are those worn by the *bes*. They bear a very strong resemblance to certain masks dating from the period of the Maya Empire. Tin rattles as described under music are employed. The dresses are tawdry and modern. The masks of the deer and the dogs are of solid wood. They are quite realistic, and are fastened onto the top of the head (Plates XVI, Fig. 2, and XIV, Fig. 2).

The dance is opened by the tiger and the two old black men, the *bes*. They kill the tiger, but he comes to life almost immediately and, chasing the deer, kills it. The tiger then retires from the stage and the deer revives. The dogs next appear. They start out to hunt the deer. Eventually they succeed in driving the deer out of the wood to the *bes*. Next the tiger reappears only to be hunted and shot with arrows by the *bes*. The deer is then caught with noose snares. The dance concludes with the *bes* kissing a number of the chorus, who are dressed up to represent women. The music is supplied by a marimba. Traditional tunes associated with the *bes*, the tiger, and the deer are played while they dance.

The dance appears to be essentially a hunting play, apparently with the object of insuring successful hunting. It may not be any more than a coincidence that the festival of the hunters was held, according to Landa, on 7 Zip at the time of the conquest. 7 Zip corresponded in the old Julian reckoning to September 1. In the course of the feast a dance was held in which the men danced with a deer's skull and an arrow painted the sacred blue in their hands. Landa also states that preparations for this feast including fasting commenced in the month Uo. Now it was the custom in Yucatan for the men to paint themselves with black soot. Black soot was used by the ancient Mayas as a sign of fasting. This might account for the black features of the hunters in the modern dance, for they certainly are not supposed to represent Negroes.

Balche (*baltše*) is occasionally manufactured. This is an intoxicating drink that was ceremonially used by the Mayas in pre-Hispanic days. Landa states that the Mayas were much given to drunkenness. However, it must be remembered that these bouts of drunkenness were purely ceremonial. The modern Maya, too, is much addicted to orgies of drunkenness, and these carousals are still in part ceremonial. The usual drink is a raw rum manufactured in the Corozal District. However the practice of making *balche* is not yet extinct in the Toledo and Corozal Districts, although it is no longer manufactured at Socotz. *Balche*, known also at San Antonio as *baluch* (Kekchi) is manufactured from fermented honey and the bark of the *balche* tree of the genus *Lonchocarpus*. Sometimes bark of the pine is substituted when there is difficulty in obtaining the *balche*. Strips of the green bark are washed and then left to dry for some time, the longer the better. Many of the older men keep the bark in this state for several months. When required, it is bruised all over with a hammer stone or some similar object. In this way the sap is released. It is placed in a jar in which are equal parts of water and fresh honey. The mixture is then left to ferment for from four to six days. At the end of this period it is ready to drink. According to Bishop Landa, the tree used in making *balche* was cultivated, although he states that the root, and not the bark, was employed. He writes, "They make the wine of honey and water and the root of a certain tree, which for this purpose they cultivate. The wine with this root becomes strong and possesses a strong odor."

A drink is also occasionally made from fermented corn and a little sugar-cane. The mixture with the addition of an equal quantity of water is left to ferment for a couple of days, at the end of which period it is ready to drink. It is only slightly intoxicating. The taste is not dissimilar to that of a slightly sour Devonshire cider. If left longer, it becomes somewhat bitter. This drink is known by the Spanish name *chicha*.

The copal (*pom*) used so frequently in all the Maya ceremonies is obtained from the copal tree (*Protium copal*) in the form of a gum. The tree is not bled in the same way as a rubber tree, but the bark is shaved. The yield is small and the gum takes a considerable time to gather. The bleeding must be carried out fasting. The only thing that can be touched before going out to bleed is the mixture of ground maize and water known as pinol. This bears some resemblance to copal, and by drinking a quantity of this it is believed that the yield of copal will be greater. The gum is also known as *sak kib* (white wax) in contrast to beeswax, which is black.

Beeswax (*kab*) is obtained from the hives of wild honey bees. It is afterwards boiled. Some say that it should be boiled fasting, but all are agreed that if the boiler should defecate while the wax is being boiled, it will turn bad.

The wick of the candle is made of cotton taken from the plant, not of imported cotton. Black wax candles are considered to be very sacred, whereas white candles have no particular value. I wished on one occasion to obtain some black wax candles from one of the workers, who had a number. He refused to sell them or exchange for white ones, saying that he needed them for All Souls' Day, and that white ones were useless as they had no soul. According to Gomara (p. 70), the Mayas did not know how to make candles, and that they were taught by the Spaniards. It is, of course, very likely that the Mayas did not use candles for ordinary illumination, as pine-wood torches served this purpose. Nevertheless I believe the Mayas used wax as an offering long before the arrival of the Spaniards. At the present time the Mayas of the Toledo District have no domesticated bees, but in pre-Spanish times the bee was domesticated in the Maya region as well as in Panama. It is not unreasonable to suppose that this great difference in the functions of the white and black wax candles has its origin in the fact that the black wax candle was used ceremonially before the conquest. In the Valley of Mexico, at least, wax appears to have been used for ceremonial purposes. Traces of beeswax have been found in some of those odd vessels typical of the Teotihuacan culture, which are generally known as *candeleros*. There is no information as to the inhabitants of the Highlands of Mexico possessing domesticated bees, although domesticated bees are reported from Vera Cruz and Jalisco (Oviedo, Book 34, chap. 2). Therefore if they used beeswax for ceremonial purposes, presumably the Maya, who had domesticated the bee, would almost certainly have made use of the wax, although again, according to Peter Martyr, the Mexicans did not make candles of beeswax.

VI. RELIGION AT SOCOTZ

The area dealt with in this and the succeeding chapter is situated
in the extreme central west of the Cayo District, British Honduras.
Socotz has been taken as the type village. During the 1928 field
season I, as leader of the Marshall Field, First Archaeological
Expedition to British Honduras, was carrying on archaeological
work in the south of the Cayo District. The labor was almost to a
man drawn from Socotz. Among these workers was one of excep-
tional intelligence, Jacinto Cunil, a Maya of mixed Peten Maya and
Santa Cruz de Bravo Maya stock. Besides being a very ready worker,
Jacinto also proved himself a good informant. A good deal of the
following two chapters is based on his information, with the exception of the *primicia* prayers.

The Socotz Mayas differ but slightly from their brothers to the
north and northeast. The material culture of the Mayas of the
Corozal District has already been dealt with by Dr. Thomas Gann
(Bureau of American Ethnology, Bull. 64), therefore I am omitting
almost all reference to this side of the life of the Mayas of the western
Cayo District.

The nominal religion of the Mayas of Socotz and the neighboring
village is the Roman Catholic faith. Nevertheless their Christianity,
like that of their fellow Indians in the Toledo District, shelters
within its somewhat expansible bosom a good deal of the degenerate
remains of the old Maya religion. They, too, are at heart poly-
theists. The Christian god is the Zeus of the Pantheon. The Virgin
Mary, the Saints of the Catholic church, and such of the old local
gods as have survived, form a less powerful, but more friendly
group of divinities (see La Farge).

The most important gods are the old agricultural deities. Each
milpa is guarded by them. They are four in number, and stand one
at each corner of the milpa. They are noted for their great size and
strength. They are known under a number of different names, of
which the most important are the following: *Nukil winkob* ("the
mighty men"), *Yum Quhob* ("the lord gods"), *Qaanan Qašob* ("the
bountiful forests"), *Halatš winkob* ("the true men"), and *Ahbehob*
("the captains, who clear the roads").

There seems to be some doubt as to whether all of these are really
names for the same group of four guardians of the milpa. In any

case to the modern Maya the names are of slight importance, yet to a man they implicitly believe in the existence of these deities, who have complete control over the milpas and their products.

The Chacs (*Tšakob*) are often confused with the milpa deities They are primarily rain and thunder deities, but from the close association of rain and the success of the crops they have come to be closely associated with the milpa. Like the lords of the milpa they are four in number and are believed to be of immense size. The title *Nukil winkob* bestowed on the milpa gods more rightly belongs to them. The same association of stone axes with the Chacs, that is met with in San Antonio, is also current in the Cayo District.

The lords of the forest are also very closely associated with the milpa deities—in fact there is some reason to believe that they are one and the same. Again the association is natural. The milpa is after all only cleared forest land, often hemmed in with virgin forest on all sides.

The guardians of the forest are very numerous. They are known as *Nukutš makob* or *Nukutš yumsilob*, meaning the mighty men or the mighty lords. Again, therefore, we find this belief in great size forming a link with the lords of the milpa and the Chacs. However they are more generally known as *Yumil Qašob* ("lords of the forest"). They are under the orders of *Ah T'up* ("last born"). When a primicia (see p. 115) is offered, the *Yumil Qašob* are present to receive it. They carry it away to the home of *Ah T'up* in the depth of the forest. He is said to be very small and not to wander about in the bush.

When a man goes into the bush three of the *Yumil Qašob* are sent to protect him. However, if a woman goes into the bush four *Yumil Qašob* are told off to look after her. She needs an extra one for two reasons: firstly, because a woman is not so strong as a man, and secondly, because she hasn't as much intelligence, and is liable to get herself lost.

The *Ladino* has a strong belief in what is known as the *duende*. He is said to be the lord of the forest too. He is a dwarf and can always be recognized by the enormous hat he wears. He is often to be met with in the depth of the forest, but appears to be quite harmless. Possibly this duende belief has been borrowed from the Maya belief in *Ah T'up*, who is also said to be small in size. Another name for him is *Ahluš* (cf. Mendez in Saville, 1927). The reception of the primicia by the lords of the forest coupled with their general similarity both in size and functions seems fairly strong evidence that the *Quhob*, the *Tšakob*, and the *Yumil Qašob* are one and the same. This is confirmed by Bishop Landa, who states that *Yum kax* was the god of agriculture. *Yum Qaš* simply means "lord forest" in contrast to the modern name *Yumil Qašob*, which means "lords of the forest."

The wind gods are said to be either three or four in number. They are known as *Iqob* ("the winds"), and are associated with the four directions. They are said to accompany the lords of the milpa. Their special function is properly to burn the milpa when it has been cleared. At times they can do harm. They are very strong and often cause sickness. For example I was questioning a man in Socotz as to a certain neighbor of his, whom I had heard was a Hmen. The man replied that this man, Juan Cocom, was not a real Hmen. He didn't know all the prayers properly and often prayed like a Christian. For example he knew how to summon the lords of the milpa and their accompanying winds, but did not know how to send them away with the result that often the winds hang around Socotz causing much sickness which in many cases is fatal (cf. p. 166).

Sak Iq ("white wind") is associated with the east. *Šaman Qan Iq* ("north yellow wind") is, as its name denotes, the north wind. *Nohol Iq* is the south wind; and the west wind, according to my informant, was known as *Norte*, which, of course, is Spanish for north. These colors are not, however, in agreement with those given by Landa. In his account of the year bearer ceremonies yellow is associated with the east and white with the west.

Where a belief in only three wind gods is held, their names are said to be *Nohotš sukunsil* (*sukunbil*[?] "elder brother"), *T'an iɔni* ("he who speaks with his nose wrinkled up"), and *T'up iq* ("the youngest brother of the winds"). In the story of the wind gods and their mother given on page 167 only three wind gods are mentioned.

The absence of all traces of a winged serpent deity, such as the Mayas apparently worshipped with such fervor in times gone by, has not received the comment it deserves. At Socotz there is said to exist a species of winged snake, who eats people. Nevertheless they are emphatically denied any divine rank or attributes.

One can only conclude that the worship of the feathered snake formed part of an exotic and esoteric cult of which the rank and file of the Maya proletariat had no knowledge. At least if they had any knowledge of the mysteries, they failed to accord this deity more than a perfunctory worship, probably under compulsion. The Maya religion, as it survives at present, is essentially naturalistic. The deities, who still hold their places in the hearts of the modern Mayas, are primarily of the soil, or, to a less extent, simple manifestations of the natural bodies. This holds true for the whole Maya ethnological area. The esoteric anthropomorphization of mathematical concepts, the divinity of time, and such involved conceptions as feathered serpents and two-headed monsters were in all probability forced on the soil-loving, loosely organized bands of Mayas by waves of invaders already molded to a theocracy. It is not suggested that these conquering bands of theocrats were necessarily of different race to the peoples they conquered, although that apparently was the case in later times when parts of Yucatan were overwhelmed by Mexican professional soldiers.

Beyond the simple deities, savoring so strongly of mother earth, that have been already mentioned, the Maya of Socotz retains none of the old Pantheon antedating the Indo-Hispanic era. San José, the patron saint of the village, is more and more usurping the functions of the old gods. San José even sets himself up now as lord of the milpa, but this heresy is so far only held by a few women, who have necessarily had little to do with agriculture, but have on the other hand come to a large extent under the influence of Catholic priests. Unfortunately the day is not far distant when the *Yumil Qašob* will have to desert their old homes to wander disconsolate over the out-of-the-way parts of the world like Anatole France's Nectaire.

The hold of magic over the modern Maya is as strong as ever. However, the *Hmen* of the present time have degenerated into little more than herbalists, although they are still believed to be capable of working great harm with their sorcery.

The widespread custom of making waxen figures of one's enemy, and maltreating them in order to harm the man in whose image they are made, is still practised at Socotz, as well as in the Corozal District. Often red seeds are placed in the eyes of the wax image in order that the victim may suffer from sore eyes.

One of the best ways of learning *brujería* is to visit an ant's nest. Each ant's nest is presided over by a master, who is inevitably an expert in brujería. The grandfather of an informant made this trip in the company of the *Hmen*, who was teaching him. The master knocked three times on the nest, and a serpent issued forth. The master had previously removed all his clothes and was standing nude. The snake came up to him and after licking him all over, proceeded to swallow him whole. A few moments later he passed him out of his body with excrement. The master didn't appear to be much the worse for his adventure. Very similar initiation ceremonies in Chiapas are described by Nuñez de la Vega (p. 133).

The belief in *štabai* is current in Socotz, as throughout the peninsula. In Socotz they are considered to be women spirits, who have faces like sopilotes (carrion crows). The backs of their bodies are hollow like a washing board. They have long hair and wear huipiles, and their homes are in the trunks of large trees, especially ceibas. When a young fellow goes out to meet his girl at the outside of the village, the *štabai* may come to greet him in her guise. Should a man embrace a *štabai* he is in great danger of losing his reason. If a woman washes in a pool, or any stationary water, the pool or lake will run dry. However, if she takes water out of the pool with which to wash, or performs her ablutions in running water, there is no danger. If one is hit or bruised an infallible remedy is to strike the spot nine times with one of the three stones of the fire-hearth.

Round tumors in the body are a cause of much illness. They occur in the belly, the heart, and the throat, and may form naturally, or may be placed there by an enemy. Fright is one of the many causes. If one forms in the heart or passes up to the heart from the stomach, it is known as *paqil*. It is treated by massaging and twisting round the navel. It is blessed nine times, and in two days is completely cured.

Earaches are cured by placing in the affected ear the entrails of a large isapod more than an inch in length (*šqulutš*). Headaches are cured by bleeding with glass, usually of an old bottle. The blood is drawn off either from the forearm or from the side of the bridge of the nose (Plate XXI). An interesting semi-magical ceremony known as *heɔ* ("the carrying on the hip") is carried out in order to insure that children grow up to be useful members of the community.

When a boy reaches the age of four months, he is carried for the first time on the hip; previous to this he has been carried only in the arms. The number of months is placed at four, because the corners of the milpa are four in number, and his future life will be bound up with the milpa. His godfather carries him nine times round the table set in the center of the hut. At each circuit he places a small tortilla in his mouth. When this is concluded he hangs a net-bag on his back, passing the band across his forehead. Placing a machete in his hand he leads him out to a small tree and, guiding his hand, causes him to chop at the tree with the machete. In this way the future of the boy as a good hard worker is insured, as he will grow up used to milpa work.

A similar ceremony takes place in the case of a girl. However, in this case, it takes place when the child is three months old; for three is the number of the hearth-stones and, as a woman, her life will be bound up with cooking and the work of the home. After she has been carried round the table nine times and given the tortillas, as in the case of the boy, her godfather places a rolling stone in her hand, and, carrying her over to the metate, assists her to grind a little corn. After this a needle is placed in her hand and she is made to go through the motions of sewing. This concludes the ceremony. From then on the mother carries her child on her hip (cf. Mendez in Saville, 1927).

The great annual fiesta at Socotz is that of the patron saint, San José. This lasts nine days, and is an occasion for much drunkenness and uproar. Fights both among the Mayas and the *Ladinos*, who flock in large numbers to the fun, are numerous. The dancing of the *mestizada* and numerous church services and processions are kept up for the whole period. On the last day occurs a ceremony which would appear to date back to pre-Spanish times. This is the bringing-in of the ceiba (*yaštše*). In the afternoon of the appointed day (March 19) all the girls who take part in the *mestizada*, together with many of the men, go out into the forest to search for a young ceiba tree. The girls are dressed in special embroidered huipiles and wear straw hats decorated with flowers, either natural or artificial (Plates XXII-XXIV). The tree is chosen by the master of ceremonies, the *tš'ik* (pisote or coati). He is dressed up as a woman and wears a straw hat decorated with flowers (Plate XXII). When the tree has been chosen, it is cut down, and the *tš'ik* is seated on top. A net-bag is slung around his shoulders in which repose a few tortillas and a small doll in human shape. The tree is then carried back to the plaza by the men with the *tš'ik* aloft. On arrival at the plaza it is placed in a hole in the ground ready to receive it, and left standing upright. Everyone taking part in this procession carries flowers.

The rest of the evening is spent in dancing alongside, but not around, the tree. In order to dance each man has to pay fifty cents to help pay the expenses of the fiesta. There is an old lady appointed mistress of the ceremonies, and one of her chief duties is to see that nobody dances without having first paid his entrance. Anyone misbehaving or caught dancing without having paid is led off by her and tied up to the *yaštše*. Here he is left until he has ransomed himself and made his peace with the mistress of the ceremonies.

The whole ceremony bears a very close resemblance to the May-pole festivals so ably described by Sir James Frazer in the "Golden Bough." Obviously this is a spring festival in honor of the spirit of vegetation. Whereas in Europe the festival is usually held later in the year, either late in April, on the first of May, or even on Mid-summer Day; among the Mayas the feast is held so as almost to coincide with the spring equinox. It appears probable that it has survived at Socotz owing to coincidence with the feast of San José, the patron of the village. The original founders of Socotz in all probability emigrated from the village of San José, of which San José was naturally the patron. There this old pagan feast would have been overlooked by the more zealous of the Catholic fathers owing to its mergence in the festivities in honor of San José, and in that way it would survive when in other villages it was prohibited.

S. K. Lothrop (1929) describes the religious ceremonies of holy week in the Quiche town of Atitlan, Guatemala. He writes, "In front of the church two posts joined by a cross-bar were erected. These they covered with pine and cedar boughs, and further adorned with all manner of fruit and vegetables. On the cross-bar were a stuffed raccoon and two live pisotes." It will be noted that the pisote is again directly associated with agriculture, and that this ceremony like that of San Antonio falls at the same time of year.

Cucumatz, the Quiche creator god, is called pisote, in addition to his other titles which include such agricultural terms as "He of the green calabash," "He of the leaves," and "He of the green plate" (Jimenez, p. 9).

Further the hero of the fights against the Chol is called Siis, which is the Kekchi name for the pisote (p. 152).

Finally, a pottery whistle from Cankuen illustrated by Maler (p. 36) depicts a pisote holding an ear of corn in his paws.

It would then appear that the pisote was formerly intimately connected with agriculture throughout the Maya area, as survivals so far apart as Atitlan and Socotz testify.

The ceiba tree was, and in many parts of Guatemala still is, the sacred tree par excellence of the Maya race.

The only other ceremony of interest still maintained by the Mayas of Socotz is the pig ceremony held on the day of Holy Cross (May 3). In the neighboring village of Arenal it is held in July. All who wish to take part in this fiesta contribute something beforehand. Some give money; others cacao, tortillas, ribbons, or any other necessity. A large hog is obtained. He is killed, and his head and shoulders removed in one piece. A stone is placed in his mouth, and the head and shoulders are placed in a large pot to cook. When it is cooked, the stone is taken out of the mouth and replaced with tortillas, tamales, and frijoles. It is then placed in a basket surrounded by all the fruits of the milpa and a bottle of rum. The basket is gaily adorned with ribbons. A man, who is supposed to represent a hog, then lifts it on his shoulders, and proceeds to make a tour of the village. In the course of his tour he visits nine houses, at each one of which he grunts like a hog. Occasionally he lies down and rolls about like the animal he represents. Aguardiente is poured over him to revive him. In short the whole business is an elaborate buffoonery. All the time the people dance around him. At the conclusion of the procession the head and shoulders were formerly placed in the church, and prayers were said to have been addressed to it, but recently the Catholic padres have objected to this practice, and the hog is now taken to a private house where it is laid out on a table. The people march around nine times, and a little later nine times more but this time in reverse order. It is said that formerly prayers were offered to the hog, but nobody was willing definitely to say that this was so or to give any information on the object of the whole fiesta. At the close of the ceremony, the head is quartered, and a piece is given to each of the four principal participants. The contents of the basket are also divided among those present with this proviso: he who receives a tortilla at the distribution must contribute two for the fiesta when it is held the following year, and the same applies to all the varieties of food that are thus divided.

In Arenal the buffoonery is carried a step farther. Half the men dress up as women and half as old men with faces blackened (see p. 104). In their net-bags they carry tortillas and plantains.

The connection between the hog and the produce of the milpa is strongly emphasized, and apparently here again we are dealing with an old agricultural festival. Probably the hog is a modern substitute for either the wild boar or the peccary. The association of the boar and the spirit of agriculture in Europe has been commented on by James Frazer (chap. 48). In various parts of Upper Bavaria a man is detailed to carry the pig around, although in this case the pig is at the best only a bundle of straw made up in the form of a pig.

In the valley of Mexico the ceremonies connected with the spirit of the corn are very close parallels to those practiced in Europe and there seems little doubt that in both cases they are survivals of customs that date back to neolithic times at least.

Prayers to the ancient deities only survive now in connection with the making of the milpa. Here alone is to be expected a strong stand against the alien beliefs forced upon the Maya by their conquerors. One is not surprised by the little that has survived, but rather by the tenacity with which the Maya, as well as the other Indian races of Central America, has clung to the beliefs that clustered about the most sacred thing in his existence—the soil. Despite three centuries of cruel tyranny, cold-blooded abuse, and heartless persecution by both the civil and religious authorities the Maya has refused to yield up his simple pagan beliefs that are so closely associated with his everyday life. The atrocities committed on the natives of Central America during these three centuries have revealed the Christian civilization in no bright light. In Yucatan only since the introduction of the semi-socialist régime has the Maya been treated as a human being rather than a beast of burden. The Maya is no longer whipped for not attending or being late for church. No longer does one hear that bitter expression "the Maya only hears through his back," save possibly among the exiled landlords, who eagerly await the return of "the good old times."

VII. AGRICULTURE AT SOCOTZ

The communal method of agriculture employed in the Toledo District is no longer practiced at Socotz. There the system is purely individualistic. Each family cultivates its own milpa, hiring outside labor at the rate of fifty cents a day when, and if, required. Each family rents land from the government. The area is usually sufficient to allow of a four year rotation of locality.

When the owner of the land is ready to start clearing to make his milpa, he sets up a small altar on the edge of the area he intends to clear. This altar consists of four forked corner posts, across which thin sticks are laid. At the back of the altar a small rough cross is placed.

The ceremony (Spanish *primicia;* Maya *u walikol*) to be described is attended by no one save the owner of the milpa that is to be made. On the morning on which he is to start work he brings with him five calabashes (*Lutš*) containing a special posol known as *sakqab* (white juice) because it contains no lime. These calabashes are placed one at each corner of the altar, and one in the center of the front edge.

This latter, which is larger than the rest, and is known as *Holtše*, represents *Quh*, who, my informant, after some thought, hazarded was the lord of the thunder. The corner calabashes represented *Qaanan Qasob* (the rain gods, meaning bountiful forests), *Halatš winkob* (the big men), *Ahbehob* (those who pass before—the captains), and *Balam winkob* (the tiger men or big men). In Yucatan the *Yumbalamob* are the guardians of the towns. They are four in number, and sit one at each of the four entrances to the town, corresponding to the four cardinal points.

When the altar is arranged the *Hmen* recites the following prayer:

| *En el nombre del Padre,* | | *del Hijo,* | *y del Espiritu Santo amen.* | |
| In the name of the father, | | the son, | and the Holy Spirit amen. | |

| *Waye* | *kin* | *watal* | *kin* | *kawatal,* | *ošwalahen* |
| Here | I | stand, | I | a second time stand, | a third time I am on foot |

| *in wemes* | *Dios Padre,* | *Dios Hijo,* | *y* | *Dios Espiritu Santo.* |
| to bow down | to God the Father, | God the Son, | and | God the Holy Ghost. |

| *Eya in yume* | *beyšan* | *u* | *yorahil* | *kin watal* | *in tane* |
| Behold my Lord | thus also | at | this hour | I stand | in your presence |

115

a ɔiki ben	*kawa ti*	*tun*	*kin watal*	*in tane*	*t' u*	*qaba*
to worship	therefore	there	I stand	in the presence of his name		

Santo Dios	*etel tulakal in nukil winkob*	*Sateešten*	*in sipil*
Lord God	with all my great men (lords of the forest).	Give me	my sins

tumen kin	*watal utial tumen*	*in wemes*	*le diosobe*
because I	stand in order that	I may bow down	to these Lords.

baš yoqlal	*tšen tuube*	*yoqlal*	*in kuhik*	*cinco lutšil*
Because	you may not forget	without cause because	I offer	five calabashes full

ukul	*utial*	*nukil*	*winkobo*	*yum quhoba,*	*le qanaan qašhobe,*
to drink	for the	big	men	the Lords Kuh,	the bountiful forest Lords,

leti tum	*halatš*	*wincobo*	*leti*	*šan*	*ahbehobe.*
these are	the true	men.	These also the ones that clear the roads.		

Ea in yume	*uɔolben*	*tan*	*Diosobe*	*Tan in betik*	*yukulil*
Behold my Lord	the good intentions	in the presence	of the gods.	I am making	his drink

in kol.	*Ea*	*satesten*	*in nukutš*	*yumsileeš.*	*Nah mateeš*
my milpa.	Lo	give it me	my great	Lords.	You must accept

tun hun pit	*siis ha ukul*	*siiskuntic a*	*woleeš.*	*U qaba*
then one	cold drink to drink	that they may cool	your souls.	The name

Dios yume	*Dios Hijo*	*Dios Espiritu Santo.*	*Amen.*
of God the master,	God the Son,	God the Holy Ghost.	Amen.

FREE TRANSLATION

In the name of God the Father, God the Son, and God the Holy Ghost, Amen. Here before you I stand. Three times do I stand before you to worship you God the Father, God the Son, and God the Holy Ghost. Behold my Lord how I stand in your presence now to venerate you. I stand in the presence of your holy name, Lord God and in the presence too of the Lords of the forests, who are mighty men. Forgive me my sins because I am here to worship these Gods. That you may not forget me without cause I offer these five calabashes of posol in order that the mighty men, the lords of the forest, who live on the mountain tops, and who are the true lords, and are those who pass before to clear the road; in order that they, I repeat, may drink. Behold my Lord my good intentions in the presence of the Gods. I am preparing the drink-offering for my milpa. Forgive me O my great masters. Accept then but one cool draught of posol that the anger that lies in your hearts toward me may be cooled. In the name of God the Father, God the Son, and God the Holy Ghost. Amen.

When this prayer is completed the *Hmen* drinks one of the calabashes of posol. The others are left standing on the altar. If at the end of a fixed period the posol has turned sour, that is a sign that the lords of the forest are not satisfied for some reason or other and have refused to receive the *primicia*. In that case the *primicia* is repeated on some other occasion. Meanwhile, if the *primicia* is received the owner of the milpa is free to go ahead with his work. The ceremony is repeated before burning, sowing, when the ears begin to form, and at harvest. No abstentions, such as obtain in the Toledo District, are practised.

About every other year, the usual harvest *primicia* is replaced by a similar thanksgiving, but on a larger scale. In this ceremony all the family together with many friends take part. The evening before the appointed day the women are busy preparing the food. This consists of tamales made with pumpkin seeds, others made with ground beans, and a chicken or turkey from which only the beak, feet and entrails have been removed. The bird is placed in a pot to cook with salt and other dressings.

An altar is erected of the same type as that used in the ordinary *primicia*, but slightly larger. On this are placed the five calabashes of posol as on the previous occasion. At the side of each is placed a lighted candle of black wax. The center of the altar is occupied by nine piles of tortillas arranged in three straight rows of three piles each. Each pile consists of nine tortillas. Just behind the center calabash is another pile of thirteen tortillas. As soon as the altar is ready the prayer given above is recited, and then the food offerings are left for a space of two hours in order that the lords of the milpa may partake of them. At the foot of the altar is placed a bottle of rum, but there seems to be some doubt as to whether this forms part of the offering. At the conclusion of the two hours the *Hmen*, approaching the altar, recites the following short prayer:

In yume	*ɔoki*	*u yora tal tun*	*Tu qaba Dios Padre*
O Lord	it is finished	the hour has come	then in the name of God the Father,

Dios hijo,	*Dios Espiritu Santo.*	*Amen.*	*Behela tun*	*ku yantal*
God the Son,	and God the Holy Ghost.	Amen.	Now if he	desires it

in	*wensik*	*okaana*	*matikeeš*	*u suyuhil.*	*Behela kin*
I am	lowering	it having finished	receiving it you	its virginity.	Now I am

in wensik.
lowering it.

FREE TRANSLATION

O Lord, the hour is come. In the name of the Father, the Son, and the Holy Ghost, Amen. As you have accepted my offering, I am about to remove it from the altar. For you have received it in all its freshness and purity. Now I am going to lower it from the altar.

Thereupon four men step up to the altar, placing themselves one at each corner, the *Hmen* standing as before in the center. He takes the bottle of rum and, scattering a little to the four corners of the earth, he takes a drink and passes the bottle in turn to each of the four corner men. Each takes a small drink without, however, scattering any to the four directions. The *Hmen* next takes up the largest calabash (the *holtše*) and, casting a little of the contents to the four corners, again drinks. The four corner men drink also from their respective calabashes. The ceremony concludes with a Christian benediction, after which the friends and relations fall to on the victuals that have been prepared both in the house and in the *pib* (underground oven heated with stones).

Often the regular *sakqab* posol is replaced by a preparation made from twenty-five handfuls of young corn straight from the milpa. Care must be taken not to lose a single grain from the ears, and the beards too must be preserved. The corn is scraped by hand, not soaked in lime, and, after it has been ground, it is mixed with molasses and the beards. In this careful preservation of every grain and whisp of beard there is a hint of a former belief in a corn spirit residing in the young corn. However, at present no such belief is retained at Socotz.

VIII. FOLKLORE OF SAN ANTONIO

THE LEGEND OF THE SUN, THE MOON, AND VENUS

The son of the first people, Adam and Eve, was placed in heaven and the crown of the sun was put on his head, but it was too hot. At the end of seven years the boy refused to stand the heat any more, so he caused a flood to cool himself and plunged into the water. Then the world was dark and flooded. When he was cool once more he resumed his duties as before. Later a messenger came to the first people, Adam and Eve, and talked to them, and the old grandfather (Adam) said, "Many people have been drowned, because my son got tired of wearing the sun's crown. In another seven years he will want to cool himself again, and there will be another flood, and more people will get drowned. Suppose we look for somebody else to take the place of my son as the sun. There are three children here on earth, whose mother and father are dead. They live with their grandmother, whose name is Xkitza. Perhaps one of them will take the place of my son, and do the work of carrying the crown of the sun."

Then the messenger talked with the second eldest of these three brothers. The boy agreed to be the sun, and the messenger asked him how long he would act as the sun. The boy replied, "I don't know, perhaps forever."

The messenger sent him to travel across the heavens to see if he liked it. When the boy turned back in the evening, the messenger asked him how he enjoyed it.

"I don't like it at all," replied the boy. "It isn't the heat; I don't feel that, but it is the earth. It is dull and flat. There are no hills or valleys—there are no seas or rivers. It is just a dead monotonous plain. If the earth were more interesting I would be the sun forever."

Then the messenger reported what the boy said, and the world became dark for a short while, and the hills and valleys were formed, the seas were made and the rivers flowed across the land. Then the boy was once more sent as the sun to travel across the heavens, to see if he liked the earth now that it had been changed. In the evening when he returned from his journey he cried,   "Now the

119

world is beautiful and I will be the sun forever. I will never grow old, but will always be strong and do my work."

But the messenger told him the time had not yet come, and for the present the first sun would continue to do the work.

This boy, Lord Kin, was the second brother. His eldest brother was Lord Xulab, or Nohoch Ich (Big Eye) who later was to become the planet Venus, and the youngest brother, the T'up, was to become one of the other planets, either Mars or Jupiter.

The three brothers used to go out to hunt birds in the forest with their blowgun (ɔontše). At night they would return home and give the birds they had killed to their grandmother, Xkitza, to cook. But the old woman used to make them sleep while she cooked the birds. She didn't give the meat to the boys, but kept it for her lover, a huge monster, some say a tapir, who used to visit her every night. When the boys were asleep she would take fat and smear it on their lips and throw the bones of the birds they had shot down under their hammocks. When the boys woke up in the morning and called for meat, she would say to them: "But you ate all the meat last night. Look at the bones under your hammocks, and see, the grease of the meat from the bones you were gnawing is still on your lips and cheeks." The boys used to believe her.

One day they met a trogon bird (Kokoh) in the forest.

"Kokoh, kokoh," the trogon cried.

"I'll kill you and put your head in a pot. What are you saying?" shouted Lord Kin.

"Kokoh, kokoh," replied the bird.

"I'm going to kill you and eat you," replied Lord Kin, raising his blowgun to take aim.

"Why do you want to kill me?" cried the trogon. "You kill off all us birds, but you don't eat us at all."

Lord Kin asked him what he meant, and the trogon thereupon explained how their grandmother used to trick the boys into believing they had eaten the meat, whereas really it was her lover who ate it. Then Lord Kin turned to Lord Xulab, and asked him what they should do. Lord Xulab, who was rather stupid, said, "I don't know what we can do."

"But I, yes, I know what we must do," answered Lord Kin. "We'll kill this monster. Leave it to me."

When they got home the Lord Kin said to his grandmother, "We couldn't get any birds. They are getting scarce and wild. Tomorrow we are going a long way away. Make us plenty of tortillas for the journey."

That night the old woman made them a big pile of tortillas and totopostes, and at dawn the three brothers went off with their blowguns. However, they didn't go far, but looked around for the trail through the forest along which Xkitza's lover used to pass. After a while they found it.

"Now how are we going to kill him?" Lord Kin asked his eldest brother.

"I don't know," replied Lord Xulab. "We have only our blowguns, and with them we can't kill this beast."

"Oh you are very stupid. Do as I tell you and we'll kill him."

Then under the Lord Kin's direction they set to work and made a deep pit in the trail. In this they placed sharp sticks, of the kind called *tontšib* in Maya, with the points upward. The top of the pit they covered over with small branches and earth. When all was ready they spoke to the thrush (*Tšiqwam*), asking him to sing to them if the monster came along and fell into the trap. The bird agreed to do so, but when he sang and the boys came running up, there was no monster in the trap nor sign of him. Then they asked the Singing Thrush (Maya *P'itš;* Spanish *Tordo Cantor*) to give them warning. He called out, but again it was a false alarm. They then asked the Magpie (*Paap*) to warn them. About sunset they heard the earth trembling. It was the noise of the monster coming out of the hill where he lived. The Magpie called to the boys. They went running and found the monster lover of their grandmother had fallen into the pit and was transfixed by the sharp stakes, called *tontšib*. Then the boys cut off and roasted the animal's penis and took it home next day to their grandmother. When they arrived they called out to the old woman that they had shot no birds, but they had got a fine fish, giving her the roasted penis. The old woman ate it.

"Does it taste good?" asked the boys.

"Yes, it is fine," replied Xkitza.

Then the boys began to laugh, and some birds that were round the house called out, "Look at her. She's eaten the penis."

Xkitza was suspicious, as her lover hadn't visited her the previous night. She called to the boys, "You must be tired. Get into your hammocks and go to sleep. I'm going down to the river to fetch water."

The boys did so, and the old woman, taking her water jar, left the house. The boys were afraid and didn't go to sleep. After some time when the old woman didn't return they asked the toad (*Muš*) to go and see what their grandmother was doing. But the toad said he was afraid as he couldn't travel fast, and if the old woman wanted to kill him he could only get away hop by hop. Then the boys asked the big crested lizard (*Baat*) to go. The lizard went off. When he got to the side of the river he saw the old woman sharpening her finger nails, and muttering, "Make my nails and the bones of my fingers grow."

When the lizard saw and heard this, he ran between the old woman's feet. The old woman was annoyed, and breaking off a piece of the pottery water jar, she threw it at the lizard. The piece lodged there in the back of the lizard's head. The lizard ran off back to the boys, and told them what he had seen, and how the old woman was going to kill the three of them. Then he asked them to take the piece of jar out of his neck. The boys only laughed and said he looked prettier like that, and they took a knife and sharpened the point of the piece of pottery.

"Now shake your head," they said.

The lizard did so, but the boys only laughed. That is how the *baat* got his crest.

The boys then took three *qaantše* ("low wooden seats made from tree trunks") and put one in each hammock, and then three cala-bashes which they put at the heads of the *qaantše*, and blankets over them, so that it appeared as though they were all three sleeping in their hammocks. Instead they climbed up into the rafters of the hut. Soon their grandmother came quietly in and creeping up to the first hammock dug her claws into the calabashes one by one, so that if the boys had been lying there instead they would surely have been killed. Then the boys laughed, and their grandmother looked up startled.

"What are you doing down there?" they asked.

"I was just playing," she replied.

Lord Kin and Lord Xulab resolved to get rid of their youngest brother, as they had decided to kill their grandmother, and the youngest boy did not approve. They went out with their blowguns to shoot birds. Presently they shot a bird, which, although killed, remained stuck in a top branch of a high tree. They made the youngest boy climb up to retrieve the bird, after first tying a blanket round his waist with the loose end hanging down behind. When the boy had almost reached the top branch of the tree, Lord Kin called out to him, "You must do as I tell you. Now call out wacwacwacwacwac" (imitating the chatter of the spider monkey, *Maaš*).

The boy did so. Then Lord Kin made the boy climb up higher still, and again imitate the spider monkey. Then the boy began to chatter just like a monkey, and to swing himself from tree to tree. The blanket round him turned into the shaggy hair of the monkey, and the end hanging down below was transformed into a monkey's tail.

"Now you must stay there, and always remain like that," Lord Kin told him.

Before this there had been no monkeys in the world. From the young boy who was turned into a monkey are descended all the monkeys one now sees in the forest.

Lord Kin and Lord Xulab returned home to Xkitza.

"Let's play at asking questions," Lord Kin said to the old woman. Now it was understood that whoever failed to answer any of the questions would be killed. The boy asked the first question. "What is the stick, from the end of which water flows?" He hoped that she would reply that it was the water liana, but she answered correctly that it was his penis. It was now the old woman's turn to ask a question. "What is the water that flows between the two hills?" she asked. Kin answered correctly that it was her urine.

"Now again it is my turn," he cried. "Tell me, what is it that makes a noise 'Trump, Trump' as it moves?"

Xkitza said it was the spindle and whorl.

"This is it," cried Lord Kin, hurling a throwing top (see p. 153) at her.

But Xkitza jumped aside, and the top did not kill her. Again it was her turn to put a question, and again the Lord Kin answered her. The question was as to what were the three hills with something flat on top. The answer was the three stones of the fireplace and the comal (griddle) on top. Once more Lord Kin put the question, "What is it that goes up into the air, travels along and drops down again?"

The old grandmother confessed she didn't know.

"Well, this is it," cried the Lord Kin. As he said this, he drew his bow and let fly an arrow which killed Xkitza.

The boys buried their grandmother, but then they found they had no woman to cook for them. Lord Kin told his brother Lord Xulab that, as he was the eldest, he must get married, so they could have a woman to cook for both of them. Lord Xulab didn't want to marry, but Lord Kin insisted, and got an old woman to arrange the marriage between his brother and the daughter of an old man that lived close by. The girl came to live with Lord Xulab, but she never saw his face as he was away all day minding his animals and only came home at night. For Lord Xulab is the owner of all the animals in the world, and he used to keep all these animals in pens—the peccary, the deer, the antelope, the gibnut, the turkey, the curassow, in short, all the animals and birds of the world. He did this so that everyone could come to him for meat. He used, too, to make a milpa to have maize for his animals. Every plant in his milpa used to yield a cob of corn for every leaf, and with two cobs of corn a day he used to have sufficient corn to feed all his animals.

However, as Lord Xulab was always away his wife got discontented. One day when the brothers were away, a man arrived at the house and began to make love to her. The girl took no notice of him, although he was a sorcerer. A second time he came, and again he was repulsed. A third time he came and said to the girl, "Why won't you take any notice of me? I'm handsome, but your husband, Lord Xulab, is as ugly as can be. His face is all covered with a big beard. If you don't believe me, look at him tonight. Put seven sticks of pitch pine by the fire; and when he comes in, light them and hold them up so that you can see his face, and you will know that I am speaking the truth."

That night when Lord Xulab was eating, the girl lit the pines and looked at her husband's face. Just as the bad man had said, she saw how ugly Lord Xulab was with his great beard (like his brother, Lord Kin). Then she began to laugh, and Lord Xulab jumped up. As he jumped up, all the animals broke out of their pens and started to scatter in all directions. Lord Xulab ran out to catch them, but he couldn't do so. Some of the animals, like the deer, the antelope, the rabbit, and the peccary, he managed to catch by the tail, but their tails broke off, and they escaped. That is why these animals either have no tails now, or their tails are very short.

Lord Xulab was very angry. "I'm going away," he cried. "I won't have anything more to do with women."

Then he called the Mam, who are also known as the Huitz-Hok, and are the earth gods, Lords of the hills and valleys, and told them they must look after his animals and plants for him.

"The people can no longer have tame animals, but if they obey my laws I will give them meat to eat and corn and other plants in their milpas. My law is this. When men want to hunt, they must keep vigil all night, and in the hours before dawn they must burn copal incense (*pom*) to me, and beg me for some of my animals. They must do this when I am at home and before I rise high above the horizon. Then when they arrive where they are going to hunt or make their milpa, they must again burn copal and pray, but this time to the Mam. For the Mam are to do my work for me, and they will release the animals from their pens and place them in the forest where they can easily be hunted. Those people who don't comply with this law will get no game except the few stray animals that don't want to live in my pens, and the crops in their milpas will be of little value, and the fish they get will be small."

Now Lord Xulab's hands were covered with blood from the animals' tails that had broken when he caught hold of them, and he wiped his hands first on the plant called *štšayuk*, and next on another plant called *štšai* (*Jatropha acontifolia*) and lastly on an old tree. Then these two plants became edible and edible fungi (*šiqintše*) grew on the tree trunks. This Lord Xulab did, so that the people might have more to eat to replace the tame animals that were no more. Then Lord Xulab went away, but the time was not yet come for him to become the Morning Star.

Lord Kin, too, wandered away, travelling far. When he came to a large mountain, he hurled his blowgun at it, and crawled through the tube of the gun. Eventually he arrived at the house of his mother. Now his mother had been unmarried when she gave birth to him, and fearing the wrath of her father, had hidden him in a box close to a stream where he had been found by the old woman, Xkitza, whom he subsequently killed. On arriving at the house, he entered, asking for food and lodging, which his mother granted him. However, she did not recognize him as her son although he knew her to be his mother. She pointed to her hammock, and told him to rest in it until the food was ready; but he sat instead in the hammock of another son of his mother. When he had finished eating, he prepared to leave; but his mother asked him to stay and live with her as she had no husband. Lord Kin was angry at this. "Shameless woman," he cried, "don't you realize you are my mother, yet you wish me to sleep with you."

When his mother understood who he was, she asked to be forgiven, begging him to stay at the hut, and promising to get a good wife. Lord Kin refused, and continued on his way.

After a time he came to a house where an old man lived, whose name was T'actani. With him lived his granddaughter, a pretty girl called X't'actani, who was a very fine spinner and weaver of cotton. Lord Kin decided this girl should be his wife, but he resolved not to employ any professional matchmaker to arrange the affair, but to win the girl by himself. The first day in that neighborhood he went out to hunt, and shot an antelope. He returned home, passing by the house where the girl lived so that she could see him. Game was scarce, so Lord Kin decided to trick the girl into thinking he was a fine hunter. Accordingly he stuffed the antelope's skin with ashes and dried grass and leaves, and every evening after dark he used to take the stuffed skin and leave it in the forest, returning to his hut. Early in the morning he would pass by the girl's house empty-handed on his way to hunt, returning a short while afterwards with the stuffed animal on his shoulder. The girl was impressed.

"Look, grandfather!" she cried. "That man shoots game every day. He must be a wonderful hunter. I would like to have him as my husband."

"Hmm," said old T'actani. "Perhaps he's just tricking you."

"No," said the girl. "He must be the one who kills the animals. Look at the blood on him."

"Hmm," grunted the old man. "Throw some water on the path next time he passes and see what happens."

The girl didn't believe him, but next time when Lord Kin was returning from hunting, she threw the lime water in which she had been soaking the maize on the path.

Lord Kin slipped and fell. The antelope skin burst, and all the ashes, grass, and leaves poured out on the ground in front of the house. The girl began to laugh, and Lord Kin, very ashamed of himself, ran off.

Lord Kin was very ashamed and vexed, but he still wanted the girl. So he went to the humming bird (ɔ'unun) and asked him to lend him his skin. But the humming bird said that he could not lend his skin as he would die of the cold. Lord Kin said he would wrap him up in cotton, and then the humming bird agreed. Lord Kin then put on the skin and, turning into a humming bird, flew off to the house where X't'actani lived. From the ashes and grass that had poured out of the antelope skin had sprung up a tobacco plant. To this sped Lord Kin, in his guise of humming bird, and darting from flower to flower sucked the honey. X't'actani saw him, and called to T'actani.

"Grandfather, look at that beautiful humming bird. How I would like to have him. Get your blowgun and shoot him for me."

The old man grumbling did so, and the humming bird fell to the ground. However, it was only stunned, and X't'actani picked it up. As she stooped down, the strap which passed round her waist and held the loom taut slipped, and the loom fell to the ground. She took the humming bird indoors and, giving it chocolate and maize, succeeded in reviving it. That night she took it to her bedroom, which was the innermost of thirteen rooms.

In the night she woke up to find a man with her. Frightened, she asked him who he was. It was Lord Kin, and he explained how he had changed into a humming bird to be able to approach her.

"My grandfather will kill me now," the girl cried.

"Well you must run away with me," replied Lord Kin.

The girl wanted to do so, but she was afraid, as her grandfather had a magic stone (*sastun*, a round pebble of jade or rock-crystal) in which he could see everything that was happening in the world. Lord Kin told the girl to fetch the *sastun*, and when she brought it, he proceeded to cover it with soot, and then told the girl to put it back in its place, and then they could flee without danger of being found. But the girl was still afraid, as her grandfather had a magic blowgun with which he could suck anything to him, no matter how far away it might be. Lord Kin bade her bring him the blowgun too, and grind some red pepper. When the pepper was ready, he placed it in the blowgun and, stopping up the muzzle, told the girl to put it back in its accustomed place. They then fled together.

In the morning T'actani saw no sign of the girl. He called her, but there was no reply. He searched for her, but could not find her. Then he reached for his *sastun* to see where she had gone. It was covered with soot and he could see nothing till he noticed a small spot that Lord Kin had omitted to cover, and looking through that he saw his granddaughter and Lord Kin in a canoe. Determined to bring the couple back, he stretched for his magic blowgun and, putting it to his lips, he sucked with all his might. Next moment he lay on his back half-choked and gasping for breath, his mouth and throat full of the ground chili Lord Kin had put in the barrel before he fled. T'actani, when he recovered, was beside himself with fury.

"Now they shall die," he cried.

He sent his son to fetch his uncle, Chac, the thunder god. When Chac arrived, he asked him to send a thunderbolt to kill the fleeing lovers. Chac protested, "No, I won't kill them. You are very angry now, and want me to kill them; but later when your anger passes, you will be sorry that they are dead, and you will then be vexed with me for killing them."

However, T'actani insisted and insisted until at last Chac agreed, and departing dressed himself in his black clothes, and took up his drum and axe.

Lord Kin saw Chac approaching. "Now your grandfather has sent Chac to kill us," he cried. "In this canoe we have no shelter."

Accordingly he turned himself into a turtle and the girl into a crab. With all speed they swam to the bottom of the sea (or lake?). But the crab swims slowly, and when the thunderbolt fell, Lord Kin was far below the surface, but the girl was only a little way down, and the thunderbolt killed her. Lord Kin, when the danger had passed, swam to the surface again, and saw the water dyed with the blood of X't'actani. He was very grieved. He called to some small fish that were swimming in the water (*suktan*), and asked them to collect the remains of the girl. The fish came, but instead of collecting the remains they began to eat the flesh and drink the blood. Then Lord Kin asked the dragon flies (*tuhluš*) to help him. They did so and collected the remains in thirteen *huhul* (hollow wooden logs). These Lord Kin left in the house of an old woman who lived by the shore. "In thirteen days I will come back for them," he told the old woman.

At the end of the thirteen days he returned for the *huhul*. "You must take them away," the old woman cried. "I can't sleep for the noise that comes from inside them, a buzzing and a humming and a creaking. Not another night must they remain here."

Then Lord Kin began to open the barrels. The first contained nothing but snakes—tommy goffs, rattlesnakes, coral snakes; in fact, every conceivable kind of poisonous snake. Lord Kin shut the lid again. He peeped into all the other barrels. The second was full of snakes, as was the third, but they were not the poisonous kind. The fourth was full of mosquitos; the fifth, of sand flies; the sixth, of big green hornets; the seventh, of yellow wasps; the eighth, of small black wasps; the ninth, of black wasps with white wings; the tenth, of hairy white caterpillars, whose hair causes an intense irritation; the eleventh and twelfth held different kinds of flies, but squatting in the thirteenth was his love, X't'actani. He sent a man to throw the other twelve *huhul* into the sea. On the way, the man became curious as to what caused all the noise in the barrels and opened them one by one. Out crawled the snakes and caterpillars, and the different insects flew away all over the world. Before this there had been none of these pests.

When X't'actani came to life again, she had no vagina. Lord Kin did not know what to do, but consulted the old woman in whose house he had left the thirteen hollow wooden tubes. Acting on her advice, he made the girl lie down in a narrow defile between two hills. Then he called the small deer (*yuk*) and asked him to run over the outstretched girl. The small deer did so, but the imprint of his hoofs between the girl's thighs was very small. Lord Kin thereupon summoned the large deer (*keh*) to his aid. The imprint of the hoof of the large deer was satisfactory. Lord Kin had connection with the girl. It seemed to him very wonderful. He thought the people would ruin themselves with this new pleasure; accordingly, he summoned the rat (*tšo*) and bade him urinate in the girl's vagina. Since then sexual pleasure has been followed by revulsion.

Lord Kin and the woman went away and built a new house, and his brother, Lord Xulab, came to live with them.

After a time Lord Kin began to suspect that his wife was not true to him, and was having relations with his brother, Lord Xulab. He was jealous and angry and determined to give the pair a lesson.

One day he went out and, meeting a turkey on the road, asked the turkey if he would give him his gall. The turkey did so. A little farther he met a fowl, and from him, too, he obtained some gall. Then he went to the hut of an old woman and asked her for some ground chili, and red dye (arnatto) that is used to color food (*kušub*, *Bixa orellana*). Then he got the old lady to make a tamal out of the mixture. When it was ready in its covering of maize paste, he put it under his arm so that the heat of his body might cook it, and returned home. When he got to the hut, Lord Xulab and X't'actani were there.

"I've got a fine tamal here," he said. "An old woman made some for me, and they are very good."

The guilty pair took the tamal and began to eat it. With the first mouthful they almost choked to death. Tears streamed down their faces, and they vomited. They drank all the water that was in the house, but could not get the horrible taste out of their mouths. X't'actani took the water jar, and went down to the bank of the river to get more.

She was sitting there sobbing with vexation and self-pity when a vulture (*tšom*) flew down. "Oh, I wish you would take me away with you. My husband is very cruel to me and I hate him," sobbed the girl.

"I'll take you away if you like," answered the vulture. "I'll take you to my master, who lives in a big white house."

X't'actani agreed to go, and getting onto the sopilote's back was carried up into the air and away. After a half-way rest on a big cottonwood tree (*yaštše*) they approached the town of the sopilotes.

"There is the fine stone house of my master," said the sopilote. "See how white it is." But the house wasn't of stone. It was made of guano droppings.

The girl went to live with the chief of the vultures. Some say he was a king vulture; others, a big devil with four eyes and four horns.

Lord Kin suspected that the girl had been carried off by the vulture. Accordingly he went to the antelope and, borrowing his skin, changed into an antelope and lay down on the bank of the river as though he were dead. Then he called the blue blowfly (*yaškatš*) and told him to put the stuff on the antelope skin that turns into worms. The blowfly did so.

"Now fly past the home of the vultures, so they smell the smell of rotten meat," said Lord Kin.

The blowfly did so, and the vultures smelt the smell of the meat and asked the blowfly where he had been feeding.

"Down by the river bank there is a dead antelope," replied the blowfly.

The vultures flew off to the feast. They alighted. All were there except the one that had carried X't'actani on his back. They waited for him, for the vultures have the custom of waiting till all are present before they start to eat. At last he arrived, and the vultures hopped toward the antelope. Lord Kin kept still till the one that had carried off his wife hopped up to pluck out his eye. Then, swiftly putting out his hand, he caught the vulture.

"Let me go. Let me go," cried the vulture.

"No, I won't let you go. You must carry me to your master," answered Lord Kin.

"You are too heavy. I can't carry you," said the vulture.

"You carried the girl, so you can carry me," replied Lord Kin.

At last the vulture consented, and taking Lord Kin on his back, started to fly home. When they were getting near the vultures' home, Lord Kin made the vulture put him down on the ground. Near-by he found two men who were cutting wood to carry to the town. One of these he persuaded to carry him, hidden in the middle of his load. The load of wood began to creak. When they were close to the town, Lord Kin got out of the wood and entered the town. He went to the house of the chief and asked lodging.

"There is no room here, but you can occupy that empty house over there," the chief's servant told him.

Lord Kin borrowed a hammock and went to the house. In the rafters he found a drum and a flute of the long kind called *šol*, and on the ground he discovered seven grains of red maize. In each grain he dug a hole, and then threw all seven of them over the house where the chief lived. Then he began to play the drum and flute.

The chief began to suffer from toothache (caused by the red corn with the holes). Gradually the pain grew worse. The chief sent his servant to ask Lord Kin if he could cure the pain, but gave orders that Lord Kin was not to be admitted inside the room. Lord Kin refused to go, saying, "How can I cure the old man of his toothache if I have to stand outside the door and cannot see him to find out what is the matter?" The messenger returned to his master, and Lord Kin resumed playing the flute and drum.

The pain grew worse, and again the chief sent to fetch Lord Kin, but still refused him admittance to the room. Again, Lord Kin said it would be useless for him to go unless he was allowed into the presence of the sick man. At last the old chief could stand the pain no longer and sent for Lord Kin, giving orders that he was to be admitted to the room. Lord Kin then went. When he entered the room, he saw his wife sitting there with the sick chief. By means of his skill he quickly cured the sick man of his toothache, and in a short while the chief fell asleep. Lord Kin turned to X't'actani and bade her flee with him. X't'actani refused, but after much entreaty at last consented to return to him. The pair then left the house and, catching two of the vultures, made these carry them back to the side of the river.

The time had now come for Lord Kin to take up his duties as the sun and to bear on his head the crown. Together with his elder and younger brother and his wife he ascended into the sky. His elder brother became the morning star. His younger brother became the evening star; and his wife, X't'actani, the moon.

Lord Kin placed a mirror in the center of the sky, and every morning he used to start out from his home in the east and travel till he got to the center. Then he used to turn back home, but the mirror reflected his light, and it appeared as though he were continuing his journey. When he got home, X't'actani, as the moon, used to walk across the heavens in the same manner. At that time she was as bright as her husband, the sun. Then there was no darkness, for the night was as bright as the day. One night when she returned from her journey, she appeared sad. Lord Kin asked her what ailed her.

"I have been looking down on the earth during my walk across the sky," she replied, "and I see the people of the world are not happy. They work all day and night, and cannot sleep as the nights are as bright as the days."

Lord Kin thought for some time, and then turning to her said, "What you say is true. The people require sleep. Your light is too bright. I will take out one of your eyes, and then you will not shine so brightly." Whereupon he gouged out one of her eyes.

"Now go and see if the people of the world are more contented," he cried. The lady U did so. With her one eye, that gave only a soft light, she looked down on the world, and saw the people there contentedly sleeping in their houses. She returned to her husband and reported that now all was well. Since that time men have been able to rest from their labors and sleep at night.

Now at that time mankind had no maize or other agricultural plants. They and the animals lived on fruits and the roots they found in the forest. However, there was maize in the world. It was hidden under a great rock, but no one knew of it except the leaf-cutting ants (sai). One day the fox was going along, when he found a number of grains of maize, which the ants had dropped when they brought them from under the big rock; for they had found a way to get down through a small crack in the rock to the hidden supply below. The fox tried the maize and thought it tasted delicious. He waited till night when the ants came again, and then followed them till they came to the rock. However, he could not get under the rock, as the hole through which the leaf-cutters passed was too small. Again he ate up the grains of maize that the ants dropped on their track. After he had eaten, he returned to where the other animals were sitting. He broke wind, and the other animals asked him what he had been eating that caused even his wind to smell sweet.

The fox denied that he had been eating anything new, but the other animals suspected him and decided to follow him and see what he ate. A little later the fox loped off. The other animals followed him secretly. The fox went back to the ants' trail, where there was more maize that had been dropped. He looked round to see if he was observed, and as he could see no other animal, he began to eat the maize. However, all the other animals were hidden in the bush without his knowing it, and as soon as he began to eat, they came out of their hiding places, jeering at him. "Now we know what you have been eating," they cried.

They tried the maize and liked it. Then all the animals waited for the ants to come along the trail to ask these to fetch them more maize. The ants agreed, but the animals were so numerous that they couldn't keep all of them supplied with maize, and refused to bring any more up except for their own use. The other animals didn't know what to do. They went to the big red ants and asked them to help, but the big red ants were too big to get into the hole. Then they went to the rat and asked him to help them, but he could not get into the cache any more than the red ants could.

Finally they told man about this wonderful new food, and man asked the Mam to help them. Now the Mam are very numerous. There are four principal ones and many others of less importance. Yaluk is the greatest of the Mam. When man asked the Mam to help, Yaluk was not present. The rest of the Mam decided to try to break the stone themselves. Now the Mam are lords of the mountains and plains, they look after the animals for the Morning Star, and they are also lords of the thunder. Then each of the other three important Mam hurled a thunderbolt at the rock to try and burst it, but all failed. At last they decided they would have to ask Yaluk after all. They sent a message to him, saying they needed his help. Now Yaluk knew all that had happened, and he refused to go. A second time they asked him to go, but again he refused.

"I am an old man," he bade the messenger tell them. "I haven't the strength. They are young men, let them do it."

Thereupon the other three principal Mam again sent to summon Yaluk, confessing that they had tried, but failed. Then at last Yaluk went. First, he sent the woodpecker (*kolonte*) to tap the stone to see where it appeared weakest. The woodpecker tapped all over the stone and told Yaluk where it was thinnest.

"Well, that is the point at which I am going to hurl my thunderbolt," Yaluk told him. "Hide there behind that ledge of the rock, and you will be quite safe, but don't thrust your head out, or you will probably get killed."

Yaluk gathered all his strength together, and hurled his thunderbolt at the spot that the woodpecker had indicated as the thinnest, and burst the rock asunder. Just as the thunderbolt fell, the woodpecker, forgetful of what Yaluk had warned him, thrust out his head; and a piece of rock, hitting him on the head, cut it open, and the blood gushed out. Ever since then the woodpecker has had a red poll. Yaluk fainted away from the tremendous force he had exerted, but the other three principal Mam rushed forward to seize the corn. Now when the thunderbolt burst the rock asunder, it had burnt much of the maize. Originally all the maize had been white, but now much of it had been badly burnt and had turned red. Other grains were covered with smoke, and they had turned yellow. This is how the red and yellow maize originated.

The three Mam, taking no notice of Yaluk, seized only the white grains and hurried away to plant them. When Yaluk recovered, he could find only the red and yellow maize. This he took, and making a milpa, planted it. He was angry with the other three Mam, and said, "They have taken all the white maize, but they will have to plant it three times before it will come up."

And so it happened. The crops of the three other Mam failed. Again they sowed, and again the crop failed to come up. Then they went to Yaluk and asked him why their crops were a failure, but his was coming up beautifully.

"I don't know," replied Yaluk, still angry with them for having left him no white maize. "Your crops ought to do better than mine as you took all the good maize and only left me what was burnt. I steeped my seed in lime for three days. Perhaps that is the reason why it has come up so well."

Now he just said this as a joke, for he knew their crop would fail in any case. The three Mam went off, and soaked the rest of their seed in lime, and then sowed it. A few plants came up, but the crop was of poor quality. Thus was maize brought into the world.

The Mam gave the maize to man to sow, but at that time there were no other plants cultivated. One day some men, wandering in the forest, found a huge mamey tree (*tšukul haas*), on the branches of which grew all kinds of vegetables and fruit such as beans, sweet potatoes, squashes, etc. The animals had known of this tree for a long time and used to go there to eat.

The men decided to cut down the tree so that they might have the seed to sow. The tree was so large that by the evening there still remained a small part of the trunk to be cut through before it would fall. Next day they returned to finish chopping it down, but to their astonishment found no trace of the cut they had made the previous day; the trunk was intact.

Once more they started to cut it down, but by evening a small portion still remained uncut, and nightfall forced them to abandon the task. On returning next morning again they found the trunk once more intact. All day again they worked chopping down the tree, and when nightfall forced them to stop work, they laid down close to the tree to see what happened. Soon all the animals of the forest began to arrive one by one. When they were all there, they began to collect the chips that the men's axes had bitten out of the trunk and to hand them to the fox who replaced them one by one in their original position. As he replaced them, he called out, *"Tente otš"* ("I am replacing it"). (There is a play on words here such as the Mayas are so fond of as the word for fox is also *otš*.) When all the chips were back in position, and the trunk healed up, the animals departed.

Next day the men started once more to cut down the tree, and this time, by working without halt day and night, succeeded in felling it. They gathered the fruits and vegetables, and taking them to their milpas, sowed them.

Since then there has been plenty of beans, squashes, and other cultivated plants in the world.

The above legend was obtained from four different informants. Two of them were Kekchis by birth; a third, Maya speaking, of Kekchi descent, who, as a boy had heard the legend in San Luis, Peten; and the fourth informant in all probability, to judge by his features, had Kekchi blood in his veins. The legend therefore may be attributed to the Kekchi, and this attribution, moreover, is strengthened by the fact that some fragments of the legend have already been published by Robert Burkitt, and are stated to have been obtained from Kekchi informants (Gordon; Burkitt, 1918). Nevertheless, the legend has now been incorporated into the folklore of San Antonio, and is known to nearly all the people, be they of Kekchi or Maya descent. The four versions show on the whole a marked uniformity. Apart from minor details, omitted probably through forgetfulness from one version or the other, there are only four marked discrepancies.

The first of these deals with the important point as to the relationship of Venus and the sun. Three of the versions make the two brothers related at the opening of the legend. The fourth informant states that the sun was only an adopted brother and that Xulab had two brothers. This version I have incorporated into the story at the point where the sun is engaged in his wanderings. Incidentally, the abandonment of the child in a box at the side of the river reminds one forcefully of the story of Moses in the bulrushes, and I strongly suspect that this version is a post-conquest mutation.

The second discrepancy arises over the question of the attempt to slay the sun and his lover when they are escaping over the sea. In the discrepant version the old man, T'actani, when he recovers from his choking with the red pepper, calls for his sons to go and kill the lovers. The sons, supported by their mother, one by one refuse to obey him. T'actani then asks his uncle to kill the pair. The latter, too, refuses. Finally he appeals to his grandfather, Chac, who agrees to carry out the task. Other minor discrepancies are that the girl is also turned into a turtle, not a crab, as in the legend given above; and the number of hollowed wooden containers is given as four, not thirteen.

In the incidents of the recapture of the sun's wife from the chief vulture one version reads as follows:

"When Lord Kin arrived at the city of the vultures, he went to the house of the chief, and seeing his wife there, told her to come along with him. She refused. Whereupon Lord Kin left and made preparations for a big dance outside the chief's house. When all was ready, dances, such as the Cortez and the Moros, were performed. Lord Kin had hoped that X't'actani would come out to watch the dancing, and then he would be able to seize her, but she stayed in the house."

There follows the incident of the toothache with the difference that Lord Kin bargains for his wife in return for the cure of the toothache. The chief vulture at last agrees. Lord Kin and X't'actani leave and pass the night together in a small hut. The chief vulture in revenge has the hut set on fire. When he finds the hut on fire, Lord Kin seizes a small bush that was lying in the hut and sets fire to it. Concealed by the fire, he and X't'actani ascend to heaven to take up their duties as the sun and the moon. Next morning the chief vulture comes to the hut, and finding the charred wood of the bush, mistakes it for the charred bones of the pair, and is convinced they are dead.

The story that there had been another earlier sun, who refused to serve longer, and in fact the whole opening incident connected with the creation of the rivers and hills is only given in one version. This seems to be related to the Aztec legends of the four previous suns, legends which were in all probability common to both the Mexican and Maya peoples.

The Xkitza with her sharpened claws appears to resemble the old hag with sharpened claws in the Dresden Codex (p. 74). According to R. L. Roys, this illustration represents the creation of the world. If this should indeed be so, and the new evidence produced by Roys (1920) points that way, further color would be added to the suggested identification.

The asking of test questions and the setting of tasks seem to have played an important part in Maya legends. They occur, too, in the story of the defeat of the Cheil (p. 152) and the defeat of the giants (p. 154). Further, the idea seems to be closely connected with the series of ordeals which the heavenly twins, Hunahpu and Xbalanque, have to pass through under penalty of death in the Popol Vuh.

The story of the origin of monkeys, according to a very intelligent informant, belongs to the legend, but none of the four versions includes it. Another version of the turning of the younger brother into a monkey states that the boy is made to climb up the tree to fetch down mamey apples. After the boy is turned into a monkey, the other two brothers return home and kill their grandmother. After killing her they go out hunting. On their return they sit down to eat the stew that has been simmering in the pot. Just as they are about to start to eat, a bird calls out to them, "He he he, you are going to eat your grandmother." Several times the bird repeats this. The two brothers eventually get annoyed, and ask the bird what he is saying that for. The bird doesn't reply, but keeps on repeating the same phrase. The brothers stir up the meat in the pot, and below they find the head of their grandmother. This fragment of the legend ends at this point. It would appear that the incident of the eating of the head of the grandmother was probably a confusion with the earlier incident when the grandmother eats the penis of her lover without knowing what it is.

Only one informant stated that the younger brother, presumably after being turned into a monkey, ascended to the sky with the sun and the moon, and became the evening star. The others ignored him beyond stating that the brothers were three in number. There is an important deity with the head of a monkey (Schellhas' God C), who occurs frequently in the codices in connection with the sky, and again in the inscriptions on stone, in particular in the supplementary series. He seems to be a celestial deity, and this would accord well with the statement in the legend that he became the evening star. The Mayas of San Antonio no longer distinguish between the different planets, and therefore for evening star one must probably substitute Mercury, Mars, or one of the other planets. The information that the story of the conversion of the youngest brother into a monkey belongs to the legend was given me too late to question any of the four tellers of the Venus and sun legend. Nevertheless I have incorporated it into the text as, for the reasons given above, I feel that it does in fact belong here.

The plucking-out of the moon's eye might well account for the form of the glyph used for the moon, which has been explained as a closed eye from which blood drops. The legend refers to X't'actani's skill at weaving, and in this connection it is interesting to note that Cogolludo (Book IV, chap. 8) states that the wife of the sun, Ixazalvoh, invented weaving.

One cannot help but realize the close resemblance between the story given above of the sun and Venus and the legend of Hunahpu and Xbalanque, as told in the Popol Vuh. Both pairs of heroes are distinguished by their skill with the blowgun. Both pairs bring in large quantities of birds as a result of their prowess, but they themselves are not allowed to eat any of the meat. One pair gets rid of their brother, or in one version brothers are implied, turning him into a monkey. The other pair turned their two brothers (or cousins) into monkeys by the same method of sending them up a tree to fetch down the birds they had killed. Both pairs undergo tests, failure to pass which, it is implied, will result in death. One pair becomes the sun and the moon. the other pair, the sun and Venus.

Most of the adventures they undergo are different in the two stories, but this could easily be explained by accepting the legends not as just two stories, but as being two groups of stories strung together haphazard, and connected only by the fact that they tell of the lives and deeds of the same personages. In fact, this is the view held by the San Antonio Mayas and Kekchis, for several of the

Indians told me that there are a number of legends about the sun and Venus; and when asked which one they knew, would proceed to relate any incident out of the story given above. Further, the fact that the story of the monkeys was told separately and that Mr. Burkitt gives two of the fragments as independent legends shows that all these stories are in truth independent one of the other.

To this group probably belongs the story of the creation of man (p. 151) which again has an element in common with the Popol Vuh. The incident of the calabash with holes in it occurs in the Popol Vuh when the twins send their grandmother to fetch water from the river, and make holes in the jar, so that they will have time to find the equipment to play the ball game. The story incorporated into the legend of the origin of beans and other fruits, obtained by cutting down with difficulty a big tree on which they grew, is closely paralleled by a creation myth of the Macusis, a Carib tribe of northern South America. The two culture heroes are shown the tree by the squirrel. They cut it down, although the younger brother caused the tree to be tough for his elder brother. From the tree were obtained all the agricultural plants the tribe now has (Farabee, p. 83). Besides the resemblance in the story, there is a further resemblance to the whole legend. This is to be found in the manner in which the elder brother is always shown to be rather unintelligent. The younger brother is much cleverer, and shows his elder brother up on several occasions as Kin shows up his elder brother Xulab.

Myths that center round two hero brothers are frequently met with all through the New World. In most cases there is either an antagonism between the pair, or one is made out to be clever, the other a fool. The myths where the younger brother is the clever one appear to occur more frequently in South America. In all probability, the whole concept goes back to very early days in the history of the New World.

The description of Xulab as bearded and ugly is interesting, as it accords completely with the Mexican picture of Quetzalcoatl, who was his Nahua counterpart as morning star. Similarly the sun god is invariably depicted on the monuments and codices of the Mayas as heavily bearded. He is thus described in the legend. There is no information as to the appearance of the morning star among the Maya peoples. Nevertheless, the Venus glyph on the monuments is frequently shown with a wing, which has been interpreted as a beard.

The finding of the maize is very closely paralleled by a myth given in the "Anales de Cuauhtitlan." Quetzalcoatl took the form of a black ant and was led under the mountain, Tonacatepetl, by a red ant to where the maize was hid. The mountain is split open by Xolotl, and the maize secured. Subsequently it was stolen from him by Tlaloc.

THE MAN WHO CURSED THE MAM

Once there were two friends. One always shot a great deal of game when he went out to the bush, but he did this because he knew how to burn copal and pray to the Mam before he started out. The other was ignorant of the offering and prayer that must be made. Consequently he shot little game.

One day the two friends went out shooting together. The first, as usual, burned his copal, and consequently they shot plenty of game. The man was impressed with the abundance of animals in the country over which his friend shot.

Another day, consequently, he thought he would try his friend's hunting ground. After hunting some time without success his dog ran under some stones and got lost. The man was vexed and began to curse the Mam, because they gave him no game and caused his dog to be lost. As he was cursing, a small boy suddenly appeared to him.

"My master sent me to summon you to him," the boy said; and the man was vexed and replied, "I don't know who your master is, and I don't care, and further I'm not going."

The boy repeated that the man must go to his master, but the man again refused.

"My master is Mam. Shut your eyes, as I am going to take you to him."

The man at first didn't want to do so, but the boy made him. When he opened his eyes again, he found himself in the Mam's home, and his dog was tied to the door. The Mam asked him why he had come to hunt game there on land where he had no right, and further had cursed him. The man replied that he had come there, because his friend always seemed to find plenty of game there.

"That is true," replied the Mam. "But your friend buys his animals from me. Look!" And the Mam showed him a big mass of copal, perhaps a hundred pounds in weight. Then the Mam, whose name is Yaluk, sent to summon the other two junior Mams, whose names are Xucaneb and Coha. When they arrived, they sent a messenger to summon the chief Mam, whose name is Kitzan. Kitzan didn't want to go. They sent for him a second time, and he told the messenger to tell the other Mams that he was very busy. However, on being summoned the third time he went to the council. Yaluk, pointing at the man, explained how he had come to hunt there without burning copal, and then had proceeded to curse him.

"We don't know him," he added. "And we think we should eat him."

Kitzan answered, "You do not know this man, but I know him. He is very poor, and he is ignorant of our ways."

Then Kitzan talked for the man and explained that his friend got plenty of game, because he burned copal and because he was known to the Mam, who ruled over that territory. Kitzan gave orders to let him go and to give him two peccary. The boy took the man back to where he had found him. The man, opening his eyes, went on a little and shot two peccary. From that time onwards he always went to his old hunting grounds, where he was known to Kitzan.

This legend makes Kitzan the chief Mam. This is in contradiction to the general Kekchi belief (see p. 59).

THE MAM

Once there was a man who never burnt copal or prayed to the Mam when he went out hunting. He was a bad shot, and many of the animals at which he shot ran off wounded. Mam was vexed about this, so he sent a boy to summon the man to his presence. The boy found the hunter in the forest and made him shut his eyes. When he opened them again, he found himself in the presence of the Mam. The Mam asked him why he wounded so many of his animals and did not burn copal or pray to him. The man said that he knew no better. As a punishment the Mam made the man live there with him and tend to the sick and wounded animals. Where the Mam lives in the middle of a mountain, there are a number of pens in which the wild animals are kept. There is one pen for the small deer, another for the large deer, and yet another for the peccary. In short there is a special pen for every kind of wild animal.

One day while the man was there, curing the sick animals, two other humans were brought up to Mam for not having burnt copal. The Mam kept them there in his house during the night. Early the next morning he took all three of them and showed them a hunter on earth who was offering copal to the Morning Star and the Mam. In this manner they learnt what they must do to get plenty of game.

When they had learnt, the Mam sent the two back to the world, but first he asked them what game they wanted. Then the Mam sent the third man to the pens and told him to release two peccaries and three curassows. As soon as the two men got back to earth and opened their eyes, they saw the two peccaries and the three curassows, and shot them. The other man remained with the Mam, curing the sick and wounded animals.

The Mam taught him how to pray and burn copal. First, he must pray to the Morning Star as it comes up above the horizon; for the Morning Star, Xulab, is the owner of all the animals. Further, when the man goes to the forest, he must again pray and burn copal to the Mam; for the Mam look after all the animals for the Morning Star. The Mam taught the man how to work a milpa, for before this the man had not known how. The Mam also taught him how to pray and burn copal so that he might get a good crop. The man tired of living with the Mam, and wanted to go back to earth and his family. The Mam wanted him to stay, but the man was so anxious to go home that the Mam consented. However, before the man went, the Mam gave him the seed of all the plants he wanted to sow, beans, maize, cassava, and others. When the man got back to earth, he remembered all that the Mam had taught him, and consequently his milpa always yielded abundantly. Whenever he went out to shoot, he always got plenty of game as he knew exactly how to pray and burn copal. Now it is said that the Mam used to wear sandals of moleskin, and his seat was the shell of an armadillo.

THE MAM AND THE CORTEZ DANCE

A very poor man used to go fishing in a river near a high hill. He always used to burn copal before he did so, and as a result he always caught plenty of fish. The village where he lived decided to make a fiesta, and he was elected *nohoch priosti* ("master of ceremonies"). He could not refuse, as that is not the custom; but as he had no good clothes or money to make the fiesta, he decided to get some fish and sell it to get the money. Next morning before dawn he arose and burnt copal to Xulab, and when he reached the river, he burnt copal and prayed to the Mam. Suddenly he saw a boy, who asked him what he wanted. The man answered that he was praying for plenty of fish.

"My father sent me to call you," said the boy, and bade him shut his eyes. When he opened them again, he was in the big house of Mam. The Mam asked him what he wanted. The man told him how poor he was and how he had no means of making the fiesta, and he thought that by obtaining fish he could sell them and have money for all the expenses.

"All right," replied the Mam. "I will give you plenty of fish, and if you agree to come and live with me here after the fiesta, I will supply you with clothes and everything necessary for the dance."

The man went away and caught plenty of fish. The next day he again came into the presence of the Mam. The Mam told him that he would give him two peccaries and two curassows, and when the feast was ready to come to him for clothes. The eve of the feast the Mam gave him clothes and sent him four of his messengers to take part in the Cortez dance. The man was the Coxol, the leader of the dance, and the four messengers were the Caxancatzal, Cutuncatzal, and Chanal, meaning the second, third and fourth *mayordomos*, the name of the fifth not being known. They were called Quiches because they came out of the mountain. The Mam told the man to teach the people the dance, as at the end of three days he was going to send a strong wind to carry off the man and his four messengers. The Mam told the man to let his wife know that he was leaving her forever and that at the end of three days she must pray to Xulab. At the end of the fiesta a great wind came and whirled the man and the four messengers up into the air and carried them off to the mountain called Tzunceh, and they were taken inside. The woman prayed, as she had been bidden. The boy came to her and told her that she would not be allowed to see her husband, but she was given presents.

THE ORIGIN OF THE RIVERS

Once there were no rivers on earth, only one big lake, which was underground in a big hill, and the people had to get their water by lowering jars down into a very deep cenote (a deep and wide natural well). St. Peter, who was the lord of the water, wouldn't allow rivers on earth, as the people would dirty them and churn them up. A messenger passed over the world and asked the people if they were contented and if they wanted anything. Adam and Eve, the first people, said, "It is bad. The people are increasing, and there is no water except down that deep hole. We would like to see the water on earth."

Then the messenger went to the water and questioned it under the ground in the mountains. The water began to talk to the messenger.

"Where are you going?" he asked the messenger.

"I am going to God," the messenger replied, "to tell Him the people are dying of thirst."

"Well," said the water, "I am getting tired of being hidden here under the mountain. The sun pours down on me through the cenote mouth, and I get very hot. Besides, I would like to see the world."

The messenger went away and told God what the water said.

"I put him there," answered God, "so that he shouldn't get dirty and angry with the people. If he is on earth, the people will wash in him and dirty him, and throw rubbish in him, and he will be angry. Tell him that if he is prepared to suffer all these indignities, he may go on earth."

The messenger went to the water and told him what God had said. The water was happy.

"I don't mind all that," he cried. "I shall be on the move all the time, and I shall clean myself, and I shall see everything."

Then the messenger smashed the rock, and the water began to pour out in four directions. As it poured out, each stream asked the Mam, the owners of the mountain, for some food to give to the people. In one stream the Mam put minnows, in another *machaca* and another *bagre*. From that time the people have had fish to eat. That is why one must ask the Mam for fish when one goes out to catch them, for the Mam have them stored in the mountains and send them to feed the people.

A CREATION MYTH

After the sun and moon rose, there was a man on earth, and the Mam wanted to help him. He told him to sit on a bench, but the man sat on the floor. He told him to eat his food on a low bench, but the man took his food and ate it on the floor. The Mam told him he would give him a tapir so that he could have a herd, and told him to get a rope to tie it. The man, instead of getting a rope, got some *tietie* (liana), and tied the tapir with that. Needless to say the tapir broke the thin *tietie* and escaped. Then the Mam said, "I am going to give you peccaries so that you may have a herd of them. Get some rope and tie their feet."

The man again tied them with the thin *tietie*, and they escaped. Then the Mam told him to get rope to tie the deer, but the man caught it by the tail, and the tail breaking, the deer escaped. That is why the deer now has no tail. Then the Mam said to the man, "Now I can't help you any more as you have let all the animals escape, but I will teach you how to pray and burn copal to the Morning Star, and then you will always have plenty of game."

Now there was another man who tied all these different animals well, and that is why there are domestic animals in the world. These were the first men, and all the Indians are descended from them. Some are descended from the first, and have no domestic animals in herds. Others are descended from the second, and they are rich and have herds of animals.

A STORY OF THE CREATION

At first Adam was alone in the garden. He was lonely and wanted a partner and asked God for one. God gave him a rooster, but Adam complained that the rooster was never there. Then God sent him a dog. Adam still was not satisfied, saying that the dog could not talk except by wagging his tail. Then when he was sleeping, God took out one of his ribs and made Eve.

There was a wall around the garden, and the snake, trying to get over the wall, split his skin. From that time snakes have always cast their skins.

Adam and Eve left the garden and found a large stone house, where they lived. They had no machetes, and the only food to eat was *tšib*. Adam wanted to make a plantation. The messenger of God gave him an axe and a machete, telling him to fell the four trees that stood at the four corners of the plantation. When he went to cut down the first tree, the tree called out to him, "Don't cut me down."

Adam made a small cut, and blood started to come out of the tree. Adam was afraid and went away. Later the messenger came and asked him why he had not cut down the four trees. Adam told him what had happened, and that he was afraid, but the messenger replied, "That is the way all over the world."

The messenger then chopped down the four corner trees, one cut to each side of the trunk. When the four corner trees fell, all the other trees in the plantation fell as well. When the plantation was dry, Adam burnt it off, but he had no seed to sow. The messenger of God promised to sow it. He took a stick and sharpened the point. He took corn in one hand, and thrust the stick into the ground. He was sweating, so he took the sweat and threw it into the hole. Then he placed a little earth on top of the hole. In this way he made holes at all four corners of the plantation, and one in the center. At the end of a week the field was full of maize, beans, squashes and all the fruits of the world.

This story illustrates both the Maya and Christian influences in the same legend. The clearing of the whole milpa by cutting down the four corner trees is closely paralleled by an incident in the Popol Vuh. The divine twins are sent to make a plantation by their grandmother, and on cutting down one tree the whole milpa falls (Popol Vuh, p. 245). The sweat poured into the hole is probably the Indian's way of treating the biblical injunction, "By the sweat of thy brow thou shalt earn thy bread."

THE MAN WHO ATE THE SNAKE

Once there was a man who was a very good shot and, whenever he went into the forest, he always shot something. One day he went out with three friends to hunt, and seeing a large snake, he shot it. He said to his friends, "I have eaten every kind of meat except that of snake, so now I'm going to try this snake. It must be good."

His comrades told him that he must not eat it, but the man cut off a large piece, and taking it home he ate it. Shortly afterwards he was overtaken with great thirst, drinking up every drop of water that there was in the house. As his thirst was still unassuaged, he went down to the river to get some water. There he came face to face with the Mam who carried him away. Next day his comrades, missing him, searched and found his trail. They followed it to a large mountain, in the middle of which they saw the man imprisoned. They prayed to the Mam to release him, but without success. Next day his wife too came and burnt copal, but the Mam would not release him, and the man has remained there ever since; for the Mam have forbidden man to eat snake's meat.

THE STORY OF THE CHAC

A man once went out to get some wax from a hive to make candles for a ceremony he was going to celebrate. He found a tree with a hive in it and climbed up, after first placing a leaf on the ground at the base of the tree to receive the honey and wax when it dropped down. As he was getting the honey, a Mahanamatz (see p. 67) came along and asked the man to give him some honey. The man thought the Mahanamatz was a human, and told him to take the honey if he liked, but to leave all the wax as he wanted it for a ceremony. When he climbed down from the tree, he found that the Mahanamatz had eaten all the honey and the wax, too, which he had thrown down. The man was very annoyed and asked the Mahanamatz why he had eaten the wax as well. However, the Mahanamatz offered to show him another tree where plenty more wax could be obtained. They walked off through the forest, and on the way the man noticed that his companion's big toe was turned backward, and by that he knew that he was a Mahanamatz, and was very frightened. They came to a large ceiba (*yaštše*). The Mahanamatz told the man to climb up into the tree, which he did, but as soon as he began to cut the tree to get at the hive, the tree began to grow taller and taller. The man was unable to climb down. Then the Mahanamatz laughed, saying that in three days he would return to eat him. And then he went away. Later a small deer (*yuk*), passed by.

"Small deer, help me," cried the man. "Help me to climb out of this tall tree."

"Why should I help you," replied the deer, "since you killed all my uncles and family?" And he went away.

A little later a peccary passed by. The man asked his help, but was again refused on the same grounds. Next a wild boar was asked for his aid and also refused. At last just before the Mahanamatz was going to return to eat him, a coati or pisote (*chiic, tšiik*) came along. The coati agreed to help him to get down from the tree, provided the man would give him as payment two milpas of new corn. The man agreed and the coati went away to fetch his comrades, returning later with a large number of them. By catching hold of each other's tails with their front paws, they made a living chain which reached from the man down to the ground. Then they told the man to climb down over them, but to take care not to put his weight on any of the pregnant females. When the man had nearly reached the ground, he put his weight on a female and she fell to the ground, breaking the living rope.

The chief coati was very vexed and told the others to put the man back once more at the top of the tree. But the man heard it and jumped to the ground. The man led the coatis to the milpa of Chac, the rain god. As he was going along, the Mahanamatz came running after him in pursuit, and the coatis, giving him one of their incisor teeth, hid him in the hollow trunk of a tree. There the Mahanamatz found him and put out his tongue to get him, but the man plunged the incisor tooth into the tongue, nailing it to the tree trunk, and fled on. He ran on till he came to three fences which he jumped over and arrived at the house of Chac. The Chac was playing on his musical bow (*tinkan*, or *paštše*). A few moments later the Mahanamatz, who had wrenched his tongue free, arrived at Chac's house in pursuit.

"Give me this man as food, or I will eat you," he roared at Chac.

However, Chac called the jaguar and puma, and they caught the Mahanamatz and tore him to pieces.

Chac told the man that he could stay there as his servant. One day Chac sent him to pull up *chicam* (*tšikam*, jicama), telling him in no case to look underneath the root. The man went out and started to pull up the jicamas. After a time he felt curious to know what there could be underneath the root that Chac forbid him to look. Accordingly he looked underneath the next root he pulled up, and there below he saw the world and right underneath him his brother and his wife. They appeared so near that the man decided to make a rope and let himself down to earth. Accordingly he made himself a long rope and tying one end round the trunk of a tree and the other round his waist began to let himself down. But the rope, although it was long, did not reach to within miles of the earth, and the man found himself there unable to climb up again. The wind swayed him about at the end of the rope, and he was very frightened. Later Chac, noticing that he had not returned, went out to look for him. Finding him hanging there on the end of the rope 'twixt heaven and earth, he hauled him up and gave him a severe scolding.

Another day Chac sent the man to fetch some pawpaws (*put*), telling him on no account to cut down any except those that were small. The man went away and, seeing a small pawpaw tree, decided that the fruit was not large enough. Consequently he cut down the largest pawpaw he could see. The tree fell on him, growing as it fell, and he was unable to get out from under it. There some hours later Chac found him and again scolded him. Chac told the man that if he wanted any tortillas to ask the metate for them, but under no circumstances to ask for more than one. One day the man was hungry and went to the metate and asked for a number of tortillas. Enormous tortillas rained down upon him and buried him under their mass. Chac extracted him after again scolding him. One day Chac told him to clean the house, the table and the *qaantše* (wooden benches), as he was going to make a feast and was expecting guests. The man thoroughly cleaned the house, but returning later found many frogs (*mutš*) seated on the benches. Annoyed that they had come in to dirty the place after he had cleaned it, he began to drive them out with his broom. Later Chac inquired if the guests and the musicians had arrived, as it was past the time for the feast.

The man answered, "No, no guests have arrived yet. The only thing was that a big crowd of frogs came into the house just after I got it all clean and tidy."

FOLKLORE OF SAN ANTONIO 149

"Well," said Chac, "those were my musicians and guests."

The man thought that he would like to play at being Chac, so he watched how Chac dressed himself when he went out to do his work. One night when Chac was asleep, he took his clothes, his windbag and water-calabash (*tšu*), his axe and his drum. Then he went out and let loose the winds. The winds went screeching off, and the man, who had not the strength of Chac, could not shut them up again. A terrific storm rushed down upon the world. Then he took the calabash to make rain. Now, by pouring out four fingers of water, Chac used to cause a heavy rain. The man upset the whole calabash, and torrents of rain poured down on the earth. He began to beat on the drum, which causes the thunder, but when he tried to stop it, he couldn't. In his effort to stop the thunder the rain and the winds, the man fell into the sea. When Chac woke up, there were no signs of his clothes and his instruments, and the man had disappeared too. He went to one of the other Chacs, for they are very numerous, and borrowed his clothes and his windbag and went out to stop the rain, and put the winds back in their bag and stop the beating of the drum. When he had controlled the storm, he went out in search of the man. At last he found him broken into many pieces; for the black wind, which is the biggest of all the winds, had utterly smashed him. Nine times Chac made passes over the body and revived him. When they got back to Chac's home, he told the man that he could not stay there any longer, as he was always getting into trouble. He gave him a calabash full of honey and a bag of black wax, which would always replenish themselves. Then he took him back to earth.

"If you want to come and see me again here is the trail, but you must not bring anyone with you," Chac told him on parting.

The man promised, and then returned home to his wife. His wife was very anxious to know where he had been, but he told her that he had been to visit his grandfather. She also became curious about the never-ending supply of honey and wax. One day the man decided to visit Chac, but he told his wife that he was going to visit his grandfather. She asked him to take her with him, but he refused. Accordingly, when he went off, his wife, who suspected him, followed him secretly. When the man arrived at Chac's house, the god said to him, "Why do you bring somebody with you?" But the man said that he had come alone. "But I know you are not alone," Chac replied, and at that moment the man's wife, who had been following him, arrived. Chac, who was very vexed, started to question her.

"What have you there?" he asked, pointing at her hair. "Hair," the woman replied. Chac asked her the names of all the parts of her body from her head to her waist. Each time the woman answered correctly. Then Chac asked her what she called her genital organs. As the woman was about to reply, there came a great wind, which swept the woman and her husband off into space.

———————

Another version of this legend omits the entire first part, which is in all probability a separate story, and commences with the arrival of the human, in this case a boy, at the home of the Chac. The only divergence is seen in the cutting of the plants. The boy is sent to cut down plantains instead of pawpaws, as in the version given above. He pulls up yams, not chicam. However, these are minor differences. After the storm the boy is sent back to earth as incorrigible. Arriving there, he asks his elder brother if he suffered much damage from the storm. The elder brother answers, "Yes." Whereupon the youngster begins to laugh, saying to his elder brother, "Well, I was the one that caused the storm. Wasn't it fun?"

The introduction of frogs into the story is of interest, as the frog is intimately associated with the Chacs. In the Chachac ceremony in northern British Honduras small boys are tied to the altar, and made to croak like frogs. The frog was also closely connected with Tlaloc, the Aztec counterpart of the Chac.

A CREATION MYTH

The Creator decided to make men, for the jaguar already existed. He took some mud and started to fashion men, but the jaguar was watching him, and he did not wish him to see how man was made. Therefore he sent him to the river to fetch some water, giving him a jar and a calabash with holes in it to scoop the water out of the river. In this way he hoped to have time to make the men, while the jaguar was vainly endeavoring to fill the jar with the leaking calabash. The jaguar tried and tried to fill the jar, but did not succeed. Then the frog called out to him, "Chohac, Chohac, Chohac! Put mud over the holes."

The jaguar did so, but by the time he had filled the jar and taken it back, the Creator had already made thirteen men of mud and twelve guns. As the jaguar came up, he saw that the Creator was making a dog too out of mud.

"That animal is going to be for me to eat," he said.

"No," said the Creator. "The dog is to be the servant of man and these guns, further, will teach you to respect him."

"I am not afraid of the gun," replied the jaguar. "I'll catch the shots that are fired at me."

"All right, let's see," said the Creator, and he made the jaguar stand some way away, and then one of the newly created men fired at him, wounding him in the paw. The man bandaged up the wound. Again the jaguar said, "The dog is for me."

But man said, "No," and sent the dog after the jaguar and drove it up into a tree, and again shot him in the paw.

"Now you have learned your lesson that you must not eat man or dog. The other animals you can eat. Go away and live in the bush."

The incident of the calabash with holes in it is paralleled in the Popol Vuh (p. 251), when the twins send their grandmother to fetch water with a leaking jar while they search for equipment to play the ball game.

HOW FIRE WAS BROUGHT

Once upon a time the people had no fire. On the edge of the land where they lived was a big river, and across the river were folk who had fire. Nevertheless, those that had the fire refused to give any to those that had not; and, although the latter had made many attempts to steal some, these attempts always ended in failure. At last they decided to send over a dog. The dog swam across with a black-wax candle, and when no one was looking, he stole up to the fire and lit the candle. The dog raced off before he could be caught and, swimming back across the river, he brought the candle safely alight to the people. Since then they have never been without fire.

AROUND THE CAMP FIRE

Not so very long ago a party of men arrived at a group of old houses in the forest. They resolved to spend the night there. After they had eaten, they sat around the camp fire a short while. Suddenly a rat ran forward, turned a somersault in the fire, and continued on its journey. It was followed by a rabbit that went through the same motions. There followed a regular procession of animals, each one larger than the preceding one. All turned a somersault in the fire and then ran on. Finally men came running through the fire. The travellers, thoroughly frightened, took refuge on the roof of the hut. Whereupon the animals tried to cut down the house-posts to bring down the roof. They did not succeed, and in the morning there was no sign of what had happened.

THE CHEILS (CHOL)

There was once a young man called Juan Siis (Kekchi for the pisote or coati). One day in the bush he came across a party of Cheil (Chol in Kekchi). He got all his friends, and they went off to try and kill all those Chols. When Juan Siis got close to where the Chols lived, he turned himself into a tree. Soon a Chol came along close to the tree. Juan Siis put out his arms and caught the Chol. The Chol called out, and all the other Chols came running up. Soon a regular battle was going on between the Chols and Juan Siis and his friends. The Chols were armed with bows and arrows, boomerangs and top slings. After fighting some time, the Chols begged for peace.

"All right," said Juan Siis. "Let us see who can do the best tricks."

The Chols then went to a big gombolimbo tree (*tšikqa*) and climbed up it. Then they turned till they were head downward, and in that position climbed down the tree.

Then Juan Siis went to the tree and climbed both up and down head downward, and the Chols were afraid of his magic, and refused to do any more tricks.

Juan Siis told them they must, and as they still refused, he turned them into trees.

The mention of boomerangs (*ɔinah*) is of peculiar interest. Without any prompting they were described by the informant as curved sticks which are thrown and return to the thrower if they do not hit the target. Boomerangs are not now made in San Antonio, and knowledge of them survives only in tradition. So far as I know, returning boomerangs have hitherto never been reported from the New World, although throwing sticks are in common use in the Southwest. Of course, there is a possibility that the idea of the boomerang may have been introduced in recent times by Spaniards or Guatemalans, who were acquainted, through literature at least, with this weapon. However, this seems improbable. Further, the boomerang is mentioned in connection with the Chols, who were, tradition implies, bearers of the old Maya culture.

The top slings were called *štrumpu*, an obvious corruption of the Spanish word *trompa*. They are described by the informant as resembling a boy's top with a point at one end and feathers at the other. A string was wound round the center, and it was thrown just as a modern top is thrown, the string remaining in the thrower's hand.

CHEIL OR CHOL

Two men (Kekchis) were walking along when they met a couple of good Chols sitting by the roadside. The two Kekchis were going to kill the Chols, but the latter said, "Don't kill us, we are harmless. We are of the same race as you. We are Indians. If you go on along that road, you will meet the bad Chols, who are called *Xacampach*, and live by the sea. They are getting ready for their big fiesta, and if you go there, they will kill and eat you. They are bad people. Their ears are very long, and at night they lie down and sleep on them. They are not Indians. Close your eyes now, and we will take you back to your home."

The two Kekchis did so, and when they opened their eyes a moment later, they were back in Cajabon.

THE STORY OF JUAN SIIS AND THE CHEILS

There was a boy who used to live with his grandmother. He used to go out to cut firewood close to the church, where he would smell the rich food that was being prepared for the priest. He wanted to taste it, and kept muttering to himself, "I wish I could eat that nice food."

One day the messenger of the Mam appeared to him and asked him why he was always muttering to himself. The boy explained that he wanted to eat all that fine food, whereupon the messenger told him to shut his eyes. When he opened them again, he was in the room of Chich (*Tšitš*). The Chichs are the wives of the Mams, and they are full-breasted. The Chich asked him his trouble, and when the boy explained, she told him that he must suckle at her breast for three days. The boy did so, and at the end of the three days Chich told him to throw himself on the ground. He did so and immediately turned into a jaguar. When he threw himself down again, he turned back into a boy. The Chich said to him, "Now you can get all the food you want," and sent him back to the world. The boy's name was Juan Siis, which is a Kekchi word meaning "coati." That evening his grandmother cooked him food, but he said he did not want to eat cooked food, only raw meat. He told his grandmother he was going to play, and throwing himself on the ground, he turned into a jaguar. His grandmother was very frightened and called all the neighbors, but when they arrived, Juan Siis had already turned back into a boy. He began to catch and eat fowls, hogs, etc., and then, becoming more ferocious, ate up his own grandmother. After that he went away to live in the forest. One day in the forest he met three men. They told him that they were out hunting, but could find nothing. Juan Siis told them he would kill meat for them, and bid them follow him. At sunset they built a camp, and after dark Juan Siis went out hunting. Just before dawn the hunters heard the roar of the jaguar and Juan Siis reappeared in camp with several peccary. Next day he said to the hunters, "Let us go and visit my friends, the Cheils."

The hunters did not want to go. "They are bad men," they said. "They will eat us." Juan Siis promised that no harm would befall them. They arrived at the home of the Cheils and entering sat down. The children of the Cheils were playing round, and scratching the bare legs of the hunters, they drew blood. The Cheils, smelling the blood, wanted to eat them. They asked Juan Siis to give them the hunters to eat, but the jaguar man refused them. Again they asked for the hunters. Juan Siis said, "I will give them to you, but you must beat me in play first of all."

There was a large gombolimbo tree (tšikqa) close by. Juan Siis climbed up the tree to the first big branch, and then dived head down to the ground unscathed. He said to the Cheils, "You must do that too if you want my friends."

At last one Cheil climbed up in the tree, but diving down broke his neck, and the rest were afraid to try the trick. Juan Siis next jumped over twelve hills (caves).

"Now you must do that if you want those men," he said.

None of the Cheils could jump that far. Juan Siis told the three hunters to go away and take the peccary he had hunted with them.

HOW THE GIANTS WERE WORSTED

Around Salana the people used to be very wise, as when they were five days old their mothers used to take them to the side of a mountain and leave them there some time to be suckled by the Santa Chich (the wife of Mam). The people used to go down from the mountains into the forests of the lowlands to trade goods, but there were three giants, who lived on the road, and used to levy tribute and kill the people, and eat them by the riverside.

An old man from the village, which is called Santiago, went that way. On the way he killed a vulture. When he got to where the giants lived, they stopped him and demanded food.

"I have no tortillas," he told them, "but here is meat," giving them the vulture which he had already cooked. Now these giants had their own star, and they could only do *brujería* when it came above the horizon. Later the star appeared, and they asked the old man if he could do any *brujería*. The old man said no, whereupon the giants told him that if he could not do as they did he would be killed. The first giant then went behind a hill and jumped over it. In the air he turned into a stone, but just before he reached the ground the old man hit him with a stick he carried, and the stone turned back into a giant again. The second giant also threw himself over the hill, turning into a jaguar, but again the old man nullified the trick by hitting him with his stick. The same happened with the third giant, who turned himself into a goat-like monster.

"You are no good," cried the old man. "You cannot do *brujería*," and he killed them.

When Zicnic, the owner of the mountain where the giants had lived, heard about this, he sent a messenger to have the old man imprisoned. They put him in a big cement house, and were going to kill him at midnight, but the old man with his *brujería* escaped and went back to his village.

HOW THE JAGUAR GOT HIS SPOTS

Once there was a jaguar cub, and his mother told him to be very careful of men as they were very dangerous. The cub did not believe her and wanted to test his strength against that of man. One day, wandering through the forest, he came to a place where a man was splitting wood.

"You are a man, aren't you?" the young jaguar said to him. "I have come to test my strength against yours."

The man agreed and told the young jaguar to put his paw in the tree trunk where it was wedged open by his axe. The jaguar did so whereupon the man pulled out his axe and the wood coming together imprisoned the cub's paw in its vise-like grip. Then the man gave the cub a thorough thrashing and let him go. The jaguar cub's body was covered with black bruises and blood, and since then its skin has always been of this color.

THE LORD OF THE BEES AND THE TABAI

A man once wanted to go out into the forest and get some honey from a hive of wild bees. He asked his compadre to go with him, but the compadre said he had no food, but agreed to go when the first man said he would take food for both of them. At midday the man was feeling hungry and suggested to his friend who had the food that they should eat, but the other said no. Later the man was very hungry and again asked for food, but his friend refused. A bit later he was famished, and again demanded food. The first man agreed to give it to him on condition that he was allowed to take out one of his eyes. The man was so hungry that he agreed and his friend, taking out one of his eyes, gave him food. Later he became very thirsty and asked for water. His friend would only give him water if he was allowed to take out the other eye. The man finally agreed and lost his second eye in return for the water. His friend told him to wait there for him, and went away, returning no more. The man waited and waited, and eventually, realizing that his friend would not return, he started to stumble along through the forest. At last he reached a tree, where, from the noise of the humming of the angry bees, he knew that men had recently been there and destroyed the hive to get at the honey. There he waited resting on a fallen tree-trunk. After nightfall the Lord of the Bees arrived. He called out to the bees, "I will cure all those who have broken wings or legs, who have been crushed or who have lost their eyes."

All the wounded bees came to him, and he cured them. The man heard all this and, groping his way to the Lord of the Bees, asked him to cure his sight too. The Lord of the Bees agreed and restored to him his sight. However, although he could now see again, he was still lost in the forest. Next night he climbed a tree close to a big ceiba tree. In the night he heard the voices of the tabais talking among themselves inside the ceiba. Now the tabais are always seeking mischief, and they were planning among themselves what damage they could do to mankind. One was saying how he was going to the village to spy at the people in their huts. Another was going to cause a man to make love to his comadre. Listening, the man learned how to open the ceiba, and after the tabais had gone away he went inside and found money, clothes, and other riches. He took some and went home. Some of the material he sent as a present to his bad compadre, who had gouged out his eyes. His bad friend asked him where he had got such fine stuff, and asked the man to take him to the ceiba. The man agreed, and taking his bad friend to the place left him there. Just before night the bad compadre climbed up into a tree, and listening he learned from the tabais the secret of how to get into the ceiba. When they had gone, he entered the ceiba and took all the material he wanted. Unfortunately for him he forgot how to get out, and so he hid inside. The tabais came back from their errands of evil.

"It is very hot inside and there is a sweet smell," said the youngest tabai.

They looked around and found the man and beat him till he died.

Another version of the same story omits any mention of the bees. The tabais are three in number, and they tell what evil they have done during the day. The first says, "I have destroyed a fine milpa. If the owner only knew he could restore the corn by strewing it with ceiba leaves."

The second says, "I have dammed a river, so the people in the village will suffer thirst. If they only knew, there is one stone that is the key-stone. Removing that the water will flow again."

The third says, "I caused a man to take out the eyes of his compadre. If the sufferer only knew he could get back his sight by rubbing the sockets with the leaves of the ceiba."

Next morning the man takes cciba leaves and regains his sight. The rest of the story is the same as in the version given above except that the man undoes the work of the tabais by restoring the milpa and river.

No name survives in San Antonio at the present time for the Lord of the Bees. However, in Yucatan they are worshipped under the name Ucananxuxob (Tozzer, 1907, p. 163).

THE XTABAI

A young man had arranged to meet his sweetheart in the forest on the edge of the village. When he arrived at the tryst, he saw what he thought was his sweetheart, but it was a xtabai in her form. He advanced to meet her, but the xtabai walked backwards so as not to show her hollow back, which was like the rough bark of a tree. The youth at last overtook her, and placing his arms around her embraced her. He felt her back to be hollow and rough and realized it was not the girl, but a xtabai. He began to pray, whereupon the xtabai turned into a heap of rotten wood. The man made a fire and burned the rotten wood, and in this way destroyed the xtabai. The

girl whom he had gone to visit and whom the xtabai had imperson-
ated took sick at that same moment, and three days later died.

Stories of the tabai, or their female counterparts, the xtabai, are
very common all through the Yucatan peninsula.   They are mentioned by Mendez (Saville, p. 171), Tozzer (1907, p. 158), and others.
The legend of the xtabai narrated by E. H. Thompson to Willard
(chap. 13) is totally at variance with Maya beliefs concerning these
spirits.   Like all the legends given in that book it must be dismissed
as a fragment of truth hidden below the fantastic embroidery of a very
vivid imagination.   The romantic mind of Edward H. Thompson
pervades "The City of the Sacred Well" to such an extent as to
make it useless for scientific purposes.

A SORCERY STORY

A man had a wife who was a sorceress and used to turn herself into
a mule.   Every Friday she would sit up late spinning cotton, and
she used to put a fire under her husband's hammock so that he
wouldn't wake up with the cold.   The man suspected his wife, so one
Friday he kept awake.   At midnight his wife put away the cotton
she was spinning, and throwing herself on the ground, after first
having taken off her head and placed it on the ground, she turned
into a mule; then she went off with a number of other mules.   The
man took some ashes and rubbed them on the severed neck of her
head.   Just before dawn the mules returned.   The woman threw
herself onto the ground and changed back into human shape, but
she could not fix her head on again because of the ashes.   Accordingly
she changed back into a mule again and, carrying the head, she followed the man wherever he went.   He tried to shake her off, but could
not.   One day he went into a very thick part of the forest, and there
succeeded in losing the mule and her head.   The mule and head
turned into an owl (buh).   That is why the owl hoots, cries, and
laughs like a woman.

THE FOOLISH WIFE AND THE TABAI (San Antonio and Socotz)

A man had a wife who was always wasting her time, and visiting
her neighbors, and consequently did not attend to her work.   He was
going away on a long journey, and to keep her busy during his absence gave her some cotton to spin.   While he was away, his wife did
nothing but waste her time.   The day before her husband was to return, she realized that the cotton had not been spun.   She threw it
into the fire saying,   "Fire, spin this cotton for me."

But the fire only burnt it up.   Then she took a machete and began
to dig in the ground under the fire.   She found a heap of gold which

the tabai had placed there. The tabai was standing at the back of the house. As there was no wood in the house, she called him, and giving him money told him to go out and cut her some wood. A few minutes after the tabai had gone off her husband arrived. He asked her what she had done with the cotton, and she replied that she had sold it, showing the money she had found. Her husband said that that was not enough, and then she explained that she had given the rest to a man to cut wood.

"I'll go after him, and get the money back. You stay here and mind the door," said the husband.

He went away to find the man. After a while the woman said to herself, "I want to see what he is doing, but he told me to mind the door. Oh, I know what I'll do. I'll take the door along with me, and in that way I can look after it all right."

After a while she overtook her husband.

"Why are you carrying that door on your back?" he asked her.

"Well, you told me to look after it, and I thought the best way was to bring it along with me."

"You are a silly woman," replied the husband. "When I told you to mind the door, I meant you to see that no one came into the hut to steal anything. Now you have taken away the door, and anyone can go in."

They wandered through the forest in search of the man until nightfall. When it was dark, they climbed up into a big ceiba tree, and placed the door across the boughs. Soon the tabais, the owners of the ceiba tree, arrived and began to make music. The woman heard the noise and began to dance. Her husband told her not to be so foolish, as the tabais would hear her and come up and kill them. His foolish wife took no notice of what he said until at last the door fell out of the tree onto the heads of the tabais below. They all ran away except one. The man and his wife climbed down from the tree, and the woman called out to the tabai that had remained, "Come here. I have something good for you to eat. Open your mouth," she said to him.

The tabai did so, and the woman thrust a knife into his mouth and cut off his tongue. The tabai ran off. Then the man and his wife went into the ceiba tree, and taking all the clothes and money they wanted, went off home.

THE DROUGHT

The sun and the clouds were having a dispute. The clouds maintained that they caused the rain when they formed themselves. The

sun denied that they caused the rain, as without his permission they
could not cross his face. The sun was so annoyed that he refused
permission to the clouds to cross the heavens. As a result there was
a terrible drought, and the people began to die of famine. They
made processions with the saints, but still there was no rain. There
was a small boy, Vicente, who lived with his grandmother. He
was very disobedient, and his grandmother decided to thrash him,
so Vicente ran away to the top of a high hill to avoid the thrashing.
He stayed there all day, and when night came, he was afraid to go
home. Shortly after sunset a small boy appeared to him, and asked
him what he was doing there. Vicente explained that his grandmother wanted to thrash him and that he had fled to the top of the
hill to avoid her. The boy said he was the messenger of Mam and
told Vicente to tell his grandmother to inform the people that it was
useless to make processions like those they had been making. The
people must make a new procession and carry Vicente instead of the
saint, and then Mam would send the rain. Vicente returned home,
and his grandmother was so pleased to see him once again that she
forgave him. Vicente began to repeat what the messenger of the
Mam had told him. "The people in the village are fools. They will
never get rain if they continue to make processions with the saint.
They must carry me if they want rain." The old lady was vexed with
him. "How can you cause the rain?" she said. "You aren't God."

Someone overheard the conversation, and told the alcalde of the
village. The alcalde summoned Vicente to his presence, and asked
him if it was true that he could cause rain. Vicente told him what
the messenger of the Mam had said to him. The alcalde was impressed, and arranged for a new procession next day, when Vicente
would be carried on the litter. Next day Vicente was placed on the
litter in the church, and everyone in the village brought a few flowers,
till Vicente was entirely buried in their mass. At midday they heard
thunder at each of the four corners of the world, and there came a
heavy wind, and the sky was full of clouds. The rain poured down
unceasingly, until at last they made the procession to stop the rain.
When the procession was finished, and they were returning to the
church, Vicente and all the flowers that surrounded him were
carried up to heaven, where he became the patron of rain.

The sun made his peace with the clouds. "I now see," he said,
"that I am not so powerful as you. In a few minutes your clouds
covered the sky, and made it so that I could not see anything. You
will be my elder brother."

This is the reason why it always becomes cool when it rains, as the sun cannot shine down on the earth.

This story, like so many others, is a mixture of pagan and Christian beliefs. San Vicente is under the orders of the Mam. The offering of flowers, an inheritance from pre-conquest times, is associated with the church. The simple legend well typifies the blending of the two religions, met with throughout Central America.

AN INDIAN VERSION OF THE LIFE OF CHRIST

Once there was a young man who went to travel with twelve other men. He arrived in the town and asked for lodging, but the owners of the house only permitted him to sleep in the henhouse. He did not want to sleep there, so he found another man who gave him lodging and who gave him a large mat on which he and the other twelve could sleep. He told the man's wife to grind corn on the metate, giving her a fistful of maize. The woman did so, and with the handful of maize made sufficient tortillas for all of them. He went away at dawn after leaving money on the mat. The man went on and saw some men sowing. He asked them what they were sowing, but they did not reply. Then he told them that trees would come up in the milpa, and it was so. There sprang up trees over a milpa, which it took three days to cross. He saw some more men sowing, who again refused to tell him what they were doing. To these he said that they were sowing water, and a great expanse of water sprang up. Yet other sowers he caused to sow stones. Passing farther on, he again met some sowers, and these he caused to sow cohune palms. Then he passed on and crossed over a river. As he was crossing the river, he stepped on some fresh-water snails. The twelve men who were coming along could not find him, and questioned the fresh-water snails. The snails replied, "Don't you see that he has trampled on us and turned us over?"

He came to a town where the people cursed him, saying that he was a witch doctor. Then he prepared a big feast, but the chief of the town wanted to kill him because of his sorcery in causing the milpas to grow trees, stones, water, and cohune palms. The man hid himself inside a harp at his feast. All the twelve young men were drunk. The chief did not know the man by sight and he asked the man's servant to point him out. The servant said, "You will know him because he is the only one who does not eat."

The chief and his soldiers looked in at the window and noted which one did not eat. They caught him and tied him and left him lying down. Then they called in a blind man and placed a machete in his hand and guided him over to where the sorcerer lay bound, and, placing the point of the machete against the sorcerer's ribs, they bid the blind man drive it in. He did so, and the blood of the sorcerer, gushing out onto the eyes of the blind man, restored his sight. They took the body of the sorcerer and buried it and made a feast. After the feast they took the bones of the chickens they had eaten and threw them on the spot where the dead man had been buried. The bones instantly became a live turkey and a live cock. They told the birds to crow if the dead man came to life again. At midnight the dead sorcerer came to life again and told the turkey and the cock not to crow. Then he took the servant who had betrayed him and placed him in a big house under the earth and said to him, "You are to be the lord of the earthquakes. You will shake the earth three times."

The man returned to the house and told the cock that he was going up to heaven at midnight, saying, "If you see me or even a bit of me or even my foot, you can crow and wake up the sleepers."

Then the man went up into heaven. The man's name was Jesus.

IX. FOLKLORE OF SOCOTZ AND COROZAL DISTRICT

THE ANTS AND THE MILPA (Socotz)

There was once an old man with three sons. When they grew up, he told them it was time they got married. Accordingly the eldest took food and, obtaining his father's blessing, set forth in search of a wife. After a while he met a man who had three grown-up daughters. He married the eldest. Later the second son arrived and married the second daughter. Lastly the youngest son asked his father for his blessing and, preparing food for the journey, set out too in search of a bride. He fell in with his two elder brothers, and soon married the youngest daughter of the old man.

Now T'up (the youngest boy) was very lazy, as his father-in-law soon found out. T'up was always being scolded for being so lazy, and his mother-in-law was always upbraiding her youngest daughter for having such an idle husband.

When the time came to make milpa, the old man called his three sons-in-law together, and told them to go out the next day and make *holche*. Next morning the three brothers started out to work. They carried tortillas and posol to last them for three days, but T'up only carried a little, for his mother-in-law would not waste corn on so worthless a son-in-law. The two elder sons started to work at one place, but T'up went farther on until he was some way beyond where his brothers had decided to work. He sat down to rest and went fast asleep. Later, when he woke it was quite late in the afternoon, so he decided not to do any work except collect some guano palm leaves to make himself a shelter. After he had eaten some of his tortillas and drunk some of the posol, he went to sleep again.

Next morning when he woke all his tortillas and posol had disappeared. Looking around, he espied a large ant (Spanish *sampopo*, Maya *sai*) which was carrying off the last piece of tortilla. He realized then that while he slept the ants had robbed him of his food. He seized the ant and threatened to kill it unless it would lead him to its nest. The ant consented. On arriving at the nest, T'up knocked three times, and the lord of the nest appeared (he was considered to be a snake; see p. 109). "What do you want?" he asked.

"Your people have stolen all my tortillas and posol," replied T'up. "Either you must return it to me or you must do my work."

163

The lord of the nest considered for a few moments, and then agreed to do the work. So T'up instructed him where to make the milpa, and said its size was to be a square league, and returned to his shelter to sleep while the forest was being cleared. All the ants turned out to work that night, and with their huge numbers and powerful jaws they had cut down all the trees and bush at the end of three days.

T'up returned to his father-in-law's hut. On the way he passed his two brothers, but instead of clearing the forest for the milpa they were busily engaged in making holes in the larger tree-trunks, for they had misunderstood what their father-in-law had said. Whereas he had told them to make *holche*, that is, cut down swathes in the forest for milpa, they thought he had told them to make *hoolche*, that is, make holes in the tree-trunks.

When T'up arrived home, his father called out, "Here comes Idle-bones, the last to go and the first to return. Don't give him anything to eat." But his wife managed to get some maize, and made him tortillas. Later the other two brothers arrived, and the old man ordered chickens to be cooked for them, as they had worked hard.

Later when he judged the milpas to be dry, the old man sent the three brothers to burn the dry felled bush. The elder brothers were given large supplies of posol and honey, but poor T'up, as he was so lazy, was only given a little of each. The two elder boys collected all the loose rubbish and burnt it, but the column of smoke that rose up to the sky was miserably thin. T'up took his honey and posol to the ants' nest, and gave it to the lord of the nest on condition he burnt the milpa. Accordingly T'up rested all day, while the ants hurried about their task of burning the milpa. The dense columns of smoke that resulted were so huge that even the sun was hidden. But the old man thought that the smoke of T'up's milpa was caused by the burning of the milpa of the other two brothers; so when T'up returned he again scolded him.

When all was ready for sowing, the elder brothers took three mules laden with maize seed; T'up took only a quart. The elder brothers sowed a little of the maize in the forest, but most of it they left in the store hut, and the rest they hid in one of the tree-trunks they had hollowed out. T'up took his seed to the ants, but they said it was not enough, for the fire had spread far beyond the cleared area, and the extent to be sown was enormous. T'up then showed them a storehouse where they could get more seed, and when they had started to work, as usual, T'up went to sleep. On the return of the brothers, T'up received his usual contemptuous welcome, while the elder brothers were feasted.

When the corn was in ear, the old man sent his three sons-in-law to their milpas to prepare the young corn in the *pib*. The elder made a small hole in the ground, into which they put the few small yellow ears that had just managed to survive in the shade of the forest. T'up again summoned the lord of the ants' nest to his assistance. They brought fifteen loads, made the *pib*, heated it, and put in the food while T'up slept.

On the following day the old man and his wife, his three daughters and their husbands set out with four mules to bring in the young corn and to eat the *pibil*. When they arrived at the milpa of the two elder brothers, the father-in-law was very angry, for there was no clearing visible and no corn except the few miserable plants that were growing in the shade of the forest, and they resembled grass rather than corn. Then he espied the heap of rotting corn in the hollow tree. "Well, where is the *pib?*" cried the old man. When the tiny *pib* had been uncovered and a mere handful of tamales shown him, the old man was still more furious, and refusing even to speak to the two elder boys, he sneeringly bid T'up show them his milpa. They started off again, T'up leading the way, until they struck the path the ants had made from their nest to the milpa. This path gradually widened as they advanced until it became a wide highway. "Where does this fine road go?" asked the old man, and T'up replied, "To my milpa." Eventually they reached a huge milpa, the end of which was lost to view in the distance, and T'up indicated that this was his milpa. But the old man, knowing full well T'up's indolent habits, was incredulous. They ascended a small hill at the edge of the milpa when his mother-in-law inquired where the *pib* was, thinking thereby to discover if this huge milpa was really the work of her youngest daughter's husband. "You are standing on it," replied T'up. "This hill is the *pib*." Then the old man said, "You've worked enough, let your two brothers uncover the *pib*."

While they were doing this, the mother-in-law started out to find the extent of the milpa, but it was so immense she got lost. Then T'up summoned his friends, the ants, who, on being informed of the loss of the old lady, began to search through the milpa until they located her. After they had all eaten, the mules were loaded, and they started off home. That night chickens were killed in honor of T'up. As for the other two brothers, they were ordered out of the house, and bidden never to return.

TRADITION OF A FLOOD (Socotz)

Often when hunting in the forest one comes upon old rubbing stones that have no legs. They are not really rubbing stones, although our people often take them home and use them as such. They are the boats of the tiny folk—the *P'us*. Long ago these little people lived very happily, for they possessed a magic chest, from which issued an inexhaustible supply of everything that they needed. On account of this they forgot to worship God. God sent a flood to destroy them. They knew beforehand that there was going to be a big flood, but they did not know when it would come. Accordingly they made themselves little stone boats, so that they would not rot in the wet season, as might have happened if they had made them of wood. When the flood came, they got into their stone boats, but they were all drowned as the stone would not float. There they lie to this day in the woods, often near holes in the ground where they sank when the big flood swept everyone away.

Another version states that everyone was drowned save Noah. According to Tozzer (1907, p. 153), the first people, who were called Saiyamwinkob (the Adjusters), were dwarfs. They built the ruins. As soon as the first sun was born, they turned into stone. The first epoch was ended by a flood.

THE SOURCE OF SICKNESS IN SOCOTZ

Formerly the people of Socotz lived happily and free from those numerous maladies caused by evil winds. These good times came to an end when a certain sorcerer became enraged with the inhabitants of the village and plotted their destruction.

In order to accomplish this, he made nine dolls of black wax (*qeš*), which he buried under the ground, one close to each of the gullies that meander through the village. Luckily for the future of the community another sorcerer divined the wickedness that was contemplated. With the help of some of his friends he searched for and found seven out of the nine dolls. Search as they would, they could not find the remaining two images. Feverishly they searched all through the night, but in vain. They knew that at dawn the two dolls, if not found and destroyed, would come to life, and start their evil tricks. When the sun had risen, and the evil was past remedy, they informed the elders of the village of the danger that threatened the community. The infuriated villagers sought out the evil sorcerer, and, dragging him and his family into the neighboring woods, murdered the lot. But the evil had been done, and to this day Socotz suffers from the two evil winds caused by the two wax images that escaped. These two evil winds are the source of much of the sickness in Socotz.

THE WIND GOD (Socotz)

A man one day set fire to his milpa, but it would not burn, because he had not burnt any copal incense (*pom*). He obtained some and offered it in the milpa. He then set fire to the dry brush. Presently he saw a huge thick-set man in a large hat descending from the hill behind the milpa. He walked into the midst of the flames, and catching up the fire in his arms, he threw it here and there so that all the milpa was soon burnt. He was the wind god.

THE THREE WIND GODS AND THEIR MOTHER (Socotz)

A man was lost in the forest. After wandering for some time, he arrived at the home of the three wind gods, but he did not know that they lived there. Their mother welcomed him, and prepared him food. Later when her three sons were due back, she hid the man in a large pottery urn. When the three wind gods arrived, there was a regular whirlwind. Everything was blown about the hut, the hammocks swung frantically, and there was general confusion. Gradually the place calmed down once more. "We smell chicosapote (sapodilla)," cried the three sons, for they were giants, and that was the term all giants use to describe human flesh. Their mother, however, assured them that no human was around. After they had eaten, they got into their hammocks. When at last they slept, their mother helped the man out of the urn in which he was hidden, and sent him on his way.

The wind gods are generally believed to be four in number. Nevertheless in Socotz they are sometimes said to be only three in number (see p. 108). This short story is incorporated into the legend of Juan and Rosalie given on page 175 with minor variations.

THE MAGIC FLIGHT (Socotz)

Once upon a time a young man started out from home to earn some money. After traveling some time, he came to a hut where there lived a giant with his three daughters. The young man was very attracted by the youngest daughter, and determined to stay there if he could. Accordingly he asked permission of the giant. The giant consented on condition that the young man completed certain tasks that he would set him.

"I have always," said the giant, "had a keen desire to take my bath immediately on getting out of bed instead of having to go all the way down to the lake. Tonight you will bring the lake up to the hut, so that when I get up in the morning I can sit on my bed and dangle my feet in its water. Here is a basket in which you can fetch the water." The young man was entirely nonplussed, but he decided to consult his sweetheart, the giant's youngest daughter, whose name was Rosalie. Rosalie told him to go to sleep and not to worry, that she would see to the transfer of the lake. That night when the rest of the household slept, Rosalie went down to the lake, and with her skirt she swept up the water to her father's bedside.

When the giant awoke, he was very surprised to find the water lapping the leg posts of his bed. Taking a large pot, he threw it into a very deep river, and bid his daughter's suitor bring it forth. The young man dived in many times, but failed to locate the pot at such a great depth. Then Rosalie came to his rescue. They arranged to go together that night, and Rosalie would dive in. The boy was to call her name when she was at the bottom, otherwise she would be unable to rise again to the surface. This they did, and the following morning the giant found the pot once more in the house.

The next task that the giant set the young man was to make a milpa of a hundred mecates, clear the forest, burn, sow, and at midnight of the same day bring him a load of corn on the cob from the same milpa. The young man set to work at daybreak, but by sunset he had achieved practically nothing. Then Rosalie stretched out her skirt, and promptly all the forest was felled. By magic too she dried the bush, burnt it, sowed the corn, caused it to grow, and gathered the young maize cobs, so that her lover was able at midnight to take the cobs to her father. The giant was now thoroughly annoyed, and consulted with his wife how they could get the best of the presumptuous youth. They decided to give him a trial of horsemanship.

They arranged that the woman should turn herself into a mare, the giant would become the saddle and stirrups, and Rosalie should be turned into the bridle. Rosalie, however, overheard this conversation and warned her lover, bidding him not to spare the mare and the saddle, but to treat carefully the bridle.

Next morning the giant bid the young man go out into the savanna, where he would find a mare already saddled. He was to mount her and bring her back to the house. Meanwhile the giant and his wife and Rosalie took a short cut through the forest, and by the time the young man arrived they had already converted themselves into the mare and its saddle. The boy, who had armed himself with a good stout cudgel, jumped onto the mare's back and before the mare had a chance to buck, he began to belabor her as hard as he could. The mare, or the old lady, whichever one cares to call her, was so benumbed by the shower of blows that the youth rained on her that she was quite incapable of making any attempt to throw her rider. After a few minutes she sank exhausted to the ground.

The boy returned to the hut, where a little later he was joined by the exhausted and belabored giant and his wife.

The boy had now completed his four tasks, but the giant, going back on his bargain, told him that there were yet other tasks to perform. That night Rosalie and her lover decided to run away, as the giant and his wife would still be suffering from the effects of the thrashing they had received. When all were asleep, Rosalie took a needle, a grain of salt, and a grain of *saskab* (white earth), and spitting on the floor, stole softly out of the house to meet her lover outside.

At daybreak the giant called to Rosalie to get up. "It's all right, Tata, I'm getting up, I'm dressing my hair," replied the spittle, which Rosalie had spat on the floor. The spittle spoke with the voice of Rosalie, so the giant suspected nothing. A little later the giant again called to Rosalie to know if she were not yet dressed. Again the spittle replied that she was dressing her hair. The old lady, however, was suspicious and, going into Rosalie's room, discovered the trick that had been played on them. By this time the spittle was almost dry and could only reply to her in a whisper.

Then the giant set out in pursuit of the fleeing couple. As the giant was rapidly overtaking them, Rosalie turned herself into an orange tree, and the youth disguised himself as an old man. When the giant reached the spot, he asked the old man if he had seen the fleeing couple.

"No," replied the youth in his disguise of old man, "but refresh yourself by eating some of these oranges." The giant did so, and promptly lost all desire to pursue farther the fleeing couple, as the oranges were magical. He returned to his hut and explained to his wife that he was unable to overtake them.

"You are an old fool," answered the old lady. "The orange tree was Rosalie." For she, too, was gifted with magical powers.

Again the giant set out in pursuit. When the giant was once more on the point of overtaking them, Rosalie turned the horse on which they were riding into a church, her lover into the sacristan and herself into an image of the Virgin. When the giant reached the spot, he asked the sacristan if he had seen anything of the missing pair. "Hush!" replied the youth in his guise of sacristan, "you must not talk here, the priest is just going to sing mass. Come in and see the beautiful Virgin we have inside."

The giant then went inside to view the statue of the Virgin, with the result that he lost all interest in the pursuit, and returning once again to his hut, explained to his wife how after seeing the beautiful Virgin he had no further desire to capture his daughter and her abductor.

"You double fool," cried the old lady, "the Virgin was Rosalie. You are too half-witted to be of any use. I'll catch them." Thereupon the old lady set out to overtake them. Rosalie and the youth travelled as fast as they could, but the old lady went faster and gradually overtook them. When she was almost within reaching distance, Rosalie cried out to her lover, "We can't fool her, we'll have to use the needle."

Stooping down, she planted the needle in the ground, and immediately an enormous thicket grew up. For the moment they were out of danger. As the old lady laboriously cut her way through the thicket, the lovers fled on. At last the old lady got clear of the thicket. Once more she set forth in pursuit, gradually overtaking the couple. When once more her mother had nearly reached them, Rosalie threw down the grain of *saskab*. Immediately a great mountain reared itself aloft. Once more the lovers fled away, as the old lady pantingly toiled toward its summit, then slowly down the far side.

At last she was clear of the mountain and once more catching up on the fleeing lovers. Just as she was on the point of reaching them, Rosalie threw down the grain of salt, and immediately an enormous sea was formed behind them. Rosalie became a sardine, her lover a shark, and the horse a crocodile. The old lady waded into the water, trying to catch the sardine, but the shark drove her off.

"All right," cried the old lady, trembling with vexation and disappointment, "I bid you remain here in the water seven years."

At the end of the seven years they were able to come out of the sea, and they returned to the town where dwelt the parents of the youth. Rosalie, however, could not enter the town because she had not been baptized. Accordingly, she sent her lover into the town, bidding him return with half a bottle of holy water, and on no account was he to embrace his grandparents; for in that case he would straight away forget his Rosalie.

The young man reached his home and greeted his grandparents, but he would not permit them to embrace him, much to their consternation. Feeling tired, he resolved to rest awhile before returning to Rosalie with the holy water. Soon he was fast asleep, whereupon his grandmother, bending over him, softly kissed him. Consequently when he awoke, he had no longer any recollection of Rosalie.

For days Rosalie waited outside the town for the return of her lover. At last one morning, seeing a small boy playing on the edge of the town, she summoned him, and persuaded him to fetch her some holy water. The boy did so, upon which Rosalie bathed herself in it and entered the town. There she heard that her lover was on the point of marrying another girl at the behest of his grandparents.

Rosalie proceeded to the home of her former lover, but he failed to recognize her. However, she succeeded in having the marriage postponed three days. Then she prepared a great feast, to which she invited all the elders of the town as well as her former lover. In the center of the table she placed two dolls she had made. One was in the image of her lover, the other had her features.

The guests arrived and sat down to the feast. In the middle of the festival Rosalie suddenly pulled out a lash, and proceeded to lash the doll in the form of her former lover.

"Don't you remember how you had to fetch the water with the empty basket," she cried, and "whang" sung the lash. But as the lash struck the doll, the man cried out with pain. Again Rosalie addressed the doll.

"Don't you remember the pot at the bottom of the river, and how I brought it up for you?"

Again the whip sung through the air as it descended on the doll's back. Again the young man gave a shriek of pain. Still the memory of his former love for Rosalie was lost.

"Don't you remember the milpa you had to make, and the corn on the cob I prepared for you?" Rosalie asked the doll.

"Whang," sung the whip, as once more it descended on the doll's back. Once more the youth cried out in agony as he felt the blow that had been given the doll in his likeness. Rosalie then asked the doll if it remembered the seven years in the sea. The whip fell once more on the doll's back. Again the youth cried out with pain; then the memory of the past returned to him, and forgetting his bride to be, with a cry of joy he threw himself into Rosalie's arms.

In another version of the story the youth is set four tasks. The first is to empty a lagoon into a hollow; the second, to move a mountain a mile; the third is to drive his fist through a ceiba tree; and the fourth, to throw a stone across a wide lake. Again the girl helps him. She bores a hole in the trunk of the ceiba, and stuffs the outside. Consequently the youth's fist passes through it without trouble. The girl gives him a little bird called *puhwi*, which is very fast. When he is told to throw the stone, he hurls the bird instead. The bird flies across over the lake, and the giant thinks it is the stone. This incident is similar to that in the Popol Vuh when a rabbit running away is mistaken for the head of the twin. In the part that deals with the flight there are five obstacles. A needle causes a thicket; a comb grows into thick vines; ash, soap, salt become a wall, a slippery mountain, and a sea respectively.

So far as I know, "the magic flight" has never been reported as far south as the Maya area, although it is frequently met with in the folklore of North American tribes. The three obstacles usually found in the myth have here expanded to four, or in the second version five, obstacles.

YUM CHAC AND THE MILPA (Socotz)

When my informant, Cocom, first arrived at Socotz from the Peten, he had no knowledge of how to make a *primicia*, for the Peteneros are a godless lot. Accordingly he set about the making of his milpa without making any offering to the lords of the milpa. Consequently, the maize on his milpa grew to a certain height, but no higher. It rained all around, but on Cocom's milpa no rain fell. Cocom could not understand this, for he knew nothing of the lords of the forest. One night he dreamt he came home from his milpa through a downpour of rain. Entering his hut, he saw a naked man lying in his hammock. Cocom started to talk to him, pointing out how wet he was and how hard it was raining. "Yes, it is raining," replied the naked man, "but not on your milpa. The lords of the milpa have sent flames to keep the rain off your milpa. *Yum Tšak* does the work after God, and he must eat, but you have given him nothing to show your gratitude and assuage his hunger."

Cocom woke from his dream, but such was his fright that for two days he could eat nothing. He consulted a sorcerer, telling him of his strange dream. The sorcerer thereupon advised him to have a *primicia* made to propitiate the lords of the milpa. He did so, and almost immediately rain fell, converting his crop from a failure into a good return.

THE NINTH HEAVEN (Socotz)

A man, sitting on a stone in the forest, was suddenly carried up into the sky, right to the ninth heaven. Brujos (*Sayam* or *Kini winik*) found out where he was by means of a *sastun* (a ball of rock-crystal or jade used for divination purposes). All the women of the village made a long cord by twisting cotton (*holkutš*), and threw it up into the sky. They pulled the man down to earth again from the ninth heaven with it. When he reached earth, the man had already begun to grow wings. It began to rain blood and ashes, and the people were very frightened. They thought the man they had rescued from the sky was the cause, so they made a large fire and burnt him.

THE LORDS OF THE FOREST (Corozal District)

Once upon a time there was a man who was too lazy and ignorant to make his offering to the lords of the forest that he might have a good harvest of corn. As a result his crops were always poor, and eventually the lords of the forest visited on him a wind (weakening fever). Greatly alarmed, he called in the local *Hmen* (sorcerer-priest), who told him that his visitation was a result of his neglect of the lords of the forest, and he would only recover if he promised to amend, and make his offerings in future.

The man promised, and accordingly rapidly recovered. However, a few years later he again began to neglect his annual offerings in the milpa. Then the lords of the forest were indeed filled with wrath, and awaiting an opportunity they stole his young son, and, taking him to their home in the depth of the forest, they brought him up among themselves.

When the boy had become a young man, they sent him back to the human world, on condition that he should never have relations with a human woman. But after a while the young man married a girl. On their marriage night he had just shut the door of the hut when he heard a series of long low whistles. Now every one knows that that is the way the lords of the forest let human beings know of their presence, but the boy, as he had been away from human beings most of his life, did not know this. Accordingly he stepped out of the hut to see what was the matter. The lords of the forest immediately seized him and carried him away with them. Since then he has never been seen by human eyes.

THE DEER-FOLK (Corozal District)

Once upon a time there was a young fellow who lived with his grandmother. One day he started out to work, and when he reached his milpa he saw a beautiful doe standing in the middle of it; but as he looked at it, it turned into a girl. The young fellow had been thinking of getting a wife for some time, and as the girl was pretty, he decided to ask her to come and live with him. This he did, and the girl consented. When they arrived at the hut, the girl would not enter. The boy went in and told his grandmother (*chichi*) of his discovery. Meanwhile the girl was hungry, so turning herself into a doe she made a good meal of grass and shrubs.   When the boy called her in to eat, she had turned back into a girl once again. However, she was not hungry any longer and would not eat the tortillas and frijoles that had been prepared.

After they had been living together some time, the girl suggested that they should visit her relations. Now, her relations were all deer. They decided to make the visit, but before they left, the grandmother gave her grandson three seeds. One was the seed of the cotton tree (*yaštše*), the second of the gourd tree (*was*), and the third of the quebracho (*tšintok*). She also set out a calabash of chicha. If that overflowed or turned into wine, it would mean that the boy was in danger, and she would loose the three magic dogs she had, and they would rush to the aid of the boy.

They set out and walked a very long way until they came to a lake. This they crossed and found themselves in a broad savanna, the home of the deer. Then the girl turned back into a doe and summoned her deer relatives, and urged them to attack the boy. On realizing his danger, the boy called out to his grandmother for aid, and remembering the three seeds, he threw down one, the cotton-tree seed. Immediately a huge cotton tree sprang up, into the highest branch of which he climbed. Meanwhile the grandmother paid no attention to his call for help, for she was drunk. Then the deer began to saw down the tree by rubbing their antlers against it. Crick, crick, crick, went their antlers, as they slowly rubbed down the trunk. The boy was frightened. At last the trunk was almost sawn through; then just as it was about to fall, the boy threw down the calabash seed, and immediately a large calabash tree sprung up beneath him. The enraged deer started to saw this down too. Along came a hummingbird. The boy called it to help him. "What can I do to help you, young man?" Then the boy asked him to go and wake up his grandmother. The humming-bird sped off to her house. When he arrived there, she was lying in a drunken stupor. He called her, but she would not wake up. Then approaching close, he hovered in front of her face and darting in thrust his tongue up the old lady's nostril. She gave a terrific sneeze, and the humming-bird was blown out through the door and far across the tops of the trees. However, he had done his work well; the grandmother was awakened. Immediately she realized what had happened. The gourd had overflowed with blood, and the floor of the hut was covered with it. She released the three dogs, who rushed off to the boy's rescue.

Meanwhile the deer had sawn through the gourd tree with their antlers, and were engaged in sawing through the trunk of the quebracho, which had sprung up from the last seed. After a while, however, the deer moved off to rest awhile. Then a tortoise came by, and in response to the boy's appeal for help, he turned the tree into stone by urinating at its base. When the deer discovered this, they were furious, and set to work with renewed vigor. Just as they were sawing through the last few inches, the dogs arrived, and rushing on the deer slew them all including the traitorous deer-woman. Thus the boy was saved.

Another version of this story makes the dogs four in number. The boy and the doe-girl take refuge in a tree, which the deer start to saw down with their antlers. The boy plays on his flute to summon the four dogs. The grandmother loosens them, and dashing up they slay the deer. The boy and the girl are rescued and get married. The four dogs figure in another legend of a combat with giants. The boy is also given three pieces of lead. As he throws each one off to stave off pursuit, a mountain grows up behind him. He sings out to the grandmother for help, and the pet toucan begins to bleed. This was the arranged signal that he was in danger. The old lady is again drunk. A neighbor comes in and wakes her up. The old lady releases the dogs, and the boy is saved.

JUAN AND ROSALIE (Corozal District)

Juan lived with his grandmother (*chichi*). Every night he dreamt a beautiful girl slept beside him. One morning he awoke and found that he had not been dreaming, but in fact there was a beautiful girl there; but she rushed away as soon as he awoke. Next night the girl again came to his side, disappearing, however, before daylight. Juan could never see her features properly, so that day he told his grandmother all that had happened.

"Well, why not light a light tonight, and then you will be able to see her," she replied.

Accordingly, next night when the girl was fast asleep by his side, Juan got up and lit a light. But the girl woke up and rushed out of the hut, crying to Juan that now he would never see her again.

Nevertheless Juan had seen her face, but he was overwhelmed with grief.

Next morning the grandmother called him. "Juan, Juan, come and eat, the tortillas are all nice and hot in the calabash."

"O go to the devil, you've lost me my girl. I don't want your beastly tortillas," replied Juan.

Then, in answer to her questions, Juan explained how badly her advice about the light had resulted. He decided to set forth in search of the girl. After he had been walking some time, he espied a tiger and a lion, who were quarreling over the division of a deer they had killed. Juan was frightened and climbed up into a tree. The lion and the tiger saw him, and called to him to climb down and arbitrate between them. Juan would only do so after they had promised not to do him any harm. The tiger and the lion were very pleased with Juan's decision, and gave him not only a piece of the deer, but also each of them pulled out one of his claws and presented it to Juan. Now these claws contained magic, for with the tiger's claw he could turn himself into a tiger and with the lion's claw into a lion.

Juan thanked his new friends and continued on his journey. Soon he met a hawk. "Juan," cried the hawk, "give me a piece of that meat you are carrying."

"All right," replied Juan. Then the hawk pulled out a toenail and gave it to Juan. This toenail also was magical, for with it Juan could turn himself into a hawk. A little later Juan met an ant who also asked him for some of the meat. Juan gave him a piece, whereupon the ant told him to take one of his legs, but to take care not to tear out his entrails as he removed the leg. Nevertheless Juan pulled too hard and tore open the ant's stomach. He traveled a bit farther until he arrived at a hut in which was an old lady. He inquired of the old lady if she had seen the girl he was seeking. The old lady said that she had not, but she would ask her eldest son. She hid Juan under four large barrels, and then proceeded to call her eldest son by whistling on her flute. "Pi piri pi piri pipi," sung the flute, and shortly her eldest son arrived with much noise, for he was one of the wind giants.

"I smell ripe chicosapote," he cried. Now chicosapote is the smell human beings have. The old lady denied that there was any human hidden there, but the wind god insisted so much that the old lady took a stick and soundly thrashed him for disrespect. Later when he was eating, she asked him if he had seen anything of the girl. Her grandson replied that he knew nothing of the girl, and wanted to know why his grandmother wanted to know. Then the old lady explained that he had been quite right, there was a man hidden away, and if he would promise not to eat him, she would bring him out. The wind god promised, and Juan was brought forth and described the girl. Then the old lady summoned her second grandson with her flute. He did not know anything about the girl either. The youngest was summoned. He said he knew where the girl lived and promised to show Juan if he was given plenty to eat on the journey, for it was a journey of two or three days, and as he was a giant, his appetite was immense.

Juan was busy for some time getting food ready for the journey, but at last all was prepared, and they set forth. After two days' traveling they reached the edge of a big lake, in the center of which was an island in which the girl lived in a large palace. Juan took the wind god's shoe, a hair from his head, and his handkerchief. The shoe served as a boat, the hair as the mast, and the handkerchief as the sail. In this Juan sailed across the lake. When he arrived at the palace, he espied the girl sitting at an upper window. With the ant's leg he turned himself into an ant and proceeded to crawl up the wall of the building and into the girl's room. As soon as he was safely in the room, he turned back into a man once again and started to talk to the girl. Later he sought out the girl's father and asked for work. The father told him he would set him four tasks to do. If he completed them, he could have the girl. The first task was to clear a piece of forest and sow it with watermelons, harvest it, and bring him the fruit within twenty-four hours. Juan was very disheartened, as he realized the task was impossible. He told the girl of his trouble, but she told him not to worry, just to think of her, and she would do the work.

Next day the girl, whose name was Rosalie, brought Juan the watermelons, and he took them to her father. The next task he was set was to make another milpa in which this time tobacco was to be planted, and within twenty-four hours fresh cigars made from the plants that were sown were to be brought by Juan to the girl's father. That night, while he slept, Rosalie did the work, with the result that next day the cigars were all ready to be taken to her father. The next task was to bring plantains sown, grown, and harvested in the same miraculous way. Again Rosalie did the work while Juan slept. The next and final task was to prepare a dish of young corn in the same miraculous fashion. Once more Rosalie succeeded, with the result that next day Juan was able to take the dish to his taskmaster and claim his reward, Rosalie, for the fulfilment of the four tasks that had been set him. This was granted him. And in the usual way they lived happily ever after.

JUAN T'UL (Corozal District)

Juan T'ul (John Rabbit) was very fond of watermelons. A neighbor of his had a very fine patch at which he used to regale himself. The owner of the patch suspected that it was Juan T'ul who used to steal the fruit. Accordingly he lay in wait, and pounced down on him, just as Juan was preparing to grab a particularly fine watermelon. Juan managed to wriggle free, but he was thoroughly incensed with the man, and determined at the first opportunity to get his own back. A few days later he presented himself at the house of the neighbor, requesting the loan of a lighted log, with which to start his fire. By means of a trick he violated the daughters of the man.

Some time later the man learnt of what had happened, and determined to have his revenge on the rabbit. An opportunity was not long in presenting itself, and he managed to catch Juan T'ul. He shut him up in a cage, informing him that he was going to castrate him. Juan was left in the cage, while the man went off to heat up a piece of iron for the operation. A few minutes later the ocelot loped up.

"Hello, Juan," he cried. "What are you doing here?"

"I'm just waiting for a cup of hot chocolate this man is preparing for me," replied Juan. "Will you take my place? I'd like very much to drink the chocolate, for I know what good chocolate he makes, but I've got an important engagement in a few minutes, and I really can't wait."

Just at that moment the man, who was heating the iron inside the house, called out to Juan, "Sorry to keep you waiting, Juan, but it isn't hot enough yet, but don't worry, it will be just right in a few minutes."

Juan turned to the ocelot and said, "There, do you see what a considerate man he is. He won't bring out the chocolate till he is sure it is just perfect. Just open the door and take my place and tell the man you are waiting for the chocolate in my place, as I have an important engagement." Now if there was one thing the ocelot enjoyed it was a good cup of hot chocolate; so unbarring the door of the cage, he let Juan out and took his place. Juan hopped off without waiting to see what would happen. A few minutes later the iron was red-hot, and the man sent out his son to bring in Juan T'ul. When the son saw that Juan had disappeared and that his place had been taken by the ocelot, he told his father. The man was still in such a towering rage that he was determined to have revenge on someone, even if it could not be Juan.

"Bring him in, whoever it is," he cried. "I'll teach him to try and play his tricks on me."

The ocelot was brought in, and the man, taking the hot iron, castrated him. The ocelot was sent on his way with a parting kick. Ocelot walked off, feeling very sorry for himself. As he was slinking along, an owl hooted at him, mocking him with the words, "What have you done with your testicles?" Ocelot swore a mighty oath to be revenged on Juan T'ul, but Juan always took good care to be out of his way. Ocelot was always on the lookout for Juan, and one day he met him in a cave. Juan T'ul had no time to escape, but as soon as he saw Ocelot coming toward him, he reached up with his front paws, and began to push against the roof of the cave. Ocelot came forward, crying out, "Now I've caught you at last! You are going to die this time."

"But you can't kill me at present," replied Juan. "Don't you see that I am holding up the roof of the world? If I let go now, the sky will fall down, and the whole world will be destroyed."

Ocelot was very much impressed, for he was very simple, and debated with himself as to what he should do to Juan without causing the sky to fall on top of them. After a minute or two, Juan piped up, "Ocelot, be a good fellow, will you? Take my place for a minute. I must relieve myself, and, as you know, if I let go for a single second, the roof of the world will come down on us."

Ocelot agreed to take his place for a minute or two. As soon as the exchange had been made, Juan hopped off as fast as he could. Ocelot called after him, asking him where he was going. Juan with a chuckle replied, "I've fooled you again. Now you will have to hold up the world till you can find someone else to take your place."

After he had been holding up the roof for some time, Ocelot began to feel tired. At last when he could hold no longer, he let go one paw with great trepidation. Nothing happened. Then very gently he began to ease off the pressure he was exerting with the other paw. Nothing happened. The sky did not fall down as he had expected, and it gradually dawned on him that Juan had again got the better of him.

Some time later Ocelot ran into Juan T'ul again. This time Juan was amusing himself by swinging on a long elastic-like liana (*štak-*

ami). As he swung on it, the liana would shoot up into the sky every time he said, "Shrink!" Every time he cried, "Stretch!" the liana would bring him back to earth. When the ocelot saw Juan, he gave a cry of triumph, for he thought that at last he had him in his power.

"This is great fun," cried Juan. "Why don't you have a shot at it?"

"I will," replied Ocelot, "as soon as I have finished with you."

"Well, in that case you won't be able to," answered Juan, "for if I once let go, the liana will shoot up into the air, and you won't be able to reach it again. Have some fun with it first of all, and then you can do what you like with me."

Ocelot thought this was a good idea. Next time Juan T'ul swung earthward, Ocelot caught hold of the liana, and crying, "Shrink, shrink!" was carried high up into the air. Meanwhile Juan had hopped off as quick as he could. When Ocelot tried to come down to earth again, he could not remember the word to make the liana stretch. He thought and thought, but it was of no avail. In the end he had to let himself drop from where he was high up in the air, and falling to earth, was badly bruised.

The next time Ocelot fell in with Juan, he found him busily engaged in collecting hay.

"Hello," said Juan. "I've got a fine offer for this hay in the village. Why don't you help me? And we will divide the profits. I am small and can't carry much at a time, but you have a big strong back, and could carry a heavy load."

Ocelot agreed, and as soon as they had cut a good quantity of hay, Juan piled it on Ocelot's back, tying it securely with a strong cord. Then before Ocelot realized what was happening, he set fire to the dry grass. The grass blazed up, and Ocelot was burnt to death. After that Juan T'ul lived in peace.

This is one of a series of tales that deal with Juan T'ul, the bre'r rabbit of Central America. Juan is always astute, and always comes off the victor, thanks to his superior intelligence. The incident in the above story of the holding-up of the roof of the world is told with somewhat different detail by Burkitt (Gordon, p. 143). He also gives another story of the rabbit, where as usual he displays his cunning to the discomfiture of his enemies. Bre'r rabbit stories are also reported by Radin from Oaxaca. Owing to the close similarity to the Uncle Remus stories, one would be inclined to suspect an African origin for these tales. However, African influence would scarcely be expected to show itself in the Alta Vera Paz, or Oaxaca; and the Mayas of the Corozal District have never been in touch to any extent with Negroes. Stories of Juan T'ul were also obtained at San Antonio, where again there has been no discernible African contact, as the relations between the Mayas and the Caribs of the coast are very slight.

APPENDIX I

LANGUAGE

No attempt has been made to make a linguistic study of the Maya dialect spoken at San Antonio. I had neither the time nor the qualifications for such work. That is a task that awaits a qualified philologist. Nevertheless, it seemed advisable to give a number of phrases in San Antonio Maya that would tend to emphasize the differences between the different dialects discussed in the text, without attempting any explanation. The different prayers, too, that are embodied in the text should prove of assistance to anyone attempting a comparison. Not everyone has a good ear for phonetics, and there are undoubtedly many mistakes in the texts of the prayers. Still, it seemed best to let them stand as they are, rather than attempt to improve them along lines based on Yucatecan grammars.

NOUNS

The plural is seldom employed. Where it is used, the Yucatecan ending *ob* becomes *o*.

TIME PARTICLES

These do not contract as frequently as in Yucatan. In prayers the uncontracted forms appear to be almost invariably used. *Tan in meya,* "I am working," is more common that *t' in meya.* The *k* compounded with the nominal pronoun is seldom used to express present time.

TENSES

These follow closely those used in Yucatan. In past time the particle *t'* is absent. *U hantah buq,* "he has eaten meat." *In kubah-tetš hode,* "I gave you something yesterday." *Utš o kaštah bašul,* "they found figurines a long time ago."

NUMERALS

The Spanish forms are now generally used above three. However, many of the old men can count up to a hundred in Maya.

ADVERBS

Ma, "no," does not contract even when used with *yan. Minan* is unknown. It is usually employed with the affix *i.*

Ma in qati.	I do not want.
Ku a meya?	What are you doing?
Ku (ku u) qaba hedaa?	What is the name of this?

182

Tan in yokol itšil a yototš.	I am entering your house. (The *y* appears to follow no rule as to whether it is to be affixed or not.)
Maka watakah?	Who came?
Tubak taletš?	Where did you come from?
Ka talaketš in etel.	You must come with me.
Bel u kah ti kah.	He is going to the town.
Bel in kah in hanal	I am going to eat.
or	
Ben kah in hanal.	I am going to eat.
Tan in liqil.	I am getting up.
Tan to in liqil.	I am just getting up.
Maaš to in liqil.	I am not yet getting up.
Walak in ɔib.	I can write.
Ma ta betik maaškui.	You are doing nothing.
Tales hai.	Bring me a small pot.
Kulen.	Sit down.
Bikiletš?	How are you?
Lailiken.	I am fine.
Yan a tetš wa?	Have you tortillas?
Yan u muk Juan.	Juan is strong.
Inene wihen.	It is I that is hungry. (Emphasis on the I.)
Ma ka wihetš.	You aren't hungry.
Ma in wel.	I don't know.
Ka wilah.	You must understand. (*Coll.*, do you get me?)
Ikta kananen.	I am very tired.
Watak ha.	It is beginning to rain. (*Lit.*, the water comes.)
Sami kalanen.	Today I am drunk.
Hode udi.	Yesterday he arrived. (Note the *d.*)
Hedo.	That one there. (Note the *d.*)
Tan u tša tube.	He is bringing a flower.
Ku yan tetš?	What is the matter?
Intšetš a kuštah.	You found it. (Emphasis on you.)
Pateto ka haniken.	I will eat later.
Biki ka betah ila?	How do you make this?
In wel in bete.	I know how to do it.
Lekalo winiki.	That man over there.
Lekila winiki.	This man here.
Bikil a be a ki?	Which road is the best?
Hoqen patš na.	Go out of the house.

APPENDIX II

NOTES ON THE PLANTS CULTIVATED BY THE
SAN ANTONIO MAYAS

Below are listed the more important plants cultivated by the modern Mayas of British Honduras. The list is divided into two parts. First, those plants that are known to be indigenous to the New World, and second, those plants that have been introduced in post-Columbian times. Where doubt exists as to whether a plant was known to the ancient Mayas or not, such evidence as can be gleaned from historical sources is given.

The alligator pear (*Persea gratissima*) is without doubt of American origin. The tree has been found in a wild state from Mexico to the Amazon, and was undoubtedly cultivated by the Mayas before the conquest. Its name in Spanish (*aguacate*) is derived from the Aztec name *auacatl*. Both in San Antonio and Socotz it is known as *on*.

Arnatto (*Bixa orellana*) is grown to a certain extent in and around the villages. It is used to color foods and chewing gum. In Honduras it was used to color chocolate (Torquemada, Book III, chap. 41). In San Antonio it is called *kušub*.

Beans (*Phaseolus vulgaris*) are, and have been for many centuries, one of the food products of most importance not only to the Maya, but also to practically every tribe practising agriculture from the United States to Argentina. Although climatic conditions in the Maya area do not permit of the conservation of such agricultural produce as may have been buried in pre-Columbian graves, beans have been identified in graves in pre-Pueblo graves in our Southwest (Kidder, p. 75) and in pre-Inca graves on the coast of Peru. The early conquerors and priests make constant reference to the bean in Central America. The first mention of beans in the area under discussion in this publication dates back to 1525. Bernal Diaz describes a foraging expedition for which he was detailed by Cortez in the course of the famous march from Mexico to Honduras. The force, after its departure from Peten, suffered considerably from hunger; and in an area which cannot be far from the modern settlements along the Toledo-Guatemalan border, Diaz (chap. 178) found supplies of food including beans.

184

"The five of us," he writes, "set out with the aid of two guides for a part of the country traversed by deep rivers. After crossing them, we reached some marshes, and immediately beyond them some isolated farms, where the majority of the villagers were gathered together. We discovered four houses full of maize, beans, about thirty hens [turkeys?], and some of those squashes of this country which are called *ayotes*."

In the Toledo District the black variety of bean (*boš buul*) is that which is most cultivated, although the red variety (*tšuk buul*) is also cultivated to a certain extent. After being spread out to dry, the beans are shelled and picked over by hand for bad or malformed beans. There is a considerable sale of beans. They are carried down to Punta Gorda, whence they are shipped up the coast to Belize. In the Cayo District the black variety is practically unknown, all the beans grown there being of the red variety (*tšak buul*).

The bread-nut tree (*Brosimum alicastrum*) is not in the true sense a cultivated plant, as there is no difference between the cultivated trees and those growing wild in the forest. Nevertheless, the plant is of such economic importance that it seems best to class it as one of the cultivated group. There is no information as to whether it was cultivated in pre-Spanish times. However, it is remarkable what large numbers of plants are to be found growing in the immediate vicinity of any group of ruins. This is probably not entirely fortuitous, when one takes into account that the modern Maya to a certain extent purposely plants bread-nut trees in and around his villages, or at least abstains from cutting down those that are already growing. The fruit possesses considerable nutritive power. It ripens in the months of April and May, when it is gathered in large quantities. The outer covering is eaten raw. The kernels are either boiled or, after being steeped in water or lime, are ground and mixed with maize to make tortillas. A secondary use of this plant is supplied by the leaves, which are employed as mule fodder in the forest, where maize or grass is not available. The Maya name for the bread-nut is *oš*.

Cacao (*Theobroma Cacao*) is a plant that has played a role of the utmost importance in the religious, commercial, and gastronomical life of the Maya. Cacao was the general currency among the Mayas before the conquest, and, in fact, still is in some of the remoter parts of Guatemala. Even in Yucatan it has not long ceased to be used for this purpose. A young Maya of Valladolid informed me that his father had told him that when he was a boy, cacao-beans still served as the general currency of that district. As cacao-beans were the general medium of exchange, it is not surprising to find that the patron deity of Maya merchants was the spirit of cacao, Ekchuah. Considerable quantities of cacao were imported into Yucatan in pre-conquest days from Tabasco, Ulua (Documentos inéditos. Relación de Motul), and Honduras (Torquemada, Book III, chap. 41), and cacao-beans formed part of the tribute paid to the rulers of Mayapan (Landa, chap. 22). There were special feasts in Yucatan to insure a successful cacao crop. Almost every early writer on the Maya area makes constant reference to cacao. The modern Maya of San Antonio prepares cacao in a manner that differs but slightly from that described by the early Spanish chroniclers. The beans, after being shelled, are placed upon a piece of bark and left in the sun to dry (Plate XIII, Fig. 1). Subsequently they are roasted upon a small pottery comal, known as šok (Plate XVIII, Fig. 2). After roasting the beans are ground on the metate in the same way as maize flour is prepared. The ground cacao is then mixed with maize flour made from tortillas, which have been previously roasted, and then soaked in water and reground on the metate. The mixture is next placed on the fire and boiled. A considerable quantity of black pepper is added, and the drink is ready to be served. Black pepper is probably a modern substitute for the "delicate spices," which were formerly one of the components of cacao. Frothed cacao, such as is described by Villagutierre and other writers, is no longer used by the Maya of the Toledo District. The bean is known at San Antonio as *kuku*, but in Socotz the name *cacao* is used.

Cassava of the sweet variety (*Manihot dulcis*) is grown by the Mayas of the Toledo District. Both the sweet and the bitter kinds (*Manihot esculenta*) are of American origin. Cassava roots are depicted on a vase of proto-Chimu culture from Chimbote in Field Museum (Cat. No. 4,788). It would appear that the sweet variety was typical of the area lying between the Andes and the Pacific Ocean, whereas the poisonous variety was that most generally used east of the Andes (see Nordenskiöld, 1924, Map 3). There have been two main cultural streams flowing northward from South America into the West Indies and Central America. The migrations of the Arawaks, and subsequently the Caribs, into the West Indies from northeastern South America brought in their train *Manihot esculenta*, and the whole complex of the expression of the poisonous juices and the preparation of cassava bread typical of the region east of the Andes. The diffusion of culture from Colombia through the Isthmus of Panama into Central America was responsible for the introduction of both varieties of cassava, but with *Manihot dulcis* in more general use. However, in Central America neither variety achieved the pre-eminence accorded it in other areas where maize cultivation was not highly developed. Cassava, too, was chewed to form an intoxicating beverage in South America in pre-Columbian times. This custom eventually spread to the Mosquito Coast (M. W.).

Oviedo (Book XXXI, chap. 11), dealing with Honduras, writes, "The ordinary foods of this country are maize, cassava, sweet potatoes, ajes, and mamey apples in such quantities that they are a very important source of supply to the Indians. The yucca (cassava) is of the kind that does not kill, the other kind also exists. From both kinds cassava and wine are made. Wine is also made from maize." Cortez, in his first letter, says that *potu yuca* was eaten roasted, but not as bread. Bernal Diaz (Book I, chap. 8), writing of the visit made by Juan de Grijalva to the island of Cozumel, the first discovery of Yucatan, says, "We gave this village the name of Holy Cross, as we came in sight of it four or five days before that feast (1517). There were some fine beehives, plenty of *boniatas* and sweet potatoes, also big herds of swine of the country, which have their navels on their backs." *Boniata* was one of the words used in the West Indies to denote the sweet mandioca. It is obvious that in this case there is no confusion between sweet mandioca and the sweet potato, as both are mentioned in the same sentence.

Aguilar (p. 98) also mentions that yucca was cultivated in Yucatan in his time, but he did not write until 1635. Cassava was presumably unknown in the valley of Mexico, owing to the high altitude, but it is reported from Colima, West Mexico, by Juan Cepeda (p. 526), one of the conquistadores, who wrote in 1581. The linguistic evidence from the Maya area tends to confirm what Diaz wrote. The word for "cassava" is the same in practically every one of the twenty-two Maya dialects from which there is information. Many of these linguistic groups have been separated from one another since the time of Columbus. In San Antonio the name is the same as in the other dialects, i.e., *ɔin*. The bitter variety is unknown in San Antonio, but is known to the Yucatecans and Lacondones. The root is eaten boiled, and is not used to make flour, although this is the practice among the Caribs of the coast.

Chaya (*Jatropha acontifolia*), known in Maya as *štšai* or *tšai*, is widely cultivated throughout the Yucatan Peninsula. The leaves are boiled and served as a kind of spinach. This plant, too, was undoubtedly known to the Maya in pre-conquest days. In the "Relación de Motul" and the "Relación de Merida" it is listed as one of the plants cultivated by the Maya. It is mentioned, too, in the legend of the Sun, the Moon, and Venus (p. 125).

The "cherry" (*Pseudolmedia cerasifolia*) is found growing wild in the Peten and British Honduras. It is also cultivated to a certain extent for its excellent fruit, the small red "cherries" having a delicious taste. The tree is unfortunately becoming scarcer every year owing to the lack of foresight of the *chicleros* (chewing gum gatherers), who, on finding a tree with fruit, invariably cut it down rather than take the trouble to climb up to reach the fruit. The Maya name both in San Antonio and Socotz is *manaš*.

Three varieties of chili are commonly cultivated by the modern Maya. The word *chili* is derived from the Nahuatl *chilli*. In Maya the generic name for all varieties of the plant is *ik*. *Šmaš ik* is a perennial growing a small seed on a low bush (*Capsicum frutescens*). The large annual (*Capsicum annuum*) is known vulgarly as *ton ɔul* in Socotz, but at San Antonio it is known as *nukutš ik* (big chili). The third common variety (*Capsicum baccatum*) is known at San Antonio as *mehen ik* (small chili). When fasting, the Mayas abstained from the use of chili in any of their dishes. This must have been a real hardship, as the Maya to this day is inordinately fond of highly flavored dishes, enormous quantities of chili being consumed. The seed is either sun or smoke dried immediately after harvesting. Afterwards it is ground as required. For this purpose small cylindrical pestles of clay with one end flattened are employed. The seed is placed in a small pottery bowl (*hai*, Plate XVIII, Fig. 7) and pounded with the pestle. Similar pestles have been found in the ruins of Lubaantun and other Maya cities. Tripod bowls with crisscross incisions on the base are very common in all collections of Aztec pottery. They, too, are met with, though less frequently, in the Maya area. It has been surmised that they were employed for grating chili.

Copal (*Protium copal*) is no longer cultivated by the Mayas. Nevertheless, at the time of the conquest, it appears to have been regularly planted. During the first *entrada* of Montejo into Yucatan, the Spaniards passed through a large plantation of copal, some two leagues in extent, near the town of Zinzinato. The plantation is said to have been well looked after (Oviedo, Book XXXII, chap. 3). Both the tree and the gum extracted from it are known in all Maya languages as *pom*. Copal trees are scarce in the vicinity of San Antonio, and a considerable quantity of the amount used there is imported from Aguacate. The method of bleeding the tree to obtain the gum is described on page 104.

Cotton was one of the few plants common to both the Old and the New World in pre-Columbian times. However, the varieties grown in the New World were different from those obtaining in the Old. The cotton grown in Central America was, in all probability, *Gossypium hirsutum*. Cotton clothing was extensively worn in both the Maya and Mexican areas, and nearly all the early writers remark on the beauty of the woven fabrics. In Yucatan cotton cloaks were paid as tribute to the ruler of Mayapan (Cogolludo, Book IV, chap. 3), and were exported to Mexico (Relación de Tecate, in Colección de documentos inéditos). The Mayas had a very high reputation as weavers. Approaching closer to the area discussed in this monograph, the Itzas of Tayasal, Lake Peten, were said to have possessed fine colored cotton fabrics. Among the Mayas of San Antonio cotton is grown only on a very restricted scale. The loom has fallen into disuse, and the cotton is employed solely for mending. However, in the Kekchi villages weaving is still a live industry. The San Antonio name for cotton is *tumun*, a dialecticism corresponding to the Yucatecan *taman*.

Custard apple. Several fruit-trees are grouped together under the generic name *Annona*. All are indigenous to Central America, and presumably all were cultivated by the Mayas with the possible exception of the guanabana. *Annona squamosa* is known in Maya as *ɔalmuy; A. purpurea* and *reticulata* are grouped together under the name *oop*. The cherimoya (*Annona cherimola*) is known in San Antonio as *tukib*. In Socotz it is called *tukib* or *poš*. The Spaniards were first known to the Mayas of Yucatan as *Ahmakopob*. This nickname was bestowed on them in the course of their famous march under Montejo from the east coast to Chichen Itza. Cogolludo (Book II, chap. 5) writes, "He (Montejo) arrived at the town of Coba, which today is deserted; and it was there that they (the Mayas) first began to call the Spaniards *Ahmakopob*, which means 'eaters of anonas,' which are a fruit of this country. The Indians were surprised to see them eat them without taking heed as to whether they were harmful or not." Cogolludo, however, has mistranslated the word in a manner that might suggest that the Mayas themselves were unacquainted with the fruit. The expression means not "eaters," but "bolters of anonas"; and what surprised the Mayas was probably not that they ate the fruit, but that they hurriedly swallowed the fruit without masticating it. *A. purpurea* is probably the commonest of the varieties now grown by the Mayas. The guanabana (*Annona muricata*) was probably introduced into

the Maya area after the first arrival of Europeans. There is no
Maya name for it, the Spanish term being employed. Anona
branches are said to have been twined for the royal seat of the
Cakchiquel chiefs (Brinton, p. 33).

The gourd vine (*Lagenaria leucantha*) is one of the very few plants
that were known to both the Old and New Worlds prior to the discovery of America. It is found in pre-Columbian graves wherever
the climate is sufficiently dry to allow of its preservation. Many
varieties are grown by the modern Maya. *Lek* is the name given to
a large round variety chiefly employed for storing tortillas after
cooking. Placed in one of these gourds and covered with a cloth,
tortillas retain their heat for a very long period. Another variety,
known in Maya as *tšu*, is very long, and is used for carrying water.
The name *tšu* is also applied to a variety that has the shape of the
number 8, which is much prized for its strange shape and for its
convenience; for it can be easily carried by looping a cord around
the narrow center.

The gourd tree (*Crescentia cujete*) is indigenous to Central America. In British Honduras and Yucatan it is found growing wild.
The tree was sacred to the Maya peoples, as the thorns of the tree
were used to draw blood for sacrificial purposes (Brinton, p. 44).
The sacred character of the tree is still retained in Guatemala at the
present time, although now that all memory of blood sacrifices is
lost, the reason for the sacredness of the tree is ascribed to the shape
of the leaves, which bear some resemblance to a cross. Bishop
Landa (chap. 21) speaks of the Mayas using vases made of the
skin of a fruit that grows on a tree. Further, pottery vessels made
in the shape of the tree gourd are not uncommon from the Mexican-
Maya area. At the present time a syrup is extracted from the pulp
of the fruit in Yucatan, but in the Toledo District, where large
numbers of the trees are grown around the villages, the fruit is only
used to furnish gourds. The San Antonio name is *lutš*, but in Yucatan
and northern British Honduras it is called *was*.

The guava tree (*Psidium guajava*) is indigenous to Central America. Popenoe (1919) writes, "One of the commonest fruits of
present-day Copan and doubtless well known to the ancients." In
British Honduras it is grown only on a very small scale by the
modern Mayas. The Socotz name is *pitši*, but in San Antonio it is
called *putah*. Cogolludo (Book IV, chap. 2) mentions it as one of
the plants of Yucatan, stating that when apple-seeds brought from
Spain were sown in the monastery, guava plants sprang up. In the

highlands of Guatemala the leaves were used by the Indians to wrap their cigarettes.

Two varieties of henequen are grown in San Antonio (*Agave sisalana* and *Agave fourcroydes*). Both of these are of American origin, and were undoubtedly cultivated by the Mayas prior to the conquest. Torquemada says that the common people in Mexico wore dresses of henequen. *A. fourcroydes* supplies the raw material for most of the sisal manufactured. In Yucatan it is known as *sak ki* ("white henequen"), but in San Antonio it is called *ki*. Sisalana in Yucatan bears the name *yaš ki* ("green henequen"), but in San Antonio is known as *ikeh*. In all the villages of the Toledo District both varieties are grown in and around the villages. The process by which the fiber is prepared is described on page 93.

The jicama (*Pachyrhizus erosus*) is largely cultivated at San Antonio. It was listed as grown by the Mayas in the "Relación de Merida" and in Ponce's "Relación breve." The Maya name is *tšikam* or *štšikam*.

Maize (*Zea mays*) was the foundation on which aboriginal American agriculture was built. Without this cereal it is doubtful whether any high state of culture would have been attained in the New World. The original undomesticated plant, from which the cultivated maize was derived, has not been identified with certainty. Probably it was of the family to which teocentli (*Euchlaena mexicana*) belongs. It is interesting to note that the method of planting in small hillocks separated from one another by a couple of feet or more has probably caused maize to develop into a tall plant of one stalk rather than a multi-stalked low plant, as would in all probability have been the case, had the original plant been sown broadcast. This argues strongly for the independent invention of agriculture in the New World. Had the original cultivators of the wild maize been acquainted with Old World methods, they would presumably have sown the wild maize grass in the way that they were accustomed to sow other Old World grasses like wheat, oats, barley, etc., that is to say, broadcast. Maize in that case would have developed along totally different lines into a plant bearing little resemblance to our modern maize (J. E. Thompson, 1928). The term for maize is practically the same in all the Maya dialects from Yucatan to the Pacific Coast and from Tabasco to Honduras. At San Antonio the name *išim* is used. This is the same as that employed in Yucatan. The maize sown in the Toledo District is very degenerate, and is the result of unsystematic cultivation. Yellow, white, and red grains are frequently found on one and the same cob.

The malanga or coco is also indigenous to America. The variety at present cultivated by the Maya of San Antonio is probably *Xanthosoma violaceum*. I have not been able to find any references that would point to this useful plant having been cultivated by the Mayas in pre-conquest times. The fact that the name for this plant in San Antonio (*munul*) is different from that employed at Socotz (*škukut makal*), would suggest that its introduction is recent. In addition to boiling the roots, the leaves and young shoots are boiled and served as we would serve sprouts.

The mamey apple (*Calocarpum mammosum*) belongs to that by no means small group of semi-cultivated plants, for which Central America is distinguished. It was cultivated by the Mayas in pre-conquest days, having been found in a state of cultivation close to Chetemal Bay on the east coast of Yucatan by the Davila Expedition (Oviedo, Book XXXII, chap. 6). Oviedo (Book XXXI, chap. 11) also states that large numbers were eaten by the natives in Honduras. The original Maya name for this tree was *haas* (Relación de Merida). On the introduction of the plantain and the banana to the New World the Mayas transferred their term for the mamey to the new fruit. Later, to avoid confusion, the mamey apple was distinguished from the imported fruit by the addition of the Maya word for "red," becoming *tšakal haas* (in San Antonio *tšukul haas*). The same process was adopted in the case of the horse and the tapir. The Maya name for the tapir, *ɔimin*, was adopted for the horse. Later, to avoid confusion, the tapir was distinguished from the horse by being called the "forest tapir" (*ɔimin qaš*, in San Antonio *ɔimin tše*).

The nance (*Byrsonima crassifolia*) was known to the Maya peoples in pre-conquest times. In the Popol Vuh (p. 189) it is related that the earthquake giant Vukup Cakix had a favorite nance tree from which he used to obtain fruit every day during the season. It was while he was in this tree that he was attacked by the divine twins. The Maya name for the tree is *tši* both in San Antonio and Socotz.

The pawpaw (*Carica papaya*) is indigenous to Central America. It is grown to a considerable extent by the Mayas of the Toledo District. The leaves are also employed to soften tough meat. Meat left wrapped some time in pawpaw leaves becomes quite tender. The Maya name both in Yucatan and San Antonio is *put*.

The pineapple (*Ananas sativus*) possibly did not reach the Mayas until shortly after the conquest. The Prospero Indians, who were entirely cut off from Spanish influence, were found to be cultivating the pineapple when first visited by Europeans in 1646 (Cogolludo, Book XII, chap. 7). This, of course, is not direct evidence that the pineapple was known to these tribes before the arrival of the Spaniards in the New World, as many of the articles introduced by them passed from tribe to tribe and were well established in remote areas long before Europeans had penetrated so far. Pineapples were certainly cultivated in the Cueva region prior to the conquest (Oviedo, Book XXIX, chap. 29), and on the Mosquito Coast (M. W.) and the Usamacintla basin (Tozzer, 1912) in the seventeenth century the same method of producing an intoxicant was in use. In view of the close relations between the Chiriqui area and the Mayas as demonstrated by the importation into Chichen Itza of gold objects from this region, it is not unlikely that food products of the two areas were interchanged. The "Relación breve" relates that Father Ponce was received, during his journey to Yucatan in 1588, at many of the Maya villages with gifts of pineapples. However, there is no Maya word for the pineapple, the Spanish *piña* being employed. This, however, does not necessarily imply that the Maya was unacquainted with the plant. In many cases Spanish names have been substituted for the old Maya terms. The toucan, for example, is at present almost invariably known under the Spanish name *pito real*, whereas there is a Maya name, though now almost forgotten save by a few of the old people. Among the Maya tribes of the Highlands there are three different terms, the same term being used by tribes which are now geographically separated. Sahagun, who wrote his history in the middle of the sixteenth century, says that the Indians used to bring, among other things, large numbers of pineapples to market. It is then obvious that if the pineapple had not reached the Maya area before the conquest, not many years elapsed before it was cultivated by the Maya tribes.

The hog plum (*Spondias purpurea*) is little grown in the Toledo District. Oviedo states that it was one of the common fruits of Honduras and that there were a number of varieties. The common name in use at the present time in Central America (*jocote*) is derived from the Nahuatl *Xocotl*. The San Antonio name is *abil*.

The squash (*Cucurbita pepo*) was undoubtedly cultivated by the Mayas. References to this useful plant are frequent among the early writers. Bernal Diaz speaks of squashes in the area contiguous to that under discussion. The reference is quoted under "beans." The general Maya term for squash is *qum*. A number of varieties of squashes are grouped together under the name *štšum*. These include a variety with short thorns and another kind that is white on the outside. A species of squash common in the Maya area is the chayote (*Sechium edule*) known to the Mayas as *wiskil*.

The sweet potato (*Ipomoea batatas*) has been found in aboriginal graves in Peru, and was cultivated as far north as Mexico, the common Spanish term *camote* being derived from the Mexican *camotli*. Among the Maya the sweet potato was undoubtedly cultivated prior to the arrival of the Spaniards. Bernal Diaz (Book I, chap. 9), an eye-witness, reports that there were large numbers of sweet potatoes grown on the east coast of Yucatan, and it is listed in the "Relación de Merida." The Maya name is *is*.

Tobacco was used by the Mayas in pre-conquest times, although there is no information as to which species they grew. Elbow-pipes have been found at Chichen Itza, Lubaantun, Palenque, and in the Ulua Valley. The tubular pipe is probably represented on one of the tablets at the side of the doorway leading into the shrine of the temple of the cross at Palenque. However, the Maya peoples probably smoked their tobacco in the form of cigars more than in pipes. Leaves of the guava tree are said to have been used to wrap cigars. The Maya name for "tobacco" is *quɔ* both in San Antonio and the north of the Peninsula. In San Antonio tobacco is used both for cigars and for smoking in imported clay pipes.

The tomato (*Lycopersicum esculentum*) is of American origin, the name being derived from the Nahuatl term *xitomatl*. It was presumably known also to the ancient Maya. The modern Maya of San Antonio cultivates the tomato to a considerable extent. It is called by them *p'aaq*, whereas the Yucatecan name is *p'ak*.

The following plants, that are used by the modern Maya, have been introduced into America since the first arrival of Europeans:

The banana (*Musa sapientum*) is stated by Oviedo (Book VIII, chap. 1) to have been introduced into America from the Canary Islands. It is grown fairly extensively around San Antonio. The usual name given is the Spanish term *guineo*, but in Yucatan it is known as *sak haas* ("white mamey apple").

The breadfruit tree (*Artocarpus incisa*) is little grown by the Indians of the Toledo settlement. There are a few plants at Aguacate and in the San Antonio *alquilos*. It has probably reached the Mayas from Asia via the West Indies. There is no Maya name, the Spanish term *mazapan* being employed.

The coconut palm (*Cocos nucifera*) is little grown around the Indian villages of the Toledo District. It was probably introduced by the Caribs, who have large plantations on the coast near Punta Gorda.

The grape-fruit (*Citrus grandis*) is very plentiful in all the Indian villages. The closely allied shaddock was grown in Yucatan in Cogolludo's time (Cogolludo, Book IV, chap 2).

The okra (*Hibiscus esculentus*) is a plant cultivated to a very considerable extent in San Antonio and the neighboring villages. There is no Maya name.

Onions (*Allium cepa*) also form an important crop among the Mayas. Again there is no Maya name.

The orange (*Citrus aurantium*) is popular in all the Maya villages. At San Antonio the Spanish word *naranja* is used for the fruit. In Socotz and Yucatan there is a Maya name, *paqal*, in use.

The plantain (*Musa paradisiaca*) was presumably introduced from Europe, but there seems to be a bare possibility that there was a cultivated variety in America prior to the conquest. It is one of the most important food-plants of the Mayas of San Antonio, every milpa having its patch of plants. The fruit is usually served roasted in its skin, or less frequently boiled. The fruit is known at San Antonio as *haas*, in Yucatan and Socotz the term *boš haas* is employed. As explained above, this term was borrowed from the mamey, the fruit of which has a slight resemblance to the plantain. In Kekchi, too, the word for mamey is made to serve for the plantain too.

Rice (*Oryza sativa*) is grown only in small quantities by the Indians of the Toledo District. To a certain extent they obtain such rice as they require from the Caribs or coolies of the Toledo settlement. There is no Maya term.

The sugar-cane (*Saccharum officinarum*) is grown extensively. The cane is chewed raw or crushed in primitive hand-driven mills of wood known under the Spanish name *trapiche*. The molasses thus obtained after solidification is bound up in plantain leaves in cakes weighing about half a pound and sold in the village. Again there is no Maya term for the plant or sugar.

Yams (*Dioscorea batatas*) form an important element in the diet of the Mayas of San Antonio. Both purple and white varieties are common. The Maya name is *payak*.

BIBLIOGRAPHY

Only the books consulted in the preparation of this publication and those to which reference is made in the text are included in this bibliography. The editions listed are those to which reference is made. A short historical bibliography of British Honduras has been included.

ACOSTA, J. DE.—Historia natural y moral de las Indias.... Madrid, 1608.

AGUILAR, P. SANCHEZ DE.—See Sanchez de Aguilar, P. 1639.

ALPUCHE, N. R.—Apuntes históricos y colección de tratados internacionales relativos a esta colonia británica. Merida, 1894.

ANCONA, E.—Historia de Yucatan. Merida, 1878-1905.

ANNALS OF THE CAKCHIQUELS.—Philadelphia, 1885.

ANONYMOUS.—The Defence of the Settlers of Honduras against the Unjust and Unfounded Representations by Col. George Arthur, Late Superintendent of That Settlement ... to Which is Added an Account of the Descent of the Spaniards on the Settlement in the Year 1798. Jamaica, 1824.

BELIZE LITERARY SOCIETY.—Magazine of, with Account of Raid on Orange Walk, Sept. 1, 1872. 1877-78.

BERENDT, D. H.—Vocabulario del dialecto (de Maya) de Peten. See Means, P. A., 1866-67.
Report of Explorations in Central America. Report of the Smithsonian Institution, Washington, 1867, pp. 420-426.

BLOM, F.—Report on the Ruins of Uaxactun and Other Ruins in the Department of Peten, Guatemala. Washington, D. C., 1924. In manuscript.

BLOM, F., AND LA FARGE, O.—Tribes and Temples. New Orleans, 1926-27.

BRASSEUR DE BOURBOURG, C. E.—See Popol Vuh, 1861.

BRETON, A. C.—Relationships in Central America. Man. Vol. XIX, 1919, No. 94.

BRINDLEY, J. B.—The Wesleyan Mission in British Honduras. London, 1916.

BRINTON, D. G.—The Folklore of Yucatan. London, 1883.
See the Annals of the Cakchiquels. 1885.
Native American Stringed Instruments. American Antiquarian and Oriental Journal, Vol. XIX, 1897, pp. 19-20.

BURDON, J.—Brief Sketch of British Honduras, Past, Present, and Future. The West India Committee, London, 1928.

BURKITT, R.—Notes on the Kekchi Language. Am. Anthr., New Series, Vol. IV, 1902, pp. 441-463.
A Kekchi Will of the Sixteenth Century. Am. Anthr., New Series, Vol. VII, 1905, pp. 271-294.
The Hils and the Corn. The Museum Journal, Philadelphia, Vol. IX, Nos. 3-4, 1918, pp. 274-289.
A Journey in Northern Guatemala. Museum Journal, Philadelphia, Vol. XV, 1924, pp. 115-145.

CAIN, H. E. C.—See Metzgen, M. S., and Cain.

CARR, A. D.—British Honduras. United Empire. N. S., Vol. XII, 1921, pp. 631-638.

CENSUS.—British Honduras. Report on the Census of 1921, Parts 1-2, London, 1922.

CEPEDA, J. SUAREZ DE.—Relación de los Indios colimas de la Nueva Granada, 1581. Anales del Museo Nacional de Arqueología, Historia y Etnología, Mexico, Vol. IV, 1912, pp. 505-529.

CODEX CORTESIANUS.—Published for the first time by Leon de Rosny. Paris, 1883.

CODEX DRESDENSIS.—Die Maya Handschrift der Königlichen Bibliothek zu Dresden. Edited by E. Förstemann. Leipzig, 1880.

CODEX TRO-CORTESIANUS.—Codice denominado Cortesiano que se conserva en el Museo Arqueológico Nacional (Madrid). Published by Juan de Dios de la Rada y Delgado and Jerónimo Lopez de Ayala y de Hierro. Madrid, 1892.

COGOLLUDO, D. LOPEZ DE.—Historia de Yucatan. Merida, 1867-68.

CANDOLLE, A. DE.—Origin of Cultivated Plants. New York, 1890.

COLLET, W.—British Honduras and Its Resources. London, 1909.

CONZEMIUS, E.—Ethnographical Notes on the Black Carib. Am. Anthr., N. S., Vol. XXX, No. 2, 1928, pp. 183-205.

COOK, O. F.—Vegetation Affected by Agriculture in Central America. Bulletin 145, U. S. Bureau of Plant Industry, 1909.

CORRESPONDENCE.—Correspondence as to Claims of Great Britain Relative to the Mosquito Coast, Honduras, and Yucatan. 1853.

CROWE, F.—The Gospel in Central America; containing a sketch of the country . . . . London, 1850.

CRUZ, PACHECO.—Compendio del Idioma Maya. Merida, Yucatan, Mexico, 1920.

DAHLGREN, B. E.—Cacao. Field Museum Leaflet. Botanical Series, No. 4. Chicago, 1923.

DAMPIER, W.—Collection of Voyages, Vol. II. Two Voyages to Campeachy. London, 1729.

DE LA ROSA, LUIS.—Memoria sobre el cultivo de maiz en Méjico. Mexico, D. F., 1846.

DIAZ DEL CASTILLO, BERNAL.—Histoire véridique de la conquête de la Nouvelle-Espagne. Paris, 1877.

DIESELDORFF, E. P.—Kunst und Religion der Mayavölker im alten und heutigen Mittelamerika. Berlin, 1926.
    Religión y arte de los Mayas. Anales de la sociedad de geografía e historia de Guatemala, Vol. V, Nos. 1-4, 1928-29.

DILLON, A. B.—Geography of British Honduras. Belize, 1923.

DOCUMENTOS INÉDITOS.—Colección de documentos inéditos . . . . 42 Vols. (See Relaciones de Yucatan.) Madrid, 1898-1900.

DONDE, JOAQUIN, AND DONDE, JUAN.—Apuntes sobre las plantas de Yucatan. Merida, 1874.

DOUGLASS, A. E.—Portrait Pipe from San Salvador, Central America. American Antiquarian and Oriental Journal, Vol. XI, 1889, pp. 348-353.

DUNLOP, W. R.—Report on the Economic and Natural Features of British Honduras in Relation to Agriculture . . . . London, 1921.

EDWARDS, B.—The History, Civil and Commercial, of the British Colonies in the West Indies. Philadelphia, 1806.

FARABEE, W. C.—The Central Caribs. University of Pennsylvania. The University Museum, Philadelphia. Anthropological Publications, Vol. X, 1924.

FIELD MUSEUM OF NATURAL HISTORY.—Annual Report of the Director to the Board of Trustees for the Year 1927. Report Series, Vol. VII, No. 2, Chicago, 1928, pp. 214-216.

    Annual Report of the Director to the Board of Trustees for the Year 1928. Report Series, Vol. VII, No. 3, Chicago, 1929, pp. 415-417, and pp. 449-450.

FOWLER, H.—A Narrative of a Journey Across the Unexplored Portion of British Honduras, with a Sketch of the History and Resources of the Colony. Belize, 1879.

FRAZER, J. G.—The Golden Bough. A Study in Magic and Religion. Abridged edition. London, 1924.

FUENTES Y GUZMAN, F. A. DE.—Historia de Guatemala o recordación florida escrita en el siglo XVII . . . . Madrid, 1882-83.

GALLATIN, A.—Notes on the Semi-civilized Nations of Mexico, Yucatan, and Central America. Translations, American Ethnological Society, Vol. I, New York, 1845.

GAMIO, M.—La población del valle de Teotihuacán. Mexico, D. F., 1922.

GANN, T.—Mounds in Northern Honduras. 19th Annual Report, Bureau of American Ethnology, Washington, 1900, pp. 639-650.

    The Ancient Monuments of Northern Honduras and the Adjacent Parts of Yucatan and Guatemala. Journ. R. Anth. Inst., Vol. XXXV, 1905, pp. 103-112.

    Reports on some Investigations in British Honduras. Annals of Arch. and Anthr., Univ. of Liverpool, Liverpool, Vol. VII, 1914, pp. 28-42.

    The Chachac or Rain Ceremony as Practised by the Maya of Southern Yucatan and Northern British Honduras. XIXth Int. Congress of Americanists, Washington, 1917, pp. 409-418.

    The Maya Indians of Southern Yucatan and Northern British Honduras. Bureau of American Ethnology, Bulletin No. 64, 1919.

    In an Unknown Land. New York, 1924.

    Mystery Cities. New York, 1925.

    Ancient Cities and Modern Tribes. New York, 1926.

    Maya Cities. New York, 1927.

    Discoveries and Adventures in Central America. New York, 1928.

GARCIA Y GARCIA, A.—Historia de la guerra de castas en Yucatan. Merida, 1865.

GATES, W.—The Distribution of the Several Branches of the Mayance Linguistic Stock. Appendix XII in S. G. Morley, The Inscriptions at Copan. Washington, 1920.

GIBBS, A. R.—British Honduras: An Historical and Descriptive Account of the Colony from its Settlement, 1670. London, 1883.

GIGLIOLI, E. H.—Una recente esplorazione dell' Honduras inglese e singolari strumenti litici ivi scoperti. Archivio per l'Antropologia e la Etnologia, Vol. XXI, 1891, pp. 411-414.

GOMARA, LOPEZ DE.—La Historia general de las Indias, y todo lo acaescido enellas dende que se ganaron hasta agora. Y la conquista de México y de la Nueva España. Antwerp, 1554.

GORDON, G. B.—Guatemala Myths. The Museum Journal, Philadelphia, Vol. VI, No. 3, 1915, pp. 103-144.

GRANT, H. T.—The Cockscombs Revisited. The Geographical Journal, Vol. LXX, 1927, pp. 504-572.

HANDBOOK NO. 133.—British Honduras. Prepared under the direction of the historical section of the Foreign Office. London, 1920.

HENDERSON, CAPTAIN.—An Account of the British Settlement of Honduras. London, 1809.

HONDURAS ALMANACK.—1827.

HONDURAS ALMANACK.—1839.

HUMMEL, C.—Report on the Forests of British Honduras with Suggestions for a Far-reaching Forest Policy. London, 1922.

HUNTINGDON, E.—Civilization and Climate. New Haven, 1915.
    Maya Civilization and Climatic Changes. XIXth Int. Congress of Americanists. Washington, 1917, pp. 150-164.
    Guatemala and the Highest Native American Civilization. Proc. Am. Philos. Soc., Vol. LII, 1913, pp. 467-487.

IM THURN, E. F.—Among the Indians of Guiana. London, 1883.

JOYCE, T. A.—Central American and West Indian Archaeology. London, 1916.
    Report on the Investigations at Lubaantun, British Honduras, in 1926. Journ. R. Anth. Inst., Vol. LVI, 1926, pp. 207-230.

JOYCE, T. A., CLARK, J. COOPER, AND THOMPSON, J. E.—Report on the British Museum Expedition to British Honduras, 1927. Journ. R. Anth. Inst., Vol. LVII, 1927, pp. 295-333.

JOYCE, T. A., GANN, T., GRUNING, E. L., AND LONG, R. C. E.—Report on the British Museum Expedition to British Honduras, 1928. Journ. R. Anth. Inst., Vol. LVIII, 1928, pp. 323-350.

KIDDER, A. V.—Southwestern Archaeology. New Haven, 1924.

LA FARGE, O.—See Blom, F., and La Farge. 1927.
    Adaptations of Christianity among the Jacalteca Indians of Guatemala. Thought, December, 1927.

LANDA, D. DE.—Relation des choses de Yucatan.... Texte espagnol et traduction française, by Brasseur de Bourbourg. Paris, 1864.

LAWS, GEOFFREY.—The Survey of the Lubaantun District in British Honduras. The Geographical Journal, Vol. LXXI, 1928, pp. 224-239.

LEHMANN, W.—Zentral-Amerika. Berlin, 1920.

LONG, E.—History of Jamaica. Contains chapters on settlements in Bay of Honduras and Campechy. London, 1774.

LOPEZ DE COGOLLUDO, D.—See Cogolludo, D. Lopez de. 1867-68.

LOTHROP, S. K.—The Museum Central American Expedition, 1924. Indian Notes, Museum of the American Indian, Heye Foundation, Vol. II, No. 1, 1925.

The Museum Central American Expedition, 1925-26. Indian Notes, Vol. IV, No. 1, 1927.

A Note on Indian Ceremonies in Guatemala. Indian Notes, Vol. IV, No. 1, 1927.

Santiago Atitlan, Guatemala. Indian Notes, Vol. V, No. 4, 1928.

Further Notes on Indian Ceremonies in Guatemala. Indian Notes, Vol. VI, No. 1, 1929.

LYNCH, T.—Ms. letter to the Secretary of State from Jamaica, September 20, describing, inter alia, logwood cutting in Campeche. 1682.

MALER, T.—Explorations of the Upper Usumatsintla and Adjacent Region. Altar de Sacrificios; Seibal; Itsimte-Sacluk; Cankuen. Reports of Explorations for the Museum. Harvard University, Peabody Museum Memoirs, Vol. IV, No. 1, 1908.

MARTINEZ HERNANDEZ, J.—La Creación del mundo según los Mayas. XVIIIth Int. Congress of Americanists, 1912, pp. 164-171.

MARTYR, P.—The History of the West Indies Containing the Actes and Adventures of the Spaniards. London, 1612.

MAUDSLAY, A. C. AND A. P.—A Glimpse at Guatemala and Some Notes on the Ancient Monuments of Central America. London, 1899.

MEANS, P. A.—History of the Spanish Conquest of Yucatan and of the Itzas. Harvard University, Peabody Museum Papers, Cambridge, Vol. VII, 1917.

METZGEN, M. S., AND CAIN, H. E. C.—Handbook of British Honduras. London, 1925.

MILLSPAUGH, C. F.—Contributions to the Flora of Yucatan. 1895-1902.

Contribution II to the Coastal and Plain Flora of Yucatan.

Contribution III to the Coastal and Plain Flora of Yucatan. Field Museum Botanical Series, Vol. I.

Plantae Yucatanae. Botanical Series, Vol. III, Nos. 1-2.

MORLEY, S. G.—The Central American Expedition for 1922. Carnegie Inst. of Washington, Year Book No. 21, Washington, 1922, pp. 310-318. (Wrongly states on page 317 that San Luis and San Antonio are Kekchi-speaking.)

Report of S. G. Morley on the Pusilha Expedition, Carnegie Inst. of Washington, Year Book No. 27, Washington, 1928, pp. 318-320.

MORRIS, D.—The Colony of British Honduras. London, 1883.

MOTUL, DICCIONARIO DE.—Ms. Sixteenth Century Missing. Copy in John Carter Brown Library.

NORDENSKIÖLD, E.—Comparative Ethnographical Studies. Göteborg, 1920.

Comparative Ethnographical Studies. Göteborg, 1924.

NUNEZ DE LA VEGA, F.— Constituciones dioecesanas del obispado de Chiappa. Rome, 1702.

OVIEDO Y VALDES, GONZALO F.—Historia general y natural de las Indias. Madrid, 1851-55.

OWER, L.— Features of British Honduras. The Geographical Journal, Vol. LXX, No. 4, 1927, pp. 372-386.

The Geology of British Honduras. Belize, 1928.

PEREZ, JUAN PIO.—Diccionario de la lengua Maya. Merida, 1866-77.

PINEDA, V.—Historia de las sublevaciones indígenas habidas en el estado de Chiapas. Gramatica de la lengua Tzel-tal. Chiapas, 1888.

PONCE, A.—Relación breve y verdadera . . . . Colección de documentos inéditos para la historia de España, Vol. LVIII, Madrid, 1872.

PONCE, PEDRO.—Breve relación de los dioses y ritos de la gentilidad. Anales del Museo Nacional de México, Vol. VI, Part I, 1892.

POPENOE, W.—The Useful Plants of Copan. Am. Anthr., N. S., Vol. XXI, 1919, pp. 125-138.
    Manual of Tropical and Sub-tropical Fruits. New York, 1927.

POPOL VUH.—Popol Vuh. Le Livre sacré et les mythes de l'antiquité américaine, avec les livres heroiques des Quiches . . . . Texte quiche et traduction française by Brasseur de Bourbourg. Paris, 1861.

PRICE, H. W.—Excavations on the Sittee River, British Honduras. Proc. Soc. of Antiquaries, 2nd Series, Vol. XVII, 1899, pp. 339-344.

RECORD, S. J., AND MELL, C. D.—Timbers of Tropical America. New Haven, 1924.

RELACIONES DE YUCATAN.—Relaciones historio-geograficas de las provincias de Yucatan. Madrid, 1898-1900.

REMESAL, A. DE.—Historia general de las Indias occidentales, y particular de la gobernación de Chiapa y Guatemala. Madrid, 1620.

REYNOSO, FRAY D.—Arte y vocabulario en lengua Mame. Mexico and Paris, 1644-1897.

RICKETSON, O.—Report on Excavations at Baking Pot, British Honduras, Carnegie Inst. of Washington, Year Book No. 23, Washington, 1924, pp. 219-221.
    Excavations at Baking Pot, British Honduras. Carnegie Institution of Washington, Publication No. 405, 1929, pp. 1-27.

ROYS, R. L.—A Maya Account of the Creation. Am. Anthr., N. S., Vol. XXII, 1920, pp. 360, 366.
    The Ritual of the Chiefs of Yucatan. Am. Anthr., N. S., Vol. XXV, 1923, pp. 472-484.

SAFFORD, W. E.—The Isolation of Ancient America as Established by the Cultivated Plants and the Languages of Its Aborigines. XXth Int. Congress of Americanists, Rio de Janeiro, 1915, pp. 167-172.
    Notre heritage des Indiens américains. Ibid., 1915, pp. 173-178.
    Food-Plants and Textiles of Ancient America. XXth Int. Congress of Americanists, Washington, 1917, pp. 12-30.
    Origin of the Banana. Science, Vol. LXI, No. 1589, 1925.

SAHAGUN, BERNARDINO DE.—Histoire générale des choses de la Nouvelle-Espagne. Paris, 1880.

SANCHEZ DE AGUILAR, P.—Informe contra idolorum cultores de Obispado de Yucatan. Madrid, 1639, and Mexico, 1892.

SAPPER, C.—Beiträge zur Ethnographie von Süd-Ost-Mexiko und Britisch-Honduras. Petermanns Mitteilungen, Gotha, Vol. XLI, 1895, pp. 177-186.
    La Lengua de San Luis (Peten). In manuscript, 1895 a.
    Das nördliche Mittel-Amerika nebst einem Ausflug nach dem Hochland von Anahuac. Braunschweig, 1897.

Speise und Trank der Kekchi-Indianer. Globus, Vol. LXXX, 1901, pp. 259-263.

Mittelamerikanische Waffen im modernen Gebrauche. Globus, Vol. LXXXIII, 1903, pp. 53-63.

The Independent States of Yucatan. Bureau of American Ethnology, Washington, Bull. 28, 1904.

Der gegenwärtige Stand der ethnographischen Kenntnis von Mittelamerika. Arch. für Anthropologie, N. S., Vol. III, 1905, pp. 1-38.

Das tägliche Leben der Kekchi-Indianer. XVIIIth Int. Congress of Americanists, London, 1912, pp. 362-371.

Die Bevölkerung Mittelamerikas. Wissenschaftliche Gesellschaft, Strassburg, 1913.

Über den Charakter und die geistige Veranlagung der Kekchi-Indianer. Seler Festschrift, 1922, pp. 401-440.

SAVILLE, M. H.—A Primitive Maya Musical Instrument. Am. Anthr., Vol. X, 1897, p. 272.

Reports on the Maya Indians of Yucatan. Indian Notes and Monographs of the Museum of the American Indian, Heye Foundation, Vol. IX, No. 3, 1921.

SKINNER, A.—Notes on the Bribri of Costa Rica. Indian Notes and Monographs of the Museum of the American Indian, Heye Foundation, Vol. VI, No. 3, 1920.

SPINDEN, H. J.—A Study of Maya Art. Memoirs of the Peabody Museum of American Archaeology and Ethnology, Vol. VI, Cambridge, Mass., 1913. The Origin and Distribution of Agriculture in America. XIXth Int. Congress of Americanists, Washington, 1917, pp. 269-276.

New World Correlations. XXIst Int. Congress of Americanists, The Hague, 1924, pp. 76-86.

The Reduction of Maya Dates. Papers of the Peabody Museum, Vol. VI, No. 4, 1924 a.

The Population of Ancient America. The Geographical Review, Vol. XVIII, No. 4, 1928.

STANDLEY, P. C.—List of the Plants Known from Yucatan, Campeche, and Quintana Roo, with Spanish and Maya Vernacular Names. In manuscript.

STANDLEY, P. C., AND CALDERON.—Lista preliminar de las plantas de El Salvador. San Salvador, 1925.

STARR, F.—The Indians of Southern Mexico: An Ethnographic Album. Chicago, 1899.

Survivals of Paganism in Mexico. Open Court, Chicago, 1899.

Notes upon the Ethnography of Southern Mexico. Proc. Davenport Academy of Natural Sciences, Vol. VIII, 1900, pp. 102-198.

Notes on the Ethnography of Southern Mexico, Part II. Ibid., Vol. IX, 1901, pp. 63-172.

In Indian Mexico. Chicago, 1908.

STEPHENS, J. L.—Incidents of Travel in Central America, Chiapas, and Yucatan. New York, 1841.

Incidents of Travel in Yucatan. New York, 1843.

STOLL, O.—Zur Ethnographie der Republik Guatemala. Zürich, 1884.

Guatemala. Leipzig, 1886.

Maya-Sprachen der Pokom-Gruppe. Vienna and Leipzig, 1888-96.

Die Sprache der Ixil Indianer. Ein Beitrag zur Ethnologie und Linguistik der Maya-Völker. Leipzig, 1887.

SWAYNE, E.—British Honduras. The Geographical Journal, Vol. L, 1917, pp. 161-179.

SWETT, C.—A Trip to British Honduras and San Pedro, Honduras. New Orleans, 1868.

TAIT, D.—Missionary Work in British Honduras. London, 1906.

THOMPSON, E. H.—The Genesis of the Maya Arch. Am. Anthr., N. S.,Vol. XIII, 1911, pp. 501-516.

THOMPSON, J. E.—A Correlation of the Mayan and European Calendars. Field Museum of Natural History, Anthr. Series, Vol. XVII, No. 1. Chicago, 1927.
    The "Children of the Sun" and Central America. Antiquity, Vol. II, 1928, pp. 161-167.
    Some New Dates from Pusilha. Man, Vol. XXVIII, 1928, No. 70.
    See Joyce, T. A., Cooper Clark, J., and Thompson, J. E.

TORQUEMADA, JUAN DE.—Monarchia Indiana. Madrid, 1712.

TOZZER, A. M.—A Comparative Study of the Mayas and the Lacandones. New York, 1907.
    A Spanish Manuscript Letter on the Lacandones, in the Archives of the Indies at Seville. XVIIIth Int. Congress of Americanists, 1912, pp. 497-509.
    A Maya Grammar.... Works Noted. Peabody Museum Papers, Vol. IX, 1921.

TREATY.—Tratado de limites entre los Estados Unidos Mexicanos y Honduras Británica. Mexico, 1897.

URING, N.—History of the Voyages and Travels of, with New Draughts of the Bay of Honduras and the Caribbee Island.... 2 Vols. London, 1725-1726.

VALLEJO, GONZALO.—Diario de ocurrencias particulares acaecidas en dos ocasiones; relaciones históricas y geográficas de Central America. Colección de libros y documentos referentes a la historia de America, Vol. VIII, Madrid, 1908.

VERSAVAL, A. F.—The Discovery of the Ruins of Mucnal Tunich, Cayo District. The Belize Clarion, May 11, 1922. (Ruins subsequently christened Minan Ha by T. A. Joyce and T. Gann without reference to the earlier discovery.)

VILLACORTA, C. J. ANTONIO.—See Ximenez, Francisco. 1929.

VILLAGUTIERRE SOTO-MAYOR, J. DE.—Historia de la conquista de la provincia del Itza, reducción, y progressos de la de el Lacandon, y otras naciones de Indios barbaros, de la mediación de el reyno de Guatimala, a las provincias de Yucatan, en la America Septentrional. Madrid, 1701.

M. W.—A Familiar Description of the Mosquito Kingdom. Churchill's Collection of Voyages and Travels, Vol. VI, p. 285. London, 1732.

WILLARD, T. A.—The City of the Sacred Well. New York, 1926.

WILLIAMS, E. W.—The Baymen of Belize. London.

WILLIAMS, M. W.—Anglo-American Isthmian Diplomacy, 1815-1915. Washington, 1916.

XIMENEZ, FRANCISCO.—Historia de la provincia de San Vicente de Chiapa y Guatemala. Edited by J. Antonio Villacorta, C. Guatemala, 1929.

YOUNG, T.—Narrative of a Residence on the Mosquito Shore.... London, 1842.

A LINGUISTIC POSTSCRIPT

After this publication was already in print, I came upon Dr. Karl Sapper's paper, "Choles und Chorties" (XVth Int. Congress of Americanists, Quebec, 1906, Part II, pp. 423–465). Dr. Sapper, after drawing attention to the phonetic change in Mopan Maya from *a* to *u*, remarks that this change also occurs among the Chontals. If Dr. Sapper really means the Chontals, it does not seem necessary to seek so far for such a change. A similar mutation also occurs among the Chols, a branch of whom was, apparently, living to the south of the Mopans until the eighteenth century.

It has been suggested (pp. 50 and 61) that certain beliefs of the Mopan Mayas may have been borrowed from the Chols, and this linguistic change tends to confirm the surmise. Lack of space precludes a fuller vocabulary, but below are listed a few words where the change may be noted. The Chol words are drawn from Starr (1901, appendices I and II), indicated by the letters *St.*, and from the vocabulary in the above-mentioned paper of Sapper's, referred to as *Sa*. Unfortunately the Moran vocabulary appears to contain a mixture of Maya and Chol words, and therefore can not be used. Some of the informants were, it would appear, Maya-speaking Lacondones. Maya words are spelt in Spanish fashion to facilitate comparison:

YUCATECAN MAYA	MOPAN MAYA	CHOL	ENGLISH
chac	chuc	chuchuk (St.)	red
kan	kun	kunkun (St.)	yellow
zac	zuc	susuk (St.)	white
kab	kub	lahkub (St.)	arm
nak	nuk	laktnock (St.)	stomach
bac or bacel	buc	b'ukel (St.)	bone
pak	puk	puk (St.)	to sow
chai	chui	chui (St.)	fish
bacal	bucul	bukul (Sa.)	Shelled ear of maize.

The resemblances are even closer than the above table would suggest, if one takes into consideration the different methods of spelling. The Chol words for the parts of the body, also, undoubtedly incorporate possessive elements, and the colors may well be reduplicated, as occurs, too, in Yucatecan Maya.

In addition a few words used by the Mopan Mayas appear to be definitely Chol. "Sleep" in Chol is *wiel* (Sa.): in Mopan, *wiyel*. "Cacao" in Chol is *cucuo* (Sa.): in Mopan, *cucu*. "Valley" in Chol, *hoktil* (Sa.): in Mopan, *hok*. Also the *d*, which is unknown in Yucatecan Maya, occurs sparingly in Chol, and in Mopan is occasionally used in place of the Yucatecan *l*. In the latter case it is alveolar.

INDEX TO MAYA WORDS

maaš, spider monkey, 87, 123

mahanamaɔ, Sisemito, gorilla-like monster, 67, 146

mam, grandfather or grandson, 80

Mam, name of Huitz-Hok, 57, etc.

manaš, cherry, Pseudolmedia Spuria, 188

mehen, man's son, 80

meknal, hell, 66, 68

mol, harvest, the stacking of the ripe ears of corn, 54

munul, the malanga or coco, 192

mutš, frog, 122, 149

na, house, 91

na, mother, 81

naatš haas, the toucan bird, 87

natšin, paternal aunt, 81

Noh Itš, "Big Eye," the Morning Star, 63

Nohotš sukunsil, a wind god, 108

Nukil winkob, "the big men," agricultural deities, 106-107

Nukutš makob, "the big men," agricultural deities, 107

Nukutš yumsilob, the great lords, agricultural deities, 107

nul, a dry ear of corn, 54

okom, posts used in houses, 91-92

on, alligator pear, 184

oop, *Annona purpurea* and *A. reticulata*, 189

op', totoposte, 100

oqot keh, the deer dance, 103

oš, bread-nut tree, 35, 185

otš, fox, 35, 135

otškan, a snake, possibly the boa constrictor, 68

paap, jay, 35, 121

pai, skunk, 35

paqal, orange, 195

paqal, seed, 54

paqil, a tumor near the heart believed to be caused by fright, 110

paš, harp, 101

paštše, musical bow, 101, 147

payak, yam, 195

peɔhol, lowest crossbeam of house, 92

peɔ', deadfall trap for animals, 87

pib, underground oven first heated with stones, 118, 165

pibil, food cooked in pib, 165

pišan, spirits of the dead, 67

pitši, guava, 190

poitše, tree, the bark of which is used for beds, etc., 98

pol na, ridge-pole, 92

pom, copal incense, 44, etc.

pootš, tamal, 99

puhwi, a small fast-flying bird, black in color, Spanish, Caballero, 172

pulia, sorcerer, 49, etc.

put, papaya, 148, 192

puta, guava, 190

puun, toucan, 87

p'aaq, tomato, 193

p'itš, singing thrush, 121

p'ul, jar for carrying water, 95

p'us, little dwarf people, who lived before the flood, 166

Qaanan qašob, "the forests on high," forest deities, 106, 115

qaan, hammock, 93

qaantše, wooden bench, 93, 122, 148

qambul, curassow, 87

qeqentše, peccary, 87

qeš, waxen image, 166

qisin, the devil, 67

qubak, two top crossbeams of house, 92

qum, squash, 194

qutš, thread, 97

quɔ, tobacco, 193

saam, three-toed sloth, identification a little uncertain, 35

sak (or suk) kib, a name given to the copal gum, 104

sak qab, posol, the grains of which have not been soaked in lime, 115

sak (or suk) šikin, ocelot, 35

sai, leaf-cutting ant, 132

saq, locust, 52

saskab, white limestone-like soft substance, 169

sastun, divination stone of jade or rock-crystal, 127

sayam, sorcerer, 173

siktše, vertical poles of the roof, 92

Siwanahwa, a monster, wife of Chentun, 66

sinaan, scorpion, 45

suk aq, white liana used in construction of houses, 92

suktan, small fish, 128

sukun, elder brother, 81

šak, basket, 96

šan, a palm, *Sabal mexicana*, 91

šanap, sandals, 98

šiqintše, fungus, 125

škantia, root from which yellow dye is obtained, 98

škukut makal, malanga or coco, 192

šmunul, green maize, 54

šnawa, tamale, 99

šok, pottery grill used to roast cacao beans, 95

šok qin, the divination of the weather, 75

šol, flute, 102, 131

šol, transversal beams that support the roof of a house, 92

GENERAL INDEX

Abstinence, from food, 55, 104-105; sexual, 49-50, 61
Accordion, 44
Achiote, 129, 184
Adam, 119, 144-145
Adultery, 80
Agave, 93, 191
Agriculture, 41-55, 106, 112-113, 124, 163-165, 168, 191; origin of, 132, 135, 139, 146; patrons of, 57, 60
Aguacate village, 36, 40, 96, 98
Aguilar, G. de, 46, 93
Aguilar, S. de, 35, 46, 55, 94, 187
Albinism, 86
Alcalde, 74, 78
Alcoser, 84
Alligator pears, 184
Allium cepa, 195
Alquilos, 69
Altars, 93
Alta Vera Paz, 49, 58, 67, 82, 87, 96-97, 102, 181
Ambition, lack of, 86
Animals, patron of, 124, 142; how lost tails, 124, 145; origin of, 144
Ants, 109, 132-133, 163, 176-177
Anteater, 35
Ananas sativus, 192
Anona, 189
Arawaks, 96
Arenal, 112, 113
Armadillo, 35, 58, 142
Arnatto, 129, 184
Arrows, 88, 90, 103, 124
Artistic sense, 95-96, 99
Artocarpus incisa, 194
Assi, F., 74-75
Atoles, 62
Attalea cohune, 33, 92
Axes, stone, 61, 128
Ayotes, 135, 139, 185, 193
Aztecs, 58, 63, 69, 102, 137, 184, 188

Bacabs, 48
Balche, 103, 104
Banana, 194
Bark, 48, 62, 97-98; cloth, 98
Basketry, 96
Beans, 54, 100, 184-185; origin of, 135, 139
Beds, 80, 93-94, 98, 168
Bees, 105, 156-157, 187
Belotia campbellii, 97
Berendt, K., 38
Bernal, Diaz, 53, 97, 184, 187, 193, 194

Birth ceremonies, 78
Bixa orellana, 129, 184
Black men, 103; paint, 103, 113; clothes of Chac, 128
Blood-letting, 61, 74
Blowfly, 130
Blowgun, 87-88, 120-122, 125, 127-128, Bol, F., 30
Bombax ceiba, see ceiba
Boomerangs, 152
Borgia codex, 58
Bow, 88, 90, 103, 124, 152; musical, 101, 147
Brachycephaly, 79
Breadfruit, 194
Breadnut, 35, 185
Breton, A., 80
Brinton, D., 101, 190
Bribri, 95
British Museum, 29
Brosimium alicastrum, 35, 185
Brujo, see sorcery
Bull-roarer, 102
Burial, 81-82
Burkitt, R., 135, 139, 180
Burning, 47
Byrsonima crassifolia, 192

Cabbage palm, 35, 91
Cabildo, 78
Cacao, 49, 54-55, 71, 80, 90, 96, 98, 101, 185
Cajabon, 35, 36, 41, 60, 153
Cakchiquels, 190
Cal, Cecilio, 64
Calabash, 71, 99-100, 102, 115-116, 122, 149, 151
Calabash tree, 174
Calcide, 95
Calderonia salvadorensis, 98
Calocarpun mamosum, 135, 187, 192
Cano, 85
Canoe, 33, 97, 128
Capsicum, see chili
Carcha, S. Pedro, 35
Caribs, 31-33, 56, 85-86, 97, 194-195
Carica, papaya, 148, 192
Cassava, 55, 186-187
Catholicism, 55, 56, 68, 80, 82, 106, 113
Caves, 60
Cayo, 40
Cedar, 35, 97, 130
Ceiba, 97, 110-112, 130, 147, 156, 159, 174
Census, 40

Lime, 74, 99, 115, 118, 126, 134, 185; chewing of, 101
Linguistics, 37, 182, 183
Litter, 161
Lizard, 122
Loche, 94
Logwood, 98
Lonchocarpus, 104
London, treaty of, 31
Loom, 96, 127
Loss of crafts, 96
Lothrop, S., 102, 112
Love, 84
Lubaantun, 35, 36, 188, 193
Lycopersicum esculentum, 193

Machaca, 36
Macusis, 139
Magic Flight, 167-172
Magic, sympathetic, 72, 74, 75, 89, 90, 104, 105, 109, 110, 127, 128, 131, 171, 176
Magpie, 121
Mahanamatz, 67, 146-148
Mahaywa, 66
Mahogany, 33-35, 97
Maize, 43-55, 70, 191; spirit of, 48, 49, 53, 63, 114; discovery of, 132-135; fermented, 104; preparation as food, 96, 99, 100, 104
Malanga, 100, 191
Maler, T., 112
Mam, see Huitz-Hok
Mamey tree, 134, 135, 187, 192, 195
Manteca tree, 91
Marimba, 44, 101-103
Marital relations, 81
Marriage, 79, 83, 85, 86, 124, 126
Martyr, P., 46, 94
Masks, 98, 102, 103
Match-makers, 126
Mats, 98
Maudslay, A. P., 36, 57
Means, P. A., 38, 85
Mecapal, 54, 78, 79, 97, 98
Meknal, 66, 68
Menche, 97
Mendez, S., 84, 107, 111, 158
Merida, 57
Metate, 96, 99, 148, 166, 186
Mexico, 43, 48, 62, 76, 105, 109, 113, 187, 193
Milpa making, 41-52, 112, 146, 163-165, 167
Mirror, 132
Mohijon, 36
Moho tree, 97
Moleskin, 58
Monkey, 35, 101; origin of, 123, 137, 138
Montejo, F., 94, 105

Moon, glyph, 138; goddess, 53, 57, 64, 82, 126-132, 138; regulates sowing, 55
Mopan, 32, 35, 36, 38, 85, 204
Morning Star, 57, 63, 64, 89, 120-125, 132, 141-143
Mosquito coast, 187, 193
Mountain Cow Water-hole, 37
Murder, 84
Music, 101, 103
Musical bow, 101, 147

Names, San Antonio, 37, 85
Nance, 192
Nets, 90, 91
Net bags, 54, 78, 79, 97, 98, 111
New year, 82
Nine as sacred number, 72, 73, 110, 113, 116, 117, 149, 166, 173
Nohoch Ich, see Morning Star
Nohoch Priosti, 83, 84, 86, 142
Nordenskiöld, E., 186
Nuñez de la Vega, 110

Oaxaca, 181
Ocelot, 35, 178, 179
Ochcan, 68
Offerings, see copal, candles, and posol; to deceased, 82
Okra, 100, 195
Old Empire, 46, 47
O'Neil, General, 31
Onion, 195
Orange, 195
Orange Walk, 40
Oviedo y Valdes, 94, 105, 187, 189, 192, 193

Pachyrhizus erosus, 148, 191
Palm trees, 33, 90-92
Panama, 91, 105
Papaya, 148, 192
Parrots, 87, 101
Patterson, T., 29
Pepper, black, 55, 72, 186; red, see chili
Persea gratisima, 184
Pestilence, 61-64, 68, 73, 74, 82, 107, 108, 110, 131, 166
Peten Itza, 37, 38, 189
Phaseolus vulgaris, see beans
Pig ceremony, 112, 113
Pig styes, 93
Pine, 34
Pineapple, 193
Pinol, 100, 104
Pisote, 111, 112, 147, 148, 152
Pit for game, 121
Plantain, 100, 150, 177, 195
Plum, 193
Po, 64
Poctun, 37, 38
Poison, fish, 90, 91

Tamales, 100, 129, 130
Tapir, 35, 120
Tehuantepec, 88
Temax, 36
Temperament, 84
Teotihuacan, 105
Tests, 123, 124, 152, 154, 155
Textiles, 96
Theobroma cacao, see cacao
Thirteen, as sacred number, 55, 127, 150, 177, 194
Thompson, E. H., 91, 158
Thompson, J. E., 42, 158, 191
Three, as woman's number, 93, 111
Thrush, 121
Thunder, 60, 61, see also Chacs
Tlaloc, 62, 140, 150
Toad, 74, 122
Tobacco, 54, 55, 101, 127, 177, 194
Toledo District, 33-40
Toothache, 131
Tomato, 194
Top, throwing, 123, 152
Torquemada, J., 93, 184, 186, 191
Tortillas, 72, 99, 110, 113, 148
Totopostes, 100, 121
Totemism, lack of, 80
Toucan, 87, 193
Tozzer, A. M., 43, 48, 53, 65, 75, 93, 95, 157, 158, 166, 193
Trade, 86, 96, 98, 99, 185, 186, 188, 195
Trapping, 87, 121
Troano codex, 52
Trogon bird, 120
Turkeys, 62, 117, 185
Turtle, 35, 128, 136
Two brother trait, 139, 140
Tzeltal, 57, 101
Tzen Huitz ceremony, 62
Tzultacaj, 57-61

U, see moon goddess
Uaxactun, 73
Ucananxuxob, 157
Uloa, 186
Underworld, 60, 66, 68
Uo, 103

Vayeyab, 60
Venus, see Morning Star
Vera Cruz, 105
Vigils, 42, 44, 49, 53, 62, 71, 72, 74, 90
Villagutierre, Soto-mayor de, 36, 186
Virgin Mary, 51
Vochysia guatemalensis, 97
Vulture, 35, 110, 130, 131, 136, 137

Water, spirit of, 65, 91
Watermelons, 177, 178
Wax, 74, 105, 117, 147, 150, 152
Wax figures, 72, 74, 75, 109, 166, 171
Weaning, 78
Weaving, 96, 126; inventress of, 138
West Indies, 94, 95, 186
Whistling, 173
Willard, T. A., 158
Williams, S., 29
Winds, carrying off by, 66, 143, 150, 161; evil, 73, 74, 107, 166, 173; gods of, 47, 48, 58, 64, 66, 108, 167, 176, 177; loosening of, 149
Witchcraft, see sorcery
Witz-ailik, 57
Wolffsohn, A., 29
Woman, intelligence of, 107; men dressed as, 103, 113; sacred number of, 111
Woodpecker, 134

Xanthosoma violaceum, 191
Xbalanque, 46, 137, 138
Xockin, 75, 76
Xolotl, 140
Xtabai, 66, 74, 110, 156-160
Xucaneb, 51, 59, 141
Xulab, see Morning Star

Yaluk, 59, 133, 134, 141
Yams, 55, 150, 195
Yaxche, village of, 38
Yaxchilan, 97
Yucatan, 46, 48, 56, 57, 65, 67, 71, 72, 75, 80, 88, 94, 95, 114, 157, 185, 188-190, 195, 204

Zea mays, see maize
Zicnic, 155
Zip, 103

1. SAN ANTONIO. VIEW FROM THE CABILDO

2. SAN ANTONIO. VIEW FROM THE CHURCH

MAYAS, SAN ANTONIO

1. FAUSTINO BOL, WIFE, MOTHER-IN-LAW, AND BROTHER-IN-LAW,
SAN ANTONIO MAYAS

2. CELESTINO PAQUUL, SAN ANTONIO MAYA

Field Museum of Natural History

AGUSTIN HOB, SAN ANTONIO MAYA

REMIJIO POP, SAN ANTONIO MAYA

1

2

3

4

SAN ANTONIO MAYAS
1. Cecilio Cal.　2. Isidro Pop.　3. Caterino Bol.　4. Caterino Bol

HUNTERS WITH PECCARY, SAN ANTONIO MAYAS

FERNANDO CHUN, SAN ANTONIO MAYA

WOMEN AND CHILDREN, SAN ANTONIO MAYAS

1. SIDE VIEW OF HOUSE, SAN ANTONIO (p. 91)

2. END VIEW OF HOUSE, SAN ANTONIO (p. 91)

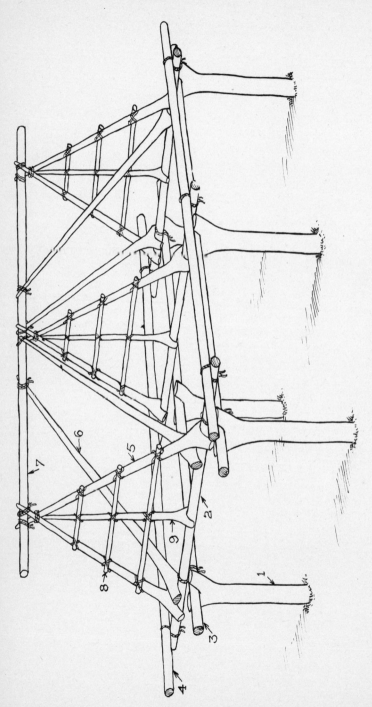

HOUSE CONSTRUCTION, SAN ANTONIO (p. 91)

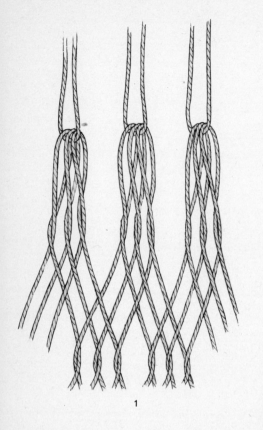

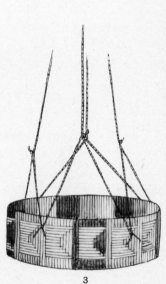

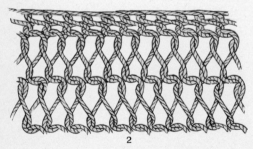

SAN ANTONIO INDUSTRY

1. Hammock Technique, San Antonio (p. 93).   2. Netted Bag Technique, San Antonio (p. 96).
3. Gourd Carriers, San Antonio (p. 100)

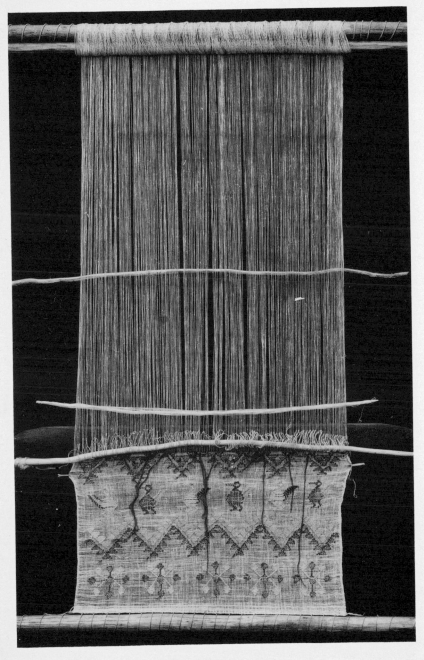

LOOM, AGUACATE (p. 96)

1. CACAO BEANS DRYING ON DRESSED BARK, SAN ANTONIO (p. 98)

2. POTTERY MAKING, SAN ANTONIO (p. 95)

2. MASK USED IN DEER DANCE, SAN ANTONIO (p. 103)

1. MAYA WOMAN, SAN ANTONIO

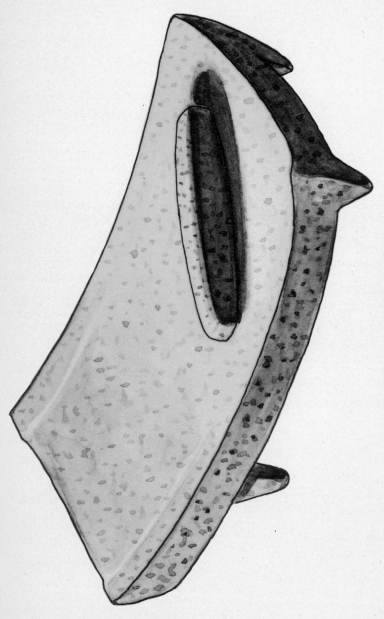

CORN GRINDER AND "HAND," SAN ANTONIO (p. 99)

1. HARP, SAN ANTONIO (p. 101)

2. MASKS USED IN DEER DANCE, SAN ANTONIO (p. 103)

1

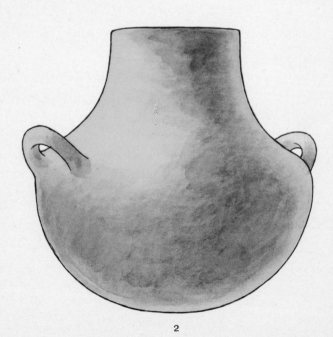

2

POTTERY, SAN ANTONIO: WATER JARS (p. 95)

POTTERY, SAN ANTONIO

3. Polished water jar.   4. Tortilla griddle.   5. Cacao griddle.   6. Cooking pot.   7. Eating dish.
8. Copal censer (p. 95)

JACINTO CUNIL, A SOCOTZ MAYA

1. FRANCISCO CUNIL, SOCOTZ MAYA

2. FELIPE PAT, SOCOTZ MAYA

1. CURING HEADACHE BY BLEEDING WITH GLASS POINTS, SOCOTZ (p. 110)

2. HMEN COCOM CURING NEGRESS OF TOOTHACHE
BY INCANTATION, SOCOTZ (p. 110)

1. THE CEIBA FESTIVAL. THE CHIIC WITH DRUM, SOCOTZ

2. THE CEIBA FESTIVAL. MAYA GIRLS DRESSED FOR
MESTIZADA DANCE, SOCOTZ (p. 111)

WOMAN DRESSED FOR MESTIZADA DANCE, SOCOTZ (p. 111)

San Antonio

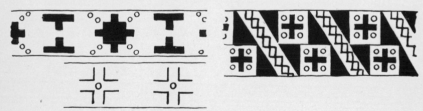

Socotz and Bullet Tree

HUIPIL DESIGNS, SAN ANTONIO, SOCOTZ, AND BULLET TREE (p. 99)

818